Comfortable Chaos

Carolyn S. Harvey and Beth E. Herrild, MA

8135

Self-Counsel Press
(a division of)
International Self-Counsel Press Ltd.
USA   Canada

Self-Counsel Press acknowledges the financial support of the Government of Canada through the Book Publishing Industry Development Program (BPIDP) for our publishing activities.

Printed in Canada

First edition: 2005

Library and Archives Canada Cataloguing in Publication

Harvey, Carolyn

    Comfortable chaos / Carolyn Harvey and Beth Herrild.

ISBN 1-55180-604-5

    1. Self-actualization (Psychology) I. Herrild, Beth II. Title.

BF637.S4H363 2005   158.1   C2005-900198-4

Self-Counsel Press
(a division of)
International Self-Counsel Press Ltd.

1704 North State Street	1481 Charlotte Road
Bellingham, WA 98225	North Vancouver, BC V7J 1H1
USA	Canada

Contents

INTRODUCTION: CHATTING ACROSS
THE DRIVEWAY   xvii

PART I: SHIFTING TO COMFORTABLE CHAOS   1

1 COMFORTABLE CHAOS: IT'S SO MUCH MORE
THAN "JUST SAYING NO"   3

The Pursuit of "Balance"   3
Life As a White-Water Raft Trip   6
The First I — Individual   7
The Second I — Imperfect   8
The Third I — Inter-Related   8

2 YOUR COEFFICIENT FOR CHAOS   11

Determining How You Are Spending Your Time   12
Aligning Your Time with Your Treasures   15
Your Coefficient for Chaos   18
    The high CFC style   21
    The mid-range CFC style   21
    The low CFC style   23
Is Your Chaos Working for You or Against You?   24
Tipping Out of the Raft   25
Recognizing the Warning Signs before Capsizing   26

3 TAKING CHARGE IN A HIGH-SPEED "SUCK
YOU DRY" WORLD   29

Controlling the Corporate Beast   31
Worrying about the Beast, Not the Economy   32
Seven Keys to Controlling the Beast   33
Give up Perfectionism   34
Remember Your Priorities   35
Know Your Worth   36
Operate in Your "Want and Can" Area   37
Learn How to Let Some Balls Drop   42
    Eliminate it   42

Redefine done 43
Delegate it 43
Create (and Keep) Your Boundaries 44
  Get out of the passive/victim mentality 46
  Diffuse the emotion 46
  Follow the pain to the problem 46
  Decide on a "trial boundary" 47
  Create a boundary support system 47
  Implement the "trial boundary" and then
  evaluate it in 30 days 47
Know How to Get Results 48

4 THE VIEW FROM THE MIDDLE 49
Self-Care Isn't Selfish 50
Why Self-Care Needs a Place on Your To-Do List 52
  You will get more done 52
  You will be around longer for your family 53
  You will be modeling life-enhancing behavior
  for your children 53
Using Transitions to Create Pools of Calm Water 56
Handling Anticipated Transitions 56
  Envision the other side 57
  Be conscious of the "one more thing syndrome" 58
  Design the improved transition 59
Handling Unanticipated Transitions 60
Comfortable Chaos: A Noble and Pioneering Effort 63
Not All Pioneers Travel the Same Road 65

5 RECLAIMING, OR CHANGING,
   YOUR CHOICE 67
Determining What's Working and What Isn't 68
The Envy Decoder 69
Which Direction Are You Moving In? 72
Where to Next? 73

PART II: THRIVING ON FULL-TIME WORK
         WHILE STILL HAVING A LIFE   75

6   FULFILLED BY FULL TIME: HOW TO MAKE
    IT MANAGEABLE AND PROTECT
    YOUR PRIORITIES   77
    Take a Dual-Centric Approach   78
    Change Your Assignment   80
    Change Your Alignment   84
    Change Your Abutment   86
    Moving Your CFC Along the Continuum   88
    Maintain Your Boundaries   89
    Ten Tips for Getting It All Done   90
        Decide on your top priority projects   90
        Use the 80/20 rule and plan   90
        Use the "project of the week" concept   91
        Get over the guilt of e-mail   91
        Develop the need for speed   93
        Avoid any meeting that doesn't help you
        with one of your critical projects   93
        Learn the tools that are pertinent for your job   94
        Be highly organized and work "lean"   95
        Think before you say "yes"   95
        Surround yourself with capable and
        positive people   96

7   FLEXTIME, COMPRESSED WORKWEEKS,
    AND TELECOMMUTING: THREE WONDERFUL
    WAYS TO DISTRIBUTE FULL-TIME WORK   97
    Flextime: Working When It Works for You   99
        How much of my time is spent in cross-
        functional collaboration?   100
        How will I accommodate communication among
        my direct reporting relationships?   100
        Can I honestly sustain the schedule I am
        proposing?   101

Compressed Workweeks: How to Not Shove
Ten Pounds in a Five-Pound Sack   101

    Do I have the physical and mental stamina
    for a longer day?   103

    Does my job realistically lend itself to my absence
    one day per week or every other week?   103

    How will the work be covered on the days I am
    not in the office?   104

    How will I communicate my schedule to others
    in order to reduce any possible resentment?   104

Telecommuting: Getting Beyond the Image of
Working in Your Pajamas   105

    How will my manager and I measure
    my deliverables?   106

    How, and how often, will I communicate?   107

    What equipment is needed and who will
    purchase it?   107

    Does my work have confidentiality or
    security issues?   108

    Am I clear on professional standards for
    telephone and e-mail etiquette?   108

    What will I do to keep feeling like
    "part of the team"?   108

    Will I feel isolated if I am working at home
    by myself?   108

    Am I the type of person who procrastinates?   108

    Do I have a workable child-care plan?   109

Telecommuting Light   109

The Common Elements of Three Wonderful Ways to
Distribute Full-Time Work   110

Your Schedule As Part of the Bigger Picture   111

8   WORKING INDEPENDENTLY:
HOW FREELANCING OR CONSULTING
COULD BE RIGHT FOR YOU   113

Work Schedules and Boundaries   115

Where Is Your Chair? Working from Home, the
Client's Office, or the Coffee Shop   117
Assessing If This Lifestyle Is a Good Fit for You   118
     Are you willing to find work by networking,
     marketing, and selling?   118
     Are you able to establish boundaries that fit your
     working style and support your goals?   120
     Are you able to accurately assess potential clients
     and avoid potential problem clients?   121
     Are you able to build positive relationships and
     develop client-specific networks?   122
     Can you work independently and manage to a
     deadline?   124
     Can you give up the traditional rewards of
     working in a corporate setting?   124
     Can you cope financially and emotionally
     during the times you don't have work?   125
Staffing Agencies: Friend or Foe?   126
     How staffing agencies bill   127
     Co-employment and length of assignment   128
     Choosing a staffing agency   129
     The three phases of an assignment   131
A New Model: Using a Mixture of Different
Employment Arrangements   133
Getting Started As an Independent Worker   135
Independent Workers: The Future of
White-Collar Work?   137

PART III: LOVING LIFE AT HOME FULL
              TIME OR PART TIME   139

9   STAYING HOME FULL TIME: EMBRACING
     THE NEBULOUS NATURE OF IT ALL   141
     Staying at Home Is Highly Individual   143
     Staying at Home Is Definitely Imperfect   144
     Staying at Home Is Intensely Inter-Related   144

Handling the Nebulous Nature of the Job 145
   Design and create your own structure 146
   Surrender to the fact that the work is never
   done and set boundaries 147
   Recognize and embrace your many daily
   transitions in new ways 147
Creating a Sense of Accomplishment and
Positive Feedback 148
   Start viewing your home as your workplace 149
   Put small, trivial-seeming tasks on your to-do
   list and check them off 149
   Delegate even though you don't have employees 150
   Give yourself a performance evaluation 150
Dealing with the 24/7 Experience 151
   Look at what you're trying to control and why 151
   Plan when to sit down and when to get out 152
   Create that Friday feeling 153
Overcoming the Isolation 153
   Hang out with "your people" 153
   Make yourself do something stimulating or
   out of the box 154
Adjusting to the Lack of Pay and the Drop in Status 154
   Work on your sense of intrinsic value and
   create your own rewards 155
   Manage the money 155
   Do some advocating 156
Allowing Time for the Transition 156

10 PART TIME: NOT JUST FOR RETAIL ANYMORE 157
Meet some Part-Timers 158
Nice Work If You Can Get It 159
   Use your current employer 160
   Create your own part-time work 161
   Job hunt for part-time work 162
Do You Have the Right Personality for
Part-Time Work? 163

Selecting the Right Ingredients for Success 165
    Selecting the right type of assignment 166
    Selecting the right type of boss 168
    Selecting the right work environment 169
Successfully Managing Relationships 170
Productivity Power: You May Actually Get More
Done in Less Time 172
Managing Your Time Off: How to Avoid
"Full Time Creep" 173
"She Just Works Part Time" and Other
Potential Perceptions 175
    You still have a career and a real job 177
    Flexibility about the exact schedule 177
    The reality of occasional work on your days off 178
    The financial balance of power 178
    Managing expectations about your
    stay-at-home days 178

11 JOB SHARING: THE POWER OF A
PARTNERSHIP HAS ENDLESS POSSIBILITIES 181
The Unique Benefits of Job Sharing 182
The Downside of Job Sharing 183
Is Job Sharing Right for You? 184
Schedules and Structure 185
Could Your Job Be Shared? 187
    Can the work be divided or can an effective
    plan for managing the work be created? 187
    Does the job have complex communication
    requirements? 187
    Does the job require heavy travel? 188
    If the job includes supervising people,
    can you develop a realistic plan for sharing
    management responsibilities? 188
    Are there quantifiable benefits to
    sell to management? 189
Assessing Your Company's Culture 190
Assessing Your Manager 191

Finding and Selecting the Right Partner 191
Which Job to Share? 195
The Importance of Being Seamless 196
Getting Started 198

**PART IV: READY TO MAKE A MAJOR CHANGE?
À LA CARTE HELP PROVIDED** 199

**12 THE ALL-IMPORTANT AFFORDABILITY
QUESTION: CAN YOUR FINANCES
SUPPORT YOUR DREAMS?** 201

Gathering Your Financial Facts: The Critical
First Step 202
    Track your spending 203
    Document your net worth 205
Assessing the Short- and Long-Term Impacts of
Change 205
    Meet current expenses 205
    Meet future expenses 207
    Medical and dental insurance 207
    Life insurance and other company-provided
    benefits 208
    Pension plans 208
    401K plans 209
    Stock options and bonuses 209
    Social security 209
Creating a Financial Plan 210
Casting Your Votes Differently 210
Spending Plans: One Piece of the Financial Plan 213
Getting Professional Help 213
    Financial planner 213
    Investment manager 214
    Stockbrokers 214
    Personal bookkeepers 215
It's Worth the Effort 215

13 CREATIVE CHILD-CARE SOLUTIONS: HOW TO CREATE THE SUPPORT YOU NEED 217

Five Keys to Finding Creative Child Care 218
    Networking, networking, networking 218
    Get creative about your advertising sources 219
    Don't be afraid to combine options 220
    Know yourself and your children, and trust
    your instincts 221
    Always be thinking about your next phase 222
Eleven Creative Child-Care Solutions 223
    Daycare centers (full time) 224
    Daycare centers (part time) 224
    In-home daycare providers (full time) 225
    In-home daycare providers (part time) 225
    Nannies (full time) 226
    Nannies (part time) 227
    Nanny share 227
    Relatives or family friends 228
    Other parents 229
    Babysitting co-ops 229
    Coworkers with opposite schedules 229
Why Finding Great Child Care Is Only the Beginning 230

14 STRATEGIES FOR RE-ENTRY: HOW TO RETURN TO THE WORKFORCE AFTER A BREAK 233

Strategies for Returning to the Paid Workforce 236
    Find the right volunteer position 236
    Network with both new and former contacts 237
    Find a full-time professional who is interested
    in job sharing 239
    Take a class in your field or do something else
    to keep current 239
    Read industry and general business/economic
    publications 240
    Participate in professional associations 240

Evaluate your former industry and consider a
new industry if the pace of change requires
up-to-the-minute skills   240

Consider going back full time even if your
preference is part time   241

View your transition as a time to reinvent
yourself by finding your passion and
identifying your skills   242

Combining Strategies   243

Résumé and Interview Tips   243

Make sure your prior work experience is
strategically placed on your résumé and is
specific and quantifiable   244

Don't try to hide your time out of the paid
workforce   244

During the interview be the consummate
professional   247

Avoid talking about your children unless
specifically asked   247

Demonstrate your up-to-date knowledge of
the industry   247

15 CREATING AN ALTERNATIVE WORK
SCHEDULE: HOW TO THINK LIKE AN
EMPLOYER AND PITCH YOUR PROPOSAL
LIKE A PRO   249

Ten Elements of a Comprehensive Proposal   251

Introductory statement and needs analysis   251

Job title   252

Schedule specifics   252

Benefits to the company   253

Benefits for the employees in the job share   254

Cost benefit analysis   255

Successful precedents   259

Strategy for managing/allocating responsibilities   259

Detailed communication plan   261

Potential issues and solutions   262

Getting the Right Equation   263
Preparing for Possible Objections   265
Making the Presentation   265

PART V: LIVING IN COMFORTABLE CHAOS   267

16 YOUR EVER-CHANGING JOURNEY   269

EXERCISES
  1 Where Does My Time Go?   14
  2 My Current Priorities   17
  3 Determining Your Coefficient for Chaos   19
  4 Determining Your "Want and Can" Area   42
  5 My Self-Care Habit   55
  6 Handling Your Worst Transition   61
  7 Determining What's Working and What Isn't   69
  8 Decoding Your Envy   71
  9 Determining Your Direction   73
10 Tracking Your Spending   204
11 Documenting Your Net Worth   206

FIGURES
  1 Determining Your "Want and Can" Area   38
  2 What Mike Wants to Control   39
  3 What Paula Can Control   41

CHECKLIST
  1 Evaluating a Staffing Company   133

SAMPLE
  1 Skill-Based Résumé   245

Notice

This book is intended to be used only as a reference guide. Application of the content to the day-to-day life choices of the reader does not guarantee a desired outcome. Most of the people referenced in the book were interviewees and seminar participants, and some profiles are composites. We have omitted last names and company names to preserve privacy.

comfortable Chaos

Acknowledgments

Back when we naively decide to write a book in "our spare time," we of course had no idea the depth of the task and the help we would need from others. Now we are much wiser to the process of bringing a book to life and have many people to thank.

We want to first of all thank "the Daves" — our supportive husbands, David Harvey and David Herrild, who just happen to have the same first name. They provided help in many forms, including weekend duty even when they were sure that "book retreat" was a code word for time away from the kids, a good glass of wine, and the occasional massage. Our children also have our gratitude because their very existence prompted our need to discover and create *Comfortable Chaos*. They were often also very patient when Mom was "working on that darn book again." Thank you Nicholas and Tessa Harvey, and Jesse, Ashton, and Zoe Herrild. We also thank our parents and sisters. Between the two of us we have five intelligent, creative, and strong sisters and each one offered her unique and helpful perspective. Thank goodness for the S.P.S. and the Schaad sorority!

We also owe much gratitude to the many wonderful people who contributed their stories and/or expertise for this book. Some, such as Paul Buboltz, Elizabeth Crary, Jennifer Easley, Karen Forner, Nancy Jones, Pam Layton, Jan Nicosia, Judy Ogden, Judi Paffenbarger, Jeanette Whiting, and Ann Zachwiegja, went beyond the call of duty and provided us with research material, articles, technical help, speaking opportunities, and their personal wisdom.

Last, we of course want to thank Self-Counsel Press for their expertise and professionalism. We were privileged to work with Catherine Plear, Richard Day, and our outstanding editor, Sharon Boglari.

Introduction

Chatting Across the Driveway

Eight years ago, I moved with my husband and two-year-old son to a bigger home in the suburbs. I first met Carolyn when she was pulling into her driveway next door. We introduced ourselves and Carolyn welcomed me to the neighborhood. A few more impromptu chats and waves across the driveway, and we were getting together with our husbands for appetizers and wine.

Later that year Carolyn excitedly told me she was pregnant. It was such a huge relief after years of stressful infertility treatments. Carolyn and her husband, Dave, were thrilled that they would soon be parents. After a few weeks, I shared my good news that I was expecting my second child. Carolyn gave me a hug and we sympathized with each other about our ever-expanding bodies and constant backaches. Our spur of the moment get togethers continued, including one memorable gathering around Christmas when we were both hugely pregnant and snowed in on our little cul-de-sac for several days (snow is an anomaly in Seattle so we don't quite know how to deal with it, especially on giant hills)!

We delivered healthy baby boys one month apart and marveled at each other's beautiful creations. After comparing notes on sleep schedules and diaper decisions, we began the inevitable discussion of how to combine work and family and what childcare plans would be best when we returned to work.

I already knew how hard it was going back to work full time after my first child was born. The memories of sneaking off to the closet to pump milk and then hurrying back to a meeting, only to struggle to stay awake once I sat down, were still fresh in my mind. But I loved my job as a sales manager and decided that hiring a new nanny would be my best option with two small children.

After spending at least half of my maternity leave scheduling and interviewing nannies, I finally found someone I trusted and went back to work three months after my son was born. Going from one to two children felt like a quantum leap. Not only was I pumping milk at work like before, but now I was even more tired because my time at home was divided between an active toddler and a hungry newborn.

Carolyn was also finding the return to work challenging. After looking at many child-care options, she decided to use a creative combination of family members to care for her son during the first six months. Recently promoted to a senior human resources manager before she got pregnant, she was eager to perform at her regular pace. But she was surprised at how nursing and caring for her son seemed to drain all of her energy. In the evenings, she gave her son her full attention, while couple time, personal time, and a decent dinner became things of the past.

Carolyn and I continued to chat across the driveway, share stories, celebrate successes, and commiserate about the challenges. Over the next two years our sleep-deprived states improved, but we faced new problems. We helped each other through several failed child-care plans including the nanny from hell, the nanny that didn't show up, and the expensive but chaotic daycare center.

We both remained committed to our careers but struggled with how to have time to enjoy our children while bringing home a paycheck and participating in the stimulating world of work. It felt like we were always going at high speed — never really enjoying each role completely — and always thinking ahead on how to get the next task done. We kept saying to each other that there *must* be a better way! As we looked around, the options didn't seem obvious.

Shortly before my second son turned two, I realized I wanted to make a change. After much soul searching, I decided that I would reduce my hours, but not my commitment to work, by creating a job share situation. I searched for an appropriate partner, developed a proposal, and strategized over when, and how, to present it to my employer. Carolyn enthusiastically cheered me on and agonized with me while I waited to see if the proposal would be accepted. Finally, I got the green light and my job sharing journey began.

Around the same time, Carolyn had a second child and was now the mother of a 19-month-old and a newborn. She too had decided to reduce her hours and was fortunate to have a very supportive boss who agreed to a part-time schedule. Carolyn worked three days a week but was essentially trying to cram her full-time job into fewer hours. She realized her mistake and was about to renegotiate her responsibilities when her beloved boss announced her retirement and a change in the organization was on the horizon. Carolyn considered her options and decided to take a first line management job that would be a better fit for a part-time schedule.

Now our chats across the driveway changed to cell phone conversations as we commuted and compared notes on our alternative work schedules. We both loved our new routines and found the mix between work and home was ideal. But we also realized that we had gone through similar processes when deciding to change our work schedules, and we both had felt like we bushwhacked into new territories at our companies. It was hard work and there didn't seem to be anywhere to turn for help. As we talked through the challenges in creating these schedules and making them work, we agreed that there was a lack of resources on this topic; there didn't appear to be any roadmaps to guide the way. We started brainstorming and dreaming of starting a business dedicated to helping people create work/life balance.

After two years of successfully job sharing, my partner and I decided to resign after the third merger in our company. This particular merger was radically shifting the company's focus and we weren't comfortable with the new direction. My job share partner and I joked that we did everything together, including resigning. I had also given birth to a third child and decided to stay home full time for a while. Carolyn and I continued to talk and loved to dream up business ideas where we could enjoy both working and less-frenzied time with our families.

One day when Carolyn was driving home from work, she called me at home and said she had an epiphany on the freeway. We could write a book! She left me an excited message about how this would be the perfect way to launch the business without raising capital and that we could do it in our "spare time." Ha!

We laughed about the spare time but couldn't let go of the idea that a "how to" book for people who wanted to create alternative work schedules was desperately needed. Our friendship grew to include collaboration and we started slowly by meeting for coffee and drafting an outline. Before long we had some concrete ideas and decided we would go for it and see what happened. We nudged each other as needed to schedule people to be interviewed for the book and we set deadlines for each chapter.

We worked this way over the next two years and the book changed as we gathered more information and solicited feedback. Our passion for the topic only grew and we started giving seminars as a method to build a business. In the fall of 2002, Carolyn also decided to leave her successful part-time position and resigned from her company. It was difficult to leave an enjoyable job and a close-knit group of employees but the new business venture beckoned. We filed for a business license and our partnership was official.

It was the following spring that we had a major breakthrough. We had started to question our frequent use of the word "balance" to describe our book and we found that focusing on alternative work schedules was too narrow. Everyone seemed to be facing the same struggle of how to create a less frazzled life and it didn't matter whether they were working full time, staying home full time, or doing something in between.

We formed a focus group and gathered people who had made different work/life balance choices but seemed to all be facing similar struggles. There was an incredible energy that evening as the group shared their choices and their challenges. When we raised the question of "balance," one woman said "don't insult me by insinuating that true balance is even possible." The room practically exploded with agreement — there was visible anger and frustration about this notion of balance that felt unreachable and tenuous.

From that evening, the concept of Comfortable Chaos was born and the book and seminars gained new life and momentum. We broadened our research to include all of the possible work/life balance choices and reflected on our own wide range of experiences. Between the two of us, we have worked just about all of the options of full time, part time, job sharing, telecommuting, and flextime. We also interviewed numerous people living these choices and discovered their strategies and tips. From our own experiences and the generously shared stories of others, we have found many common threads that tie us together. We also marveled at the infinite ways people have crafted unique solutions to fit their personalities and lifestyles.

This book will bring you both the common threads and the creative approaches to various work arrangements and lifestyle choices so you can use what works for you. Speaking of using what works for you, this book is designed with your crazy life in mind. We know that you rarely get a chance to sit down and read a book cover to cover and although we hope you do get to enjoy everything in *Comfortable Chaos*, the book is designed so you can read the sections that most apply to you or jump to the topic where you need the most help. We also have lots of exercises so you can get right to the solutions. Whether you read while a child is crawling all over you, sneak a few moments of peace in the bathroom, or glance at a couple of pages during soccer practice, we hope your copy is well used and survives spilled milk and raspberry jam.

In Part I, you will learn more about your personal preference when it comes to chaos and discover many tools and strategies for dealing with the frenzied pace of life. You will also find help in assessing your current work/life choice and determining whether it needs changing or adjusting. In Part II, we look at some strategies and options for working full time and maintaining balance, while Part III covers staying home full time and the various options of part-time work. Part IV gives you à la carte help by providing solutions for everything from finding child care and returning to the workforce after a break, to assessing your finances and writing a proposal for an alternative work schedule. Part V reminds you that Comfortable Chaos is a journey, not a destination, and prepares you for the reality of constantly reinventing yourself.

We wish you well on making your chaos more comfortable!

Part I

Shifting to Comfortable Chaos

comfortable Chaos

Chapter 1

Comfortable Chaos: It's So Much More Than "Just Saying No"

The Pursuit of "Balance"

"Let me tell you what's going on in my world today," Marisa tries to explain to her friend. "I just found out my daughter doesn't have a place to live at college so I need to fly back east to find her a studio apartment. My 88-year-old mother is refusing to get on the plane in Louisiana because she thinks she is in Seattle and is waiting for me to pick her up. My son has soccer practice at 4:00 p.m., which is the same time I am supposed to pick up my husband at the airport and then get to my daughter's school." Marisa's friend pauses a moment and then says, "You have so much going on in your life — you just need to learn how to say no."

Wouldn't it be great if life were that simple? Anyone with multiple responsibilities understands that there is no magical solution that will make life calm and easy. Whether you are working and juggling family life, staying home full time, or doing something in between, it often feels like one constant race to get to the next commitment, only to barely regroup and do it again.

What happened to the pace of life? When did it get so bad that we sacrifice sleep, time to ourselves, and therapeutic sessions with friends? In the workplace, the major shift seemed to start around 1997 with the proliferation of e-mail and voicemail. Who knew that these very helpful tools would also dramatically increase the pace of work? Instead of receiving a memo and carefully crafting a reply that would be received days later, we are now susceptible to an unspoken expectation for an instant response. Add to this the effects of corporate downsizing that reduced the number of employees but not the workload, and it's no wonder people feel so overwhelmed.

The problem becomes even more challenging when you factor in any type of family responsibilities. In fact, 64 percent of Americans report that time pressures on working families are getting worse, not better. Not only is the stress higher at work, the responsibilities of home life continue to become more complex. A primary example is today's child-centric parenting style. Typical parents are very involved in raising, educating, and coordinating their child's activities — whether they are babies, school-aged, college-aged, or beyond. The drivers for this phenomenon are numerous but the bottom line is that parents face high expectations (their own and others) when it comes to raising their children. As a result, parents often feel torn between their many priorities and end up feeling guilty.

Dan, a senior aerospace engineer with two young children at home, summed it up by saying, "My biggest frustration is that when I'm at work, I'm always pushing myself to get the job done quickly so I can get home. And then when I try to spend quality time with my family at home, I'm often rushing through the routines with the kids so I can get some private time. It feels like I am always pushing the limit."

In addition to the challenges of parenting, many of us face elder care responsibilities. Even if you are not currently caring for your parents, there is a very good chance that you will be in the future. According to the Children of Aging Parents Organization (CAPS), in 1995 there were 33 million Americans older than 65, and this number is projected to be almost 70 million by the year 2020. This translates into an estimated 22 million caregiving households nationwide. So if you thought that your days of juggling work and family would be over once your children are grown — think again. Whether you look after your parents in your home or manage their care across town or across the country, you will continue to need to find creative ways to keep the chaos comfortable.

Another factor contributing to the feeling of being overwhelmed is the vast number of choices we face in all walks of life. In today's workplace there is rarely a clear career path to follow. Instead, we need to individually design and implement a career plan. This could mean making lateral moves, changing industries, and nurturing relationships with a variety of mentors and peer organizations.

The choices involved in running a home and family are no less simple. More so than in our parents' generation, today, we make much more conscious decisions about where to live and the corresponding lifestyle choices such as what car to drive, commuting options, and services for our families. Heck, we don't even send our kids out to play in the yard without deciding if we will go outside to keep an eye on them or be hypervigilant by peering out the windows.

And then there's the issue of school. No longer do we simply send our children to the neighborhood school. Instead, we research schools and test scores before deciding on a school that best meets our children's individual needs. This is of course a good thing — but it's also a new thing. Our parents simply sent us off to school without any research because that was the norm of the time and they weren't exposed to the infinite options and possibilities available today, especially via the Internet. Today, choosing the right school is a common conversation topic among parents — just one example of how our culture and the vast availability of information make life so challenging. As you may know, once you have decided on a school, the decisions never stop. Simply emptying your child's backpack at the end of the day will produce a flood of flyers on activities, field trips, and school events that await your decisions!

We can certainly celebrate the fact that we have so many choices and that information is readily available. But it's also important to realize that these choices are a contributing factor to our chaos and that many of us are operating without clear role models of how to best create a life that combines work and family. It's not that previous generations didn't work hard, because they most certainly did. But they didn't have the wildly divergent priorities and possibilities that we are faced with today and that can overshadow our ability to create a rich and satisfying life.

So with the incredible pace at both work and at home, and the infinite number of choices, is there any hope for achieving peace of mind? The answer is a most definite yes! Comfortable Chaos is a realistic and attainable state of being. You no longer need to guilt trip yourself over the need to find "balance." This word seems to imply that you must get everything lined up just right and then stand on one foot, like a challenging yoga pose, to keep it there. While we will occasionally use the word "balance" in this book, we are not referring to the pursuit of perfection. It's time to throw out your preconceived notions of what your life is supposed to be like, and get ready to learn the techniques that will bring you to Comfortable Chaos.

Life As a White-Water Raft Trip

The concept of Comfortable Chaos is best explained by using a metaphor: Think of 21st-century life as a wild ride on a white-water raft. There are times when you are riding the rapids and feeling out of control. Instead of doing the impossible, like trying to tame the river, achieving Comfortable Chaos is about learning how to make the most of your trip:

- *Enjoy the thrills.* Making quick turns with the water rushing all around you is like multitasking with a paddle. The feeling can be exciting and invigorating when you are flying through your tasks, getting a sense of accomplishment, and enjoying your various roles. Comfortable Chaos teaches you how to enjoy the ride.

- *Avoid capsizing in the rapids.* Sometimes the pace of multi-tasking, along with a hole in your raft (like too little sleep or an overcommitted calendar), can cause you to tip right out of the boat. Since righting yourself in rapids can be very difficult, Comfortable Chaos teaches you how to keep your raft on a more even keel.

- *Paddle to a few pools of calm water.* A calm pool of water is a necessary change from the rushing of water. Without taking a break to relax and reflect, you lose your ability to paddle effectively in the rapids. Comfortable Chaos teaches you how to create your own pools of calm water and visit them frequently.

Comfortable Chaos is further explained by three concepts: *individual, imperfect, and inter-related.* We call these the three "I"s and will refer to them throughout the book.

The First I — Individual

The first I in Comfortable Chaos is *individual.* In our society, comparisons and the need to "keep up with the Joneses" are rampant and destructive. We compare our houses, our cars, our haircuts, our children's accomplishments, and, not least of all, our work/life choices. Our research shows that women have clearly emerged as the worst gender at making disparaging comments about other women's choices and lifestyles as a way to attempt to become more comfortable with their own.

We must put an end to the vicious cycle. Comparing your choices to others' is never a winnable proposition. We firmly believe in what Socrates once said, "Know thyself." The key to being comfortable with your own work/life choices, otherwise known as your "chaos," is in knowing yourself and realizing that what works for one person does not necessarily work for another. Situations that are overwhelming for some people may be energizing and delightful for others. Likewise, what is tedious and boring to some of the population, may be perfectly enjoyable to the rest. Comparisons only create a false sense of superiority at best and make you feel discouraged and inferior at worst.

The *individual* in Comfortable Chaos means taking the time and energy to understand your own personal preferences and tolerances and honoring them regardless of the choices of others. The more you understand yourself, the better able you will be to make conscious, realistic choices that work for you. In the next chapter we offer several tools to help you to better understand yourself.

The Second I — Imperfect

The second I in Comfortable Chaos is *imperfect*. The concept of Comfortable Chaos recognizes and embraces the fact that nothing, and no one, is perfect. Of course you have heard this before but have you really accepted it and learned to live in imperfection? We will talk much more about the problems with being a perfectionist in Chapter 3 and give you some strategies to overcome this tendency.

One challenge of celebrating imperfection is rejecting the artificially high standards that are thrust upon us by the media. The magazine and television images of a glamorous kitchen with flowing granite counter tops and an impeccably dressed woman talking with her clean and happy children are not realistic. Don't let those images mess with your head! Real houses with real families have mail and toys on the counters, dings in the wall, and dog hair on the floor. And if you happen to have some friends who seem to live the life in the magazine, just keep in mind that the appearance they project when you are visiting is not necessarily the one they live every day. Even if by some chance it is, remember that everything has a cost. So get over the image of the perfect house, perfect children, and perfect work and begin to enjoy the life you have by using the techniques you will learn in this book.

The Third I — Inter-Related

The last I is *inter-related* and it means having a holistic or big picture approach to life. Instead of thinking of your life in its various pieces (such as work, parenting, relaxation, and housework), think of everything as being interconnected.

We like to poke fun at some of the traditional "get balance" advice that says things like "fit in some exercise or quiet time by getting up earlier in the morning." Well, that might work if you are already getting enough or too much sleep. But if you are already shortchanged on rest, reducing it even further will most likely have negative consequences on your work, your parenting, your safety behind the wheel, and your ability to resist Krispy Kreme donuts.

A great example of the importance of a holistic approach comes from learning to fly an airplane. If you are working on getting your instrument rating, there is an exercise you go through to learn to rely solely on your instruments in inclement weather. You don a hood that allows you to see the instruments but not out the windshield or side windows of the plane. You are essentially flying with tunnel vision, without the ability to have a sense of perspective. Your instruments could be telling you that you are relatively level, but when you take off the hood you invariably realize that you are not oriented exactly as you thought you were to the horizon. This can produce quite a sense of disequilibrium because you had no perspective of the big picture. Once you are allowed to again view both the instruments and the sky and horizon outside the airplane, it becomes much easier. You may even decide that you don't need to vomit after all!

Keep this in mind as you go through your day. Being able to see, and realizing how each thing is oriented in relation to other things, will keep you flying steady. Seeing the big picture is paramount for thriving in today's world. You'll learn some techniques for doing this in Chapter 4.

You now have a basic understanding of Comfortable Chaos, and it's time to dig deeper into *individual,* the first I, by learning more about your preferences, priorities, and tolerance for chaos.

f o m C
o r
f r t
a l b e
C a h o
s

Chapter 2

Your Coefficient for Chaos

Lindsey and Nicole work in the same office as recruiters for a software company. Both enjoy their jobs but they often wonder if they are from the same planet! Lindsey's desk is covered with copies of the positions she is trying to fill, along with résumés and sticky notes covering the various piles. She jumps on the telephone and goes back and forth between the openings she is working on — happily intermixing calls to candidates with e-mails to the hiring managers. She runs her personal life in much the same way. Her three kids are enrolled in numerous activities and she is constantly coordinating the family's complex social calendar and is quick to add anything that sounds interesting. At the end of the workday it is not uncommon for her to be dashing out, always slightly late, to three or more evening commitments.

Nicole works in the cubicle next to Lindsey and her space has a much different appearance. She keeps all the material for each job opening in neat folders and although she may have several on her desk at the same time, they are all in three-step pending files so she can clearly see where each opening is at in the process. She likes to make all her candidate calls in the morning when she feels most energetic and she groups her data entry tasks to do in the afternoon. At home she has two children but she is very selective about any evening activities and prefers to have the kids take turns participating in a sport. She recognizes that she needs a certain amount of downtime so she and her husband religiously have dinner completed by 6:30 p.m. and get their kids to bed by 8:30 p.m.

Lindsey and Nicole are both top recruiters in their office and even tied last month for the elite performance award. As friends they have lots to talk about, but each secretly wonders, with a tiny bit of judgment, how the other can work like that. The reason they have such dissimilar work styles is because they each have very different "coefficients for chaos." What is comfortable and enjoyable for Lindsey may be a nightmare for Nicole, and vice versa.

As you remember, the first I of Comfortable Chaos is *individual*. By individual, we mean "know thyself," and the first step in shifting toward Comfortable Chaos is to get a clear picture of your uniqueness. Only you will know what is right for you. In this chapter you will discover your personal coefficient for chaos, which will provide a glimpse into your authentic preferences.

Determining How You Are Spending Your Time

Before you can determine your coefficient for chaos, you need to know how you're spending your time and determine if it is in alignment with your priorities. So let's start with a simple, but powerful, exercise.

In Exercise 1, you will create a pie chart that reflects how you spend your time. Each piece of the pie will represent the average amount of time that you are spending on that activity.

Start by deciding on your main categories. Many people choose things such as work, home maintenance activities, caring for children — but only you can determine the categories that are meaningful to you. Do this quickly without overthinking the categories. Follow your gut feeling about where you spend your time in general. Obviously there will be specific days or periods of time that are not "typical," but this is intended to be a high-level view. Next, draw relative sections of the pie to roughly indicate the percentage of your time devoted to each category. Don't get caught up being too exact.

In this example, Joan has chosen her categories rather broadly:

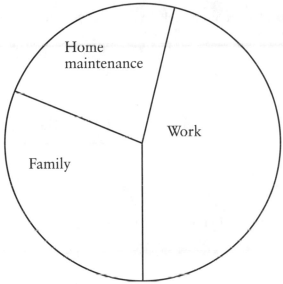

In this example, Susan made her categories a little more detailed:

Now go ahead and decide on your categories and complete your pie chart.

Once you have completed your "as is" pie chart, move on to the circle below and draw how you would spend your time in utopia. Suspend your rational mind for a moment and think how you would ideally like to divide your time.

EXERCISE 1
WHERE DOES MY TIME GO?

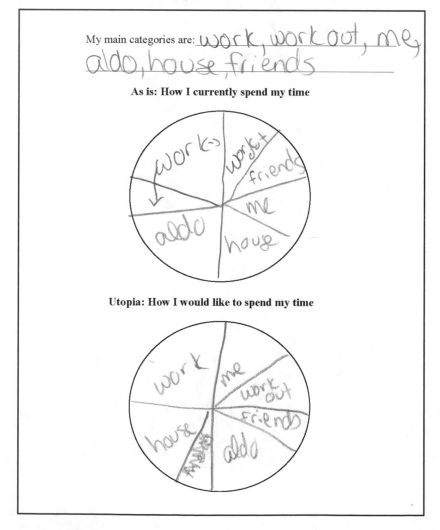

My main categories are: work, workoot, me, aldo, house, friends

As is: How I currently spend my time

Utopia: How I would like to spend my time

Now that you have completed both views of your time, what do you notice? Here are some specific questions to ask about your results:

1. *When you look at the categories you chose for the "as is" pie chart, is anything missing?* Some of our seminar participants have been a bit embarrassed to admit that time with their spouse or partner didn't show up on either chart! Many people notice with interest that sleep was not on their first chart.

2. *Which slices of your pie are too small?* Maybe it's time with friends or time for you. How much time would you need to add to each of these slices to enjoy the benefits?

3. *Are there any chunks of time on your "as is" chart that feel like they are too big?* Some people look at the significant amount of time they spend on something like home maintenance and make the decision to hire a housecleaner or someone to mow the lawn. At the same time, other people find joy and great satisfaction in caring for their home and/or yard.

4. *Looking at your "utopia" chart, what new categories did you add and which "as is" categories did you expand or contract?* The utopian chart isn't just in case you win the lottery — you can take some steps to get your "as is" chart to look more like the utopian version. Making even small changes will feel great. For example, if your utopian chart has time to exercise but your "as is" chart is missing it altogether, look for ways to add a small slice of exercise to your day. If two things like exercise and time with friends are both missing, perhaps you can find some creative ways to combine them.

The overall goal is to be honest with yourself about where you want to be spending your time. After all, you only get one life!

Aligning Your Time with Your Treasures

Now that you have an understanding of where your time goes and your vision of utopia, the next step is to make the link to priorities. A great deal has been written about identifying your values and priorities but the Comfortable Chaos approach is to give you a shortcut.

Picture yourself at about age 85 and imagine yourself looking back on your current phase of life. You are of course healthy, vibrant, and, thanks to new youth-enhancing beauty treatments, looking quite lovely. As you remember this time with young children, or whatever phase you are in, what memories do you want to have? Maybe it's family dinners. Maybe it's achieving a certain career goal. Maybe it's the time you spent curled up on your window seat reading. Maybe it's vacations to exotic parts of the world. Or maybe it is stress-free summer vacations with lots of time for everyone to do nothing.

If you have children, also think about what memories you would like them to have. They may overlap with some of yours but there could also be some uniquely kid-inspired ones. What are some of your favorite childhood memories? What do you wish they were?

This "memories" exercise can help you clarify your priorities for this point in your life. What will be really important in 10 years and 20 years? Keep in mind that not all your goals, ambitions, and hopes are likely to be satisfied in one segment of your life. For example, you may have a goal to climb Mount Everest. However, if you currently have young children, this may not be a realistic priority right now. But it doesn't mean it can't be a priority when they get older. Perhaps you can find another goal for the short term, such as joining a rock-climbing gym and taking a class.

When asked about her priorities, Nancy, one of our interviewees who is a parent, grandparent, and working professional, said, "My priority is to have the time and money for relationships. For most people, there is a trade-off between time and money. You never have enough of each — and in the end it isn't going to matter. You will run out of time and you will die penniless. Relationships and what you did to contribute are what matters."

Nancy's statement is one person's high-level view on priorities. As you think about your current priorities, try and be specific to this period of time and include the details. For example, you may list "children" as a priority. But *what* about raising children is a priority? Is it a private school education? Is it a certain parenting style? Or perhaps a specific value system? The implications of each are different so be precise about each priority. Use Exercise 2 to jot down your current priorities. You don't need to be 100 percent sure that this is your "final answer." You can change and update them whenever you want to, but it is important to periodically put them down on paper.

EXERCISE 2
MY CURRENT PRIORITIES

The next step is to look back to your "as is" circle chart from Exercise 1 and see if your time is being allocated in a way that supports your priorities. You may look at some of the larger pieces and question their relevance. Don't get too discouraged. For example, working may be a large slice of your pie, but it certainly supports your priority to feed and clothe your family, and hopefully it also supports a desire to use your skills and talent for tangible benefits. The question may be: Am I spending the right amount of time on working? That's a complicated question and the answer will be tied to your unique characteristics, finances, and lifestyle choices. The rest of the book will help you with this issue.

Household chores may be another major portion of your day and for good reason. It takes an enormous amount of time to maintain a home and, possibly, a yard, not to mention performing the role of schedule manager for the family. If these duties are preventing you from spending time on your priorities then this is an area to scrutinize.

If you have any inspirations for ideas that would better align you with your priorities, then go back and jot them next to one of your circle charts. We'll do more work on this throughout the book and you will gain new insights and ideas that will further shape your plan for spending your time.

Now that you have completed the circle chart exercises and thought about your priorities, it's time to move on to your co-efficient for chaos.

Your Coefficient for Chaos

What is your personal tolerance for chaos? Maybe you only feel really alive and energized if you are doing several things at once and have a lot going on around you. In other words, you love the thrill of the rapids and will seek them out whenever possible! Maybe you are someone who prefers to work on one project at a time, and keep your surroundings calm and orderly. You really enjoy the pools of calm water and will paddle your way out of the rapids as quickly as possible. Neither of these styles is good or bad or right or wrong. They just *are*. Different people simply have different levels of tolerance for all of life's frenetic activity. We call this level of tolerance your "coefficient for chaos" or CFC.

Your personal coefficient for chaos is probably a result of your genetic makeup and the environment in which you grew up. Many people cite their childhood as the factor that shaped their tolerance for chaos and noise. The interesting thing is that the same environment seems to affect different people in a variety of ways. Some people will say that since they grew up in a large and noisy family, they are very used to and comfortable with chaos. Others who came from a similar environment have chosen to have no children, or only one, and are very clear that a noisy chaotic environment is not what they want.

Exercise 3 will help you to plan your ideal course down the river by learning about your coefficient for chaos. Once you know your threshold of chaos, you can make choices and plan your time in a way that best fits your style.

EXERCISE 3
DETERMINING YOUR COEFFICIENT FOR CHAOS

In the quiz below, simply circle your answer to each question. Typically, your first reaction is the best indication of your personal tolerances. Try not to overthink your responses as you may end up with an unrealistic picture.

Also, remember that your answers today represent a snapshot in time. You may answer the questions differently on another day or in a different phase of your life. Nevertheless, today's answers will provide you with some valuable insight.

1. When you get time to yourself, do you tend to:

   a) call a friend and chat

   b) retreat into solitude

   c) a little of each

2. When the phone rings, do you often:

   a) hurry to answer by the second or third ring

   b) let the machine or voicemail get it

   c) depends on what you are doing

3. To relax, do you prefer:

   a) going out for a walk or being with friends

   b) lying on the couch or reading a book

   c) depends on your mood that day

4. When you are in a crowd:

   a) you find the people around you fun and energizing

   b) plan to leave as soon as possible

   c) may stay if it is an enjoyable event

5. When you turn on some music do you:

   a) play it loud and often have other things going on

b) play it as background music and prefer it soft

c) depends on your mood

6. Do you:

   a) enjoy the freedom of being spontaneous

   b) feel best when you have a plan for your day and follow it

   c) like some of each

7. Are you usually:

   a) late for appointments

   b) early

   c) right on time

8. Do you prefer having:

   a) several projects going at once

   b) one project going at a time

   c) a couple projects going at once

9. When you sit down at home to watch a movie, do you:

   a) have to be doing several other things at the same time

   b) sit and only watch the movie

   c) sometimes also do another task

Scoring Your Quiz

For each "a" that you circled, give yourself 3 points.

For each "b" you circled, give yourself 1 point.

For each "c" that you circled, give yourself 2 points.

- If your total was 21–27, you are a high CFC.
- If your total was 15–21, you are a mid-range CFC.
- If your total was 9–14, you are a low CFC.

When you total your scores at the end of the quiz, you'll determine your coefficient for chaos. Keep in mind that these labels are not meant to pigeonhole you. Your current environment and stress level can affect your score on a particular day. Also, bear in mind that the demarcations are not hard and fast as your CFC falls within a continuum. If your score is near the cutoff point for a particular CFC, you may exhibit tendencies for two CFC types. The CFC score is just meant to give you insight into your preferences and provide you with valuable information when making work/life choices.

The high CFC style

If you scored as having a high CFC, you undoubtedly have a high need for busyness and excitement. You like to have several projects going at once and enjoy the rush of deadlines and commitments. "Everything in moderation" is *not* your mantra. In fact, if there is not enough chaos, then you will create your own!

Cathy has five children, works at a full-time job, attends school at night, and has a very high CFC. She says, "I have a high tolerance for chaos because I have a low tolerance for boredom!" There definitely is an inverse relationship between a person's tolerance for boredom and his or her tolerance for chaos.

However, one danger of being a high CFC is that you may also have an overinflated view of what you can handle and are therefore more at risk to crash and burn. You are typically so afraid you are going to miss something that you often don't hear your inner voice when it is telling you to pull back. It's all busy, fast-paced fun until it becomes absolutely draining and overwhelming to the point of sheer exhaustion. High CFCs typically don't pay attention to their inner voice until they have physical or behavioral manifestations. As a high CFC, you want to harness the energy of your style and use it to your advantage. But you also want to learn to pay attention to the signs that you are approaching the edge of your tolerance.

The mid-range CFC style

If this is you, your mantra is "all things in moderation," including chaos and excitement. You multitask well and can handle a fairly high level of chaos for short periods of time, but prefer moderate levels on an ongoing basis. You may be able to handle heavy chaos in one area of your life as long as you have order and calm in the others.

Carolyn is a classic example of a mid-range CFC. Working from her home, she likes the exhilaration of having multiple projects and enjoys hustling to meet deadlines. But she also is very aware of her need for pockets of time during the day where she can restore order to her desk and home and take a break from her to-do list. In fact for her, updating her to-do list is a form of taking a deep breath — as is cleaning up the kitchen countertops.

This way of operating now feels completely natural to Carolyn. But when she first took the CFC quiz, she was surprised because she had thought she would score as a high CFC. She realized that she had operated as a high CFC in her corporate jobs, but it was hard to get the pools of calm water she craved. Although she could operate as a high CFC, the mid-range is her natural preference.

Many mid-range CFCs tell us that if they get their "excitement quotient" met in one area of their lives, like work, they will purposely shift into a low CFC mode in another area, like home. We have also found in our interviews, that some mid-range CFCs were actually low CFCs who had moved their CFC along the continuum because of the fast pace and current norms of our society. They realize that in order to feel successful in this environment, they need to deal with a certain amount of chaos. They do what they need to, but may not necessarily like it.

Whether you are a true mid-range CFC or have moved your tolerance to this level, pay attention to your mood and energy level when planning your day. You may feel like working without interruption and laying the groundwork for upcoming tasks. Or if you are in a high CFC mood, tackle lots of projects and go full steam ahead. For day-to-day planning, structure your time with alternative periods of high intensity and low intensity. This way you will create the pools of calm water you need so that you can handle, and enjoy, your time in the rapids.

The low CFC style

If you are a low CFC, you may have a purposeful and methodical approach to your work and your life in general. You aren't crazy about surprises and feel most energized when your day is planned without overlapping commitments. You enjoy focusing on one task at a time and get a great deal of satisfaction out of a job well done. At home, you prefer a serene environment although it may be a challenge to get your family members to respect your wishes.

It's possible that you are also somewhat introverted. By definition, extroverts get energy from other people around them. Introverts get energy from within, so the only way that they can recharge their battery, so to speak, is by having the time and space to go within themselves.

Ken is a therapist in private practice and he is married with one child. He is very deliberate about allowing enough time between clients to complete his notes and shift gears before seeing his next client. He says that others in his field are able to get more done, but he needs to structure his life this way in order to maintain the quality of work and parenting that he requires of himself.

Ken may be mistaken that others in his field get more done. By scheduling his activities to take full advantage of his CFC style and by focusing intently on each client, he avoids mistakes and rework. Chances are Ken rarely, if ever, spends 40 minutes searching for a misplaced file! His style is just not the one currently reinforced by our popular culture.

Another plus of the low CFC style is that you are more likely to be in tune with your innate boundaries, even if it isn't on a cognitive level. You sense in both mind and body when you are getting too close to your threshold of chaos. Unlike the "more is better" high CFC type, you do not have an overinflated sense of what you can accomplish in a day, month, or year. In fact, you may not give yourself enough credit in this area. Don't sell yourself short just because your style is not the one celebrated in our frenzied society.

Is Your Chaos Working for You or Against You?

Like stress, chaos is a double-edged sword. It can be quite positive at times and be a necessary part of your current priorities. But it can also be just as destructive. How do you know if your current chaos is too much?

One key way is to assess whether, despite all the mayhem, you feel like you are making an impact on something, or someone, that you care deeply about. For example, Cathy says, "I need to feel like all my children are taken care of and are happy. It's important that I am doing something positive and that makes a difference in order to feel like all the chaos is worth it!"

Most people need to feel that what they are doing makes a difference in some way. How individuals define "making a difference" varies vastly. For some people, it may mean doing something that is socially conscious and affects the greater good. For others, it may mean doing a job in which they feel they are a "player" and can impact the business. Still others need to always feel they are learning something. Ask yourself if your priorities are being addressed. Are you clear on what those priorities are? If not, go back to the earlier section on identifying your priorities.

In addition to being able to name the positive force that is keeping you going, it's normal to want to feel like you are making strides in the right direction. Liz is a stay-at-home mom with two children. Her CFC is in the mid to low range. She puts a lot of energy into conscious parenting and child-centered activities. She says that she can handle a fair amount of chaos, but "I need to feel like I'm making progress, meeting some goals." Like Liz, most people need to feel some sense of forward movement.

Only you can really know if your chaos is supporting or sabotaging your priorities. We all have to put up with certain tasks, situations, and struggles to live the life we have chosen. Having children is a perfect example. If our priority is to raise healthy and well-adjusted children, we accept that sick days, cranky days, and sibling rivalry are part of the package. The trick is knowing whether you have orchestrated the right environment and approach for your coefficient for chaos. Before you can do that, let's assess one more aspect of your current chaos.

Tipping Out of the Raft

You know the feeling: You start your week with a fine-tuned plan without much margin for error, and it all works great until something unexpected happens. As soon as a child-care plan blows up, the dog gets sick, or an aging parent needs help, the whole world is upside down and it feels as though it will take a miracle to right yourself. Even seemingly minor events such as heavy traffic or an unexpected telephone call can tip you over. If you are always teetering on the edge of overwhelmed, then when something unexpected happens you simply don't have any reserve brain space, energy, and of course, time, to handle it without great physical and emotional stress.

Katherine is involved in a start-up software company with her husband. She has two young children and was making everything work reasonably well despite a horrendous schedule until her babysitter quit unexpectedly and her children got ringworm. "I felt as though my whole world had caved in," she recalled. Katherine is a low CFC. She had been operating past her threshold for chaos for quite a long time, but, given the progression of events, she was making it work pretty well and really did not want to pull back — until it was too late and she was tipped out of the raft. Now she is slowly recovering, but the toll it has taken is visible when she speaks. She still believes in what she is doing but she is tired, both physically and emotionally, and a little bit of the spark that was there when she first described her new venture in the software company has been temporarily dimmed.

Not only do we schedule ourselves to the maximum, like Katherine, and fail to leave room for problems and delays, but many of us have also fallen prey to the contemporary social pressure that busyness equals importance and status. We book an exhausting amount into every day, relying on adrenaline and drive (and sometimes caffeine) to get it all done. Where is the point where busyness tips over to insanely out of control and unhealthy? That point is different for everyone. But a key question to ask is, "How often am I tipping out of the raft?" Because it takes a great deal of energy to right yourself while in the rapids, this is an area to really scrutinize. Would you rate yourself as a frequently tipped out of the raft? (At least once a day.) Occasionally tipped out of the raft? (Once or twice a week.) Or are you rarely tipped out of the raft? (Once or twice a month.)

If you are frequently soaked to the bone with cold water and have to go through the process of righting your raft, bailing out the excess water, and then drying your clothes and gear, then it's time to learn how to recognize the warning signs that you are about to capsize.

Recognizing the Warning Signs before Capsizing

It's very easy to get caught up in the activity of the moment, and not notice that you are close to capsizing. Another way to think of this is learning to read the signals that you are reaching the edge of your tolerance for chaos. Again, your coefficient for chaos can play a role. High CFC people will take longer to reach their tolerance level than low CFCs, but everyone has limits and signals. High CFCs have to be a little more careful in this area because they tend to ignore the signals and push on because of the sheer excitement of what they are doing.

People have a variety of signals that let them know they are reaching the edge of their tolerance. Scott, a manager at a high-tech company and father to two elementary-aged children says, "I know I'm reaching my threshold when I start losing track of what needs to be done. Whether it's work related or personal, I need to stop and try and get organized again. I will sit down and reprioritize my task list."

For other people, the signs can be physical. Mark is an attorney at a telecommunications company with two small boys at home and says one of his signals is a muscle pain in his back. Mark also has nonphysical signs. "I get in a total reactive mode and am not doing anything proactive. I find myself flitting around putting out lots of little fires but not really completing anything." This feeling of being like a hamster on a wheel, running but not actually accomplishing much, is a common response to feeling overwhelmed.

In place of feeling physical symptoms or focusing on tasks, some people show their frustration in their interactions with others. Instead of calmly answering a question they may respond abruptly or with sarcasm. Many of the people we interviewed cited "being snippy" as one of their most common reactions to surpassing their tolerance for chaos.

What are your personal signs that you are about to tip out of the raft? You may have one signal in particular or feel it on many different levels. If you are not clear what your signals are, then make an effort to observe them next time you start to get overwhelmed. Recognizing these warning signs can be a huge help because next time you notice them you can stop what you are doing and regroup. Take a five-minute break and ask yourself, "What can I do to stabilize my raft?" Try to calm yourself and step back from the situation for a few minutes. This may mean getting up from your desk and taking a walk, going to the restroom, breathing, or whatever else works for you. By shifting your focus, the next steps will seem more obvious and you can congratulate yourself on avoiding being capsized.

In this chapter, you have discovered where your time goes, where you would like it to go, and your coefficient for chaos. Understanding your own personal preferences and tolerances, all part of *individual,* is the critical beginning for moving along the continuum toward achieving Comfortable Chaos. In the next chapter, we shift our attention to the pressures and challenges of today's world and learn some tools that fall under the second I, *imperfect.*

f o m C
f o r t
a l b e
C a h
a o
s

Chapter **3**

Taking Charge in a High-Speed "Suck You Dry" World

Carolyn will never forget the time she was working in a very challenging job and learned the hard way that more work does not equal more appreciation. She was in a unique job called skill team support manager — a human resources position where she was required to coordinate staffing issues with managers from various programs by bringing them together in weekly or biweekly meetings. The problem with this job was that every manager considered himself or herself to be a customer and a critic. As you can imagine, it was nearly impossible to satisfy all of them since they represented very different programs and agendas.

At one of the weekly meetings, a discussion occurred about the need for a selection process and succession plan for the second-level managers. This topic had come up in the past but Carolyn had always held it off since the group was barely able to get through the processes for first-level managers. Carolyn had also worked on executive succession planning and found it frustrating due to personality challenges and lack of control.

This particular Friday she relented and did what all good skill team support people did — offered to draft a process. "We'll need that right away so that we will be prepared for upcoming promotions," came a familiar and annoying voice from the back of the room. "I'll call a special meeting to review it next week," Carolyn committed. This was late afternoon on a Friday, and she was swamped with other work and priorities so she resigned herself to working on the weekend.

She researched and she drafted and she fine-tuned an elaborate process. She worked on other projects as well and ended up having to come in on Sunday to finish the second-level management plan. The draft process was finally sent to the skill team members and a meeting scheduled for Monday afternoon. Leaving the office Sunday afternoon, Carolyn felt tired but had some satisfaction in having completed an unpleasant task.

On Monday morning she arrived at her tidied desk and diminished to-do pile but didn't feel energized for the week. Instead, she felt cheated of her weekend and sick of the four walls that surrounded her. Oh well, she told herself, at least the skill team members will be grateful.

At the meeting that afternoon, Carolyn expected a relatively uneventful review of the process with some minor revisions. She was totally shocked and instantly defensive when the meeting took a different turn. One manager commented that he thought the process was more detailed and bureaucratic than needed. Another added that he really didn't see the need for a process at this time — there were other priorities. And other managers failed to even show up for the meeting after insisting it had to be scheduled right away!

As the meeting deteriorated and Carolyn's anger grew, she managed to remain mostly professional, although her demeanor was much more abrupt than usual. She ended the meeting, walked back to her office, and threw all of her materials on her desk. Without even thinking, she grabbed her purse and headed for the car. By this point she was outraged and on the verge of tears. She left without telling anyone and once in the car, started cursing and crying and ended up driving home.

Looking back, Carolyn knows that her extreme reaction was directly related to her physical and emotional condition when she entered that meeting. She was tired, but more significantly, she was mentally and emotionally depleted. She vowed to never over-sacrifice again.

Controlling the Corporate Beast

You are about to be introduced to a metaphor we will use throughout this chapter. It may appear that we are picking on companies by using the terms "corporate" and "beast" together. We chose the word "corporate" because we view corporations, and many other organizations, as very powerful forces in our country, our economy, and our personal lives. Whether you work for a corporation or are a stay-at-home parent, the analogy works equally well because it is a way to put a name to that economic and social force that drives so much of how we spend our time. So think of the "corporate" in "corporate beast" as a powerful force that sometimes pushes against your efforts for a sane and meaningful life. Sometimes it takes a gritty metaphor to help drive home a point.

For those of you working in a traditional employer-employee relationship, think of your company as a wild and consuming animal. If you're the visual type, choose a particularly ferocious animal and imagine it with your corporate logo on its chest. It's a rather primitive analogy but bear with us (no pun intended). The beast's constant hunger is fed by the time and work of employees and its appetite is never satiated. The more it consumes, the more it desires. And the beast is not picky about the quality of its meal. It doesn't matter if you slaved and produced a quality product or were asked to stay late for meaningless busy-work. The beast likes gorging on steak as much as junk food. The beast also quickly forgets you when you are gone — it simply seeks its next victim.

If you are a stay-at-home parent or are self-employed, you will need to envision your corporate beast a little differently. The corporate beast of the stay-at-home parent is the media-driven image of the super parent who maintains a spotless and inviting home while raising incredible children and serving as a leader in their schools and the community. This corporate beast can seem to come at you from all angles. It could be those telephone calls you receive asking for your volunteer time. Or it could be your own high standards for everything from housekeeping to Halloween costumes. Just when you think you have mastered some aspect of the stay-at-home role, the beast tempts you with a new expectation and raises the bar.

For the self-employed person working from home or an office, the corporate beast is the pressure to succeed and grow. Even if you started your company as a means to better balance work and family, the endless possibilities of the marketplace beckon. There are the professional associations that want more than your membership — they want you to chair a committee. And there are the vendors and suppliers that urge you to use their marketing, web, or computing services with the subtle suggestion that what you have isn't good enough. The American dream itself can even be a companion of the corporate beast.

Whatever your situation, know that you can't tame the beast. You can only control how much it takes from you. If you are not constantly on alert, you will find the beast sucking your energy, your time, and, in the end, your life. Naturally you will need some defense strategies: the Comfortable Chaos warrior's version of a sword and a shield. You must have a plan for those times when you are presented with some new task that will give more of you to the beast and leave less of you for yourself and family. You also need strategies that will help you put up barriers and defenses against the beast. We'll cover this a little later in the chapter but first we need to get over a common stumbling block: fear of the economy.

Worrying about the Beast, Not the Economy

In our society, there is an incredible focus on the state of the economy. We are collectively addicted to checking the fluctuations of the stock market, the business section of the newspaper, and the plumpness of our portfolios. It's not wrong to care, but it is a mistake to completely relinquish the quality of your life to the fate of the economy.

The fact is that the beast thrives in a boom economy as well as in a bust economy. Think back to the boom years of 1999 and 2000 when the dot.com phenomenon was at its peak. The corporate beast was ravenously hungry during this time. People were working up to 100 hours per week in the hopes of riding a star and striking it rich in stock options. They completely sacrificed their personal lives and practically lived in their offices. Companies responded with onsite dry-cleaning, meals, and concierge services, and were touted for making their employees' lives easier.

Ha! Instead, most people gave thousands of hours to the beast and have nothing to show for it. Only a small percentage got rich and converted their paper money into hard assets before the economy started to slow and then nose-dived. Many others were victims of mergers and "re-orgs" that eliminated their jobs despite their hard work and dedication. And let's not forget the stay-at-home spouses who essentially ran the household and raised their children single handedly!

Now flip the coin and consider the typical situation during a recession — employees get nervous about the potential of lay-offs. Rightfully so, since the corporate world has become a slave to quarterly earning reports and quickly dumps people as a way to boost its stock value. Sadly, few companies recognize that real growth occurs through the long-term development of its people.

But for now, it's important to avoid the trap of blaming the economy. The tendency to overwork and give too much of your life to a corporation exists whether we are in an upward or downward economic trend.

It's also time to let go of the outdated notion that if you look after the company, it will look after you. We have slowly moved down the continuum, from our parents' era where the company took care of its people, to today's world where there are no guaranteed rewards for hard work. You are much better served by viewing yourself as "me incorporated." Whether you work for a company, run your own business, or run the family, it's only smart to package your skills and abilities effectively and use them to create the life you want to live. This doesn't mean we suggest a pure "look out for number one" attitude. Instead, we advocate having a realistic picture of your needs and the needs of the employers and family members in your life, and find a way to work with integrity to benefit all parties.

Seven Keys to Controlling the Beast

Remember how we said that the second I in Comfortable Chaos is *imperfect*? The essence of controlling the corporate beast lies in acknowledging that no matter how much you do or give, it will never be enough. You will never attain perfection and the beast will always ask for more. The remainder of this chapter outlines seven strategies to help you shift your mindset away from the "I have to do it all" mode to a more objective approach.

Give up Perfectionism

Succumbing to the pressure of the corporate beast is what creates perfectionism and it's not all it's cracked up to be. Contrary to popular opinion, perfectionism is different than striving for excellence. In fact, true perfectionism is often the enemy of excellence.

Take the example of Teri, who is working on her bachelor's degree. She is a pure perfectionist when it comes to her standards for herself and her grades. She takes the required classes for her major and maintains nearly a 4.0 grade point average and a place on the dean's list every semester. When the opportunity arises to take a couple of advanced classes that are not required, she chooses not to take them for fear that she may not do as well in them and bring down her grade point average.

She is not alone in this tendency. Many perfectionists will shy away from risks and consequently do not grow and learn to become the best person they can be. Fear of achieving something less than perfection can inhibit and paralyze. It can also prevent you from having fun — a definite element of Comfortable Chaos! Many people won't even try new sports or recreational activities that could enrich their lives because they are afraid that, at least initially, they won't be very good at them. Their mantra is, "If I can't do it well, I won't even try."

Perfectionism can also drive you crazy and cause you to end up feeling perpetually stressed and angry. You may actually perseverate on certain things while not allowing time to attend to other key priorities. The net effect prevents us from achieving excellence.

Do any of these scenarios sound familiar? You are working on a huge and high-visibility project at work. You stress and worry over it far beyond that point at which you could have said to yourself, "I did my best, I need to move on to other things now." You continue working and reworking the numbers and your presentation. In the meantime you have missed deadlines and dropped the ball on several less important projects. The result is that the coworkers involved in the other projects begin to view you as a person who is not always on top of everything and not always reliable. In the end, the high-visibility project is received moderately well, but all the extended work did not pay off. Was it really worth damaging your relationships for the sake of an only marginally improved presentation?

This same phenomenon can occur in family and parenting choices. Let's say your daughter's class is having a party at school. You've been asked to bring in some treats on Friday. You know that Thursday is going to be a busy evening, but instead of giving a little on your standard of being the "perfect cookie Mom" and purchasing a treat, you stay up way too late baking these incredibly complex, cute little cookies. The next day, your daughter takes them to school and you never hear a word of thanks or praise from the teacher or any of the other parents involved. You fulfilled your self-perpetuated "perfect cookie Mom" image but got very little gratification. Instead, you are tired and cranky the entire next day, which prevents you from being as efficient as you would like at work and causes you to snap at your children. Is this really excellence?

Remember that perfectionism is not a badge of honor — it only feeds the corporate beast. Let go of the perfectionist approach and you will take back a good chunk of your life.

Remember Your Priorities

"You can say 'no' and smile only when there is a bigger 'yes' burning within you." This wonderful quote was spotted on a desk calendar and the author is unknown. The message is so right on — you'll never know when to say "no" unless you have clearly identified your personal "yesses."

By identifying your priorities in Chapter 2, you have made them conscious and therefore more powerful. To make sure they stay fresh in your mind, consider displaying them in places where you need a reminder before taking on new commitments. For example, jot them in your calendar or daily planner or enter them in your personal digital assistant (PDA). Maybe you will just need a key word like "priorities" to serve as your cue.

Don't feel bad if you find you constantly have to return to focusing on or updating your priorities. Donna, who is a school psychologist and has extensive training on identifying values and priorities, recently found herself out of sorts. She was running at full speed and realized that her commitments had become overwhelming. So she made time to sit down and review her priorities. "I feel so much better," she later said. "I knew I wasn't spending my time where my priorities lie, but until I really took the time to compare my commitments to my priorities, I was unable to get off the hamster wheel." Donna is still performing her job duties well, but she is now making the time to eat more healthily and exercise.

To prevent yourself from reaching a crisis like Donna, don't answer immediately when you are asked or tempted to take on a new project or opportunity. Instead, ask yourself, "Does this time commitment support or detract from my priorities?" This is the essence of many time management programs but we all need to be reminded of this simple step. It's too easy to get caught up in the excitement of something new or the seduction of helping out and being a team player. These are all definite attractions but unless they fit with your current priorities, you may later feel resentment about the task and frustration about not having the time for what really matters to you.

Know Your Worth

If you know your strengths, skills, and priorities, it's much easier to play give and take with the beast. Of course, "tooting your own horn" is not something that comes naturally for most people, especially for many women who were taught to downplay their strengths and talents. But it's well worth it to overcome the good girl syndrome. This is critical in all of your roles as a parent, spouse, employee, and employer — because only when you know your value are you able to leverage your reputation to get more of what you need.

For example, if you work outside the home, you have probably negotiated something at one time or another — whether it was for a modification to your work assignment or for the opportunity to go to a professional conference. Some of these negotiations may have felt relatively easy but your success was tied to your past behaviors and results more than you probably realized. Your ability to get things done is your negotiating strength. Sometimes you don't even have to play this card, but other times you may need to tie your past success to a new request. Be prepared with an inventory of your skills and accomplishments. Update your résumé just for the practice of putting it on paper. Having a mental picture of your résumé will allow you to draw on key points during your negotiation.

If you are a stay-at-home parent, you might be thinking that this doesn't apply. But if you reflect on all the roles you play at home and what it would cost if someone had to pay for all the services you provide, your worth suddenly has a dollar value. Just knowing this can boost your self-esteem and will carry over to how you perform your job at home. You can also inventory your skills just like you would on a professional résumé. As a stay-at-home parent it is easy to lose your sense of equality in the partnership when you are not the one bringing home the paycheck. Help yourself, and your partner, to see your contributions to the family by listing them on paper. You can use this as a tool in a discussion with your partner to jointly decide on which tasks are not critical and are not deserving of your time.

Knowing your worth is an essential part of controlling the beast. By feeling confident about your strengths, you can march ahead with confidence and pride.

Operate in Your "Want and Can" Area

If perfectionism had a cousin, it would be control. You probably know exactly what we're talking about since we all have at least some desire to control things. But what we choose to control has a huge impact on our quality of life.

If your days are jammed packed with activities and commitments, how do you describe your life? Do you say "my life is full, busy, and happy," or do you say, "I'm always so stressed, busy, and tired." On the one hand, if you are choosing the right things to control, you are probably enjoying the "life is full and happy" feeling. On the other hand, if you have a high need to control and expend a lot of energy regulating everything all the time, you will be worn out and frustrated.

So how do you know if you are controlling the right things? Part of the answer lies in determining your "want and can" area. Take a look at Figure 1.

FIGURE 1
DETERMINING YOUR "WANT AND CAN" AREA

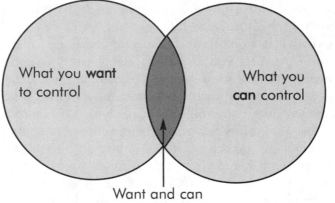

What you **want** to control

What you **can** control

Want and can

The circle on the left represents everything you *want or believe you need* to control in order to have a happy and fulfilling life. The possibilities are numerous. Wouldn't it be great to control everything from your schedule to your manager to your children's behavior? The circle on the right represents what you actually *can* control. This is the reality circle. It contains only the things you actually have the ability to control.

The shaded section, where the circles overlap, is ideally where you should be spending your time. These are the things you both want to control and have the ability to control. We call this the "want and can" area or WaC for short. Notice that this is a much smaller area than either of the circles and that's why it can be challenging to stay in the shaded area. It's very easy to get out of WaC! To further illustrate this concept, we will use two examples and then invite you to analyze your own tendencies about control.

First, let's take a look at someone who is operating primarily in the left-hand circle (what you want to control). Mike is a project manager at a software company and also has a wife and three children. He has a high need for control both at work and home. At work he is often frustrated when a change in the software requirements causes him to get off schedule and have to completely redesign the project. He also has a new manager who is eager to merge his department with another one — a plan that Mike disagrees with. Mike has spent lots of time diplomatically countering his boss's proposals. At home, Mike prefers a neat and tidy house, while his wife is much more comfortable with clutter and mess. When he is home he often spends most of his evening picking up the toys and feeling resentful about it.

Mike's situation is depicted in Figure 2.

FIGURE 2
WHAT MIKE WANTS TO CONTROL

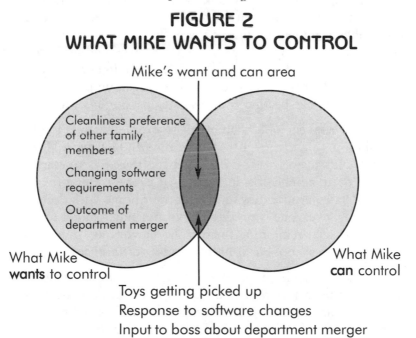

Mike's want and can area

Cleanliness preference of other family members

Changing software requirements

Outcome of department merger

What Mike **wants** to control

What Mike **can** control

Toys getting picked up
Response to software changes
Input to boss about department merger

Mike is spending most of his time in the left-hand circle and only a few things are falling into his shaded area. He could save himself a great deal of frustration if he identified what he can truly control and focused his time in the shaded area where the two circles overlap. He should also decide to let some left-hand circle items go or redefine them so they are in his "want and can" area. For example, Mike could have a discussion with his wife about what areas of the house he feels most strongly about neatness and together they could find a way to keep that minimum standard. Maybe his wife and kids will partially clean up that area before he gets home and Mike can do the finishing touches.

If you suspect you are like Mike, operating primarily in the "want" circle, make a list of all of the things that you feel are vital for you to exert some control over in order to be a happy, healthy, and successful person. As you think of them you could jot them down in the appropriate circle in Exercise 4. If the item is something you want to control, put it in the left-hand circle. If it is something you definitely want to and *can* control, list it in the shaded area.

What does your diagram look like? Take a look at the things that are in your left-hand circle, but not in the overlap area. You may be able to influence some of these things, but not totally control them. If you are operating outside your "want and can" area by trying to finesse the outcomes of things that you don't actually have control over, the results are stress, fatigue, anger, unhappiness, and depression. It is like beating your head against a brick wall.

Now let's take a look at an opposite example. Paula is a freelance photographer who works from home and has twin 11-year-old boys. Her major frustration is getting the boys to start and complete their homework. It seems as if every evening the boys are up too late because they didn't get their homework done earlier and then everyone is tired the next morning. Paula's strategy has been to start reminding them of homework as soon as they get home from school but it hasn't made a difference.

Paula's own style preference is impacting the entire family. She enjoys the rush of a deadline and often stays up late herself to complete her work. Structure and schedules are definitely not her preference. Her situation is depicted in Figure 3.

She is not operating in either circle, but there are some strategies she could try that are in the "can" circle. However, because of her aversion to structure, she hasn't wanted to try them and therefore they remain in her "can" circle where they are ineffective without the desire to act.

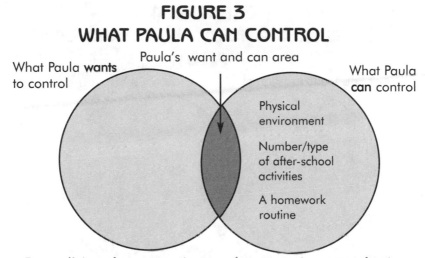

FIGURE 3
WHAT PAULA CAN CONTROL

Paula's want and can area

What Paula **wants** to control

What Paula **can** control

Physical environment

Number/type of after-school activities

A homework routine

By realizing that suggestions such as creating a productive physical environment for studying, increasing time for homework by reducing other activities, and implementing a homework routine would help her reach her goal, Paula may be able to move these suggestions to the "want and can" area. Once she is in the WaC area she will be able to end her homework headaches.

Are there items in your right-hand circle that are not in your "want and can" area? Maybe another priority or your style preference is causing you to not "want" to take some action that will improve a particular problem. This may be perfectly okay as long as you are cognizant of the fact. You can't force yourself to want to do something unless you see the payoff and are willing to alter your behavior. In Paula's case, the homework frustration had gone on for so long that she was willing to adjust her style preference in order to end the battles and get everyone to bed on time. Only you can control what is a "want" for you. But remember the powerful combination of "want and can" if you truly are seeking change. In Exercise 4, give some thought to one of your most difficult challenges and see if you are truly out of "WaC."

By consciously choosing to operate in your WaC area, you are building up another defense against the corporate beast. Your efforts are now concentrated both where you believe they are important and where they can truly make a difference. And you now have energy left over for nurturing your desire for a more satisfying life.

EXERCISE 4
DETERMINING YOUR "WANT AND CAN" AREA

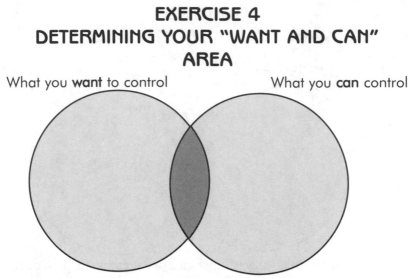

What you **want** to control   What you **can** control

Learn How to Let Some Balls Drop

One of the biggest challenges in achieving Comfortable Chaos and controlling the corporate beast is to let some balls drop on the ground. Yes, we mean let them drop and possibly not ever pick them up again! This is a tough leap in thinking if you are a perfectionist or someone who is trying to manage beyond your "want and can" area. But even if you do not have these tendencies, it can feel like a failure when something you are juggling lands on the ground. Maybe it will help you if you think of the "item on the ground" as a perfectly acceptable solution. When something lands on the ground, take it as a sign that the ball needs some adjustment or possibly a new home. And be sure to contemplate whether some of the balls you are keeping in the air with great difficulty may also belong on the ground. Consider the following three strategies for letting some balls drop.

Eliminate it

You may have a ball that needs to be deflated and put on the shelf. These are the tasks that just plain need to go away. Scrutinize every one of your regular tasks and decide if it really needs doing. For example, do you really need to dust every week or iron certain clothes? At work, is there a report you are doing just because it has always been done? Look for any opportunity to stop doing something or to do it less frequently. Try it for a few weeks and see what happens. Chances are you, and the people you thought would be impacted, do not notice the change or can at least live with the change.

Redefine done

You may need to swap your ball for something smaller and lighter. For example, let's say you have seven or eight voicemail messages. Two of the callers have requested specific information and the rest have asked that you call them back. You get the information needed for the two callers and start returning the calls. Three of the callers you were able to reach and the rest you got their voicemails and left messages. Are you done? For some people the answer is no — they don't feel like their task is complete until they have actually talked with the person. This isn't necessarily wrong, but it's much more freeing to consider the task done for this point in time. Look for other situations where you can redefine "done." Break the task into smaller pieces and revel in "done" for each step of the task.

Redefining done can also mean lowering your standards for certain tasks. For example, instead of only having one definition of a clean bathroom — the one that includes a thorough scrubbing of everything — adopt a "mini clean" definition and every other week do the mini clean. This should be a lower standard of clean that you can finish much faster and still declare "done." It's all in how you define it. And whenever you are getting too obsessive about bathrooms and closets, remember what Ann Richards, the former governor of Texas, said, "I don't want them to put on my tombstone: She kept a very clean house."

Delegate it

When you delegate, instead of dropping the ball, you are tossing it to someone else. There's no need to feel guilty about doing this. If you are delegating to your children, you are helping them become more self-sufficient. If you are delegating at work, you may also be enabling someone to learn new skills.

So how do you know if a task is something you should delegate or do yourself? There are two simple strategies when evaluating your to-do list. The first one is to ask yourself, Which of these things can *only* I do? In other words, you are looking for the tasks that require your unique skills and knowledge, and it would take significant time to train someone else. All other tasks are fair game for delegation.

The second strategy is to look for the items on your list that have been there for two or three days or longer. These are the tasks that linger on your list and are not getting started or completed. Why is this happening? Often there is an underlying reason why you are not able to check them off. It could be that you don't really value the task or you don't like the task. It could also be a signal that you need more information or are unsure how to proceed. Whatever the reason, make these tasks candidates for delegation. Your true energy and passion is not behind them and someone else may be better suited for the job. If you are worried that it is an unpleasant task that no one really wants, see if you can swap it with someone else's undesirable task.

One last thought on delegation: be mindful of the delegate's situation. At work, check to see that the new task won't cause the employee to drop other balls. Help the employee assess his or her responsibilities to see if he or she needs to drop, redefine, or delegate other tasks. At home, make sure your family members have the tools to do the job. Delegation may take an upfront time investment, but it can free up buckets of time down the road.

Create (and Keep) Your Boundaries

Boundaries are our own "lines in the sand" that help us keep other people and things from encroaching on our space. They also help us not to encroach on others. Boundaries are excellent tools for reigning in perfectionism and dealing with an imperfect world. When boundaries are lacking, everything can feel out of control. Having boundaries does *not* mean that you can't occasionally take work home or let the lines between work and home blur a little. You just need to make sure that it is a conscious choice.

How do you know what your boundaries are? As you get to know and listen to yourself, your boundaries often emerge.

Other times, you don't know you have created a boundary until it feels wrong to step over it.

Sheila negotiated a situation with her employer to have flexible hours so that she could be home early enough to pick up her daughter from the bus stop after school. She got to work between 6:00 a.m. and 6:15 a.m. so that she would be able to leave by 2:45 p.m. She isn't a morning person, but felt that getting up early was a worthwhile adjustment so she could be with her daughter after school. She also realized that late meetings or last-minute telephone calls would occasionally prevent her from leaving on time, so she worked out a back-up plan with her neighbor for those days. Things went pretty well for a month or two but then the back-up plan became the norm and her neighbor was picking up her daughter three or four days each week. Sheila started to feel angry and resentful about her early morning start when she wasn't getting the payoff she had envisioned. These feelings made her realize that she had a boundary — she just hadn't nailed it down. She now knew that having her neighbor pick up her daughter three to four days a week was too much and this shed light on where the line should be in order for her not to feel angry and resentful. She decided that her line in the sand was calling upon her neighbor a maximum of one day per week and a new boundary was born.

Sometimes other people help us define our boundaries. Beth remembers an incident that had a whopping impact on how she set her boundaries. She had agreed to meet her sister at a restaurant after work. Beth's last meeting of the day at work was running long and she kept anxiously looking at her watch. A key internal customer was talking endlessly. Although it had been an impromptu meeting late in the day that she did not have to attend, Beth didn't honor her own boundaries and get up and leave. Finally, the meeting ended and she rushed to her car and drove aggressively to the restaurant. By this time, she was about 30 minutes late and her cell phone rang. It was her sister who calmly informed her that she was tired of waiting — her time was valuable too — and she had left the restaurant. Beth was frustrated, embarrassed, and angry with herself for not leaving on time. But she realized her sister wasn't being unreasonable. This incident helped her create a new boundary between work and her personal life.

What makes a boundary beautiful? When it empowers you and improves your quality of life. Whether a need for a boundary is emerging on its own or being triggered by an event with someone else, the six steps for creating beautiful boundaries are the same:

Get out of the passive/victim mentality

Let's say you are finishing up the latest revisions on a major project. Your level of stress and frustration has skyrocketed because it has to be done by tomorrow morning and the constant stream of interruptions is making it impossible to get any work done. With personal plans for the evening, you don't want to be working late. Since this type of scenario happens quite frequently, your frustration is even higher.

It's very easy to say "my time is not my own," or "there is no way I can control my workload." This is a tempting thought pattern but one that needs to be broken if you are going to make changes. Who is in charge of your time and your life? You always have choices even if they are choices you are not willing to make. Shift your thinking from "I can't believe this is happening to me" to "what can I change?" The possibilities will be more likely to emerge once you have let go of the victim mentality.

Diffuse the emotion

While anger, frustration, and hurt can be clues that lead you to establish your boundaries, you need to diffuse them so you can plan an effective boundary and implement it well. You have probably run into situations where others have let their emotions interfere with managing their boundaries. The classic example is a sales clerk who tells you with an attitude, "I can't help you right now because I am off in five minutes." It's not the schedule we object to, but the way the sales clerk projected her emotion about her boundary. So before you define and implement your boundary, talk to someone about your feelings, role-play with a friend or partner, or write in a journal.

Follow the pain to the problem

Before you can define a boundary, you have to clearly understand the problem. In the case of the heavy workload that is bleeding into your personal time, you feel like you don't have control over anything and it impacts your satisfaction with your work. This feeling of frustration and lack of control are the pain, and the pain means there is a problem. Writing down the problem is a great way to make sure you have clearly identified the true issue. Perhaps the real issue is how you schedule your day with meetings right up until the end of the day with no time for wrap up. So, one idea would be to try not to book any meetings after 4:00 p.m. unless they meet certain criteria.

Decide on a "trial boundary"

In the case of the frustrating workload, a trial boundary might be to stay late only one day a week. To do this, you will need to define the criteria that would cause you to stay late. Is it a certain project or assignment that is critical to your boss? You will need to strategize on how you will be selective and what will happen with the work you aren't going to stay late to finish. Naturally, this takes some planning and may include your overall work priorities and responsibilities. You may have to negotiate with your boss or others but remember that the frustration that got you to this point isn't healthy for your company either.

Create a boundary support system

Recruit a friend or coworker to be your sounding board and support system when you are implementing a new boundary. Just like new habits take time to develop, new boundaries will feel awkward at first. You may even feel guilty about implementing them, but remember that you are worth it. If it is a reasonable boundary and it is implemented well, it will be a win-win for you and your employer. In most cases, those around you will respect you more for having a boundary.

Implement the "trial boundary" and then evaluate it in 30 days

Successful implementation is the result of all the planning you have done in the previous steps. It also means that you inform others of your boundary with tact and diplomacy. Let's say you work a compressed workweek and someone is trying to set up a meeting with you on your day off. Instead of saying angrily, "That is my day off!" You could say, "I'm not available that day, would the following day work?"

Once you have implemented the boundary, don't consider the process complete. Jot notes in your calendar to indicate which days you stuck to the boundary and which days you didn't. Reflect back on the times when you couldn't stay with the boundary. Was the boundary too stringent or is there something you are doing to sabotage your success? Debriefing on your own, or better yet, with your boundary support system, will help you to correct any problems.

Although many of the examples given for boundaries were work related, these steps work just as well for other aspects of life. Boundaries are also very necessary in family life and volunteer roles.

Know How to Get Results

Remember that the beast feasts on your time and efforts. So the longer you take to do a task and the more exhausted you become, the more the beast wants to include you in its dining experience. Don't buy into the belief that being frazzled is a status symbol!

Instead, you need to work quickly and efficiently. Do a good job and do it in a way that is enjoyable and satisfying to you. In some cases this may mean working very hard and giving considerable effort. That's okay when you see the payoff. The payoff can be knowing that the work helps others, knowing that you have achieved a significant accomplishment, or knowing that it was important to your family or the organization. We're not saying that all tasks must be self-serving — but you should be able to see and feel some benefit. Look for a win-win situation. Otherwise you just fed the beast for no reason.

You have now learned the seven keys for controlling the corporate beast. Use them to keep the insane, fast-paced world from taking over your priorities and your life. The next step on the journey to Comfortable Chaos is to learn about the third I, *inter-related*.

Chapter 4

The View from the Middle

You have undoubtedly heard the expression "the view from the top." What picture does this create in your mind? It may conjure up a vision of someone at the top of the career ladder, the mountain, or the world. Looking up, it can sure seem like a long and endless journey. It can also appear linear — meaning that everything is one-dimensional, simple, and sequential.

The Comfortable Chaos approach is to view life from the middle, rather than the top. When you view life from the middle it doesn't imply a final destination. Instead, it implies a well-rounded image with all the facets of your life surrounding you. One mental picture that came up at one of our focus groups was of a Zen-like woman (but not too thin) who was juggling lots of things and some of them were on the ground. She is okay with that, as we talked about in the last chapter when dishing perfectionism, but she is also rather happily in the center of all the interesting and challenging experiences in her life.

Another circular image is the pie chart of priorities you created in Chapter 2. Think back to the utopian version — the one that expanded the time for the activities that were too small or nonexistent in your "as is" pie chart. One of the reasons your utopia pie chart is so appealing is that it recognizes your life as inter-related and allows you to decide what elements should be included in relation to others. It's the right combination of all your activities and responsibilities that make for a rich and fulfilling life.

In this chapter, we focus on the third I, *inter-related*. The success and health of each piece of your life has a contribution to the whole. Living in Comfortable Chaos means having a big picture view of your life and being able to recognize how all the pieces fit together. In a nutshell, you will learn to redesign your pie chart into an appealing whole and create your own personal Zen-like image. You will also receive several techniques that will help you to easily move between your various roles and responsibilities.

Self-Care Isn't Selfish

One of the biggest challenges for most people is creating or expanding their time for self-care. Self-care means taking care of yourself physically, emotionally, and spiritually. This includes the amount of sleep you get, the quality of your nutrition, your physical activity, and how "well fed" you feel from an emotional and spiritual standpoint. All of these aspects have a direct impact on how you perform and enjoy the other areas of your life. They also play a critical role in your ability to cope and take life as it comes.

In the interviews we conducted for this book, getting enough sleep was the single biggest struggle for women, whether they worked full time or part time or were stay-at-home moms. Chronic sleep deprivation, even if it is only being shorted an hour or two per night, is a huge problem in our country. It affects everything from health and safety to sanity and can permeate a person's entire world. When we sleep well and for a long enough period, our bodies recharge on a physiological level and we produce chemicals that fight disease, depression, and even fat cells!

Sleep isn't the only area where people tend to shortchange themselves. "Personal time" was the number one sacrifice listed for fathers that we interviewed. Pat, a marketing executive with two children said, "The only thing missing in my life right now is free time to do some of the few things I really enjoy. I think this is one of the downsides to having kids later in life. While many of my peers and associates have relatively self-sufficient children in high school or college and can get away to play golf or attend a ball game on week nights or weekends, that luxury is impossible for me with a nine- and five-year-old."

Let's not forget the other two backbones of good health: nutrition and exercise. Because both of these take time, people often turn to fast food or heavily processed food as a way to save time, and skip the exercise entirely. What if in the end, all that time you saved didn't matter because poor nutrition, sleep, and exercise habits have shortened your life? We don't have any easy answers for improving nutrition and exercise other than to suggest that you work on adding one good habit at a time, instead of taking the "all or nothing" approach. The longest journeys begin with one step at a time. We don't know anyone, ourselves included, who feels like they have the ideal eating and exercise habits. But we do know lots of people who have added a little bit of exercise to their lives and recognize that it is better than nothing. High CFCs, in particular, need the physical release of energy and adrenaline. Medium and low CFCs also benefit greatly from exercise but may choose different types of exercise and feel the benefits differently.

All CFC styles can find a way to make at least one positive nutrition change such as drinking more water, replacing their afternoon candy bar with fruit and an energy bar, or cutting out one fast food meal a week. By defining any positive change as success, you can pat yourself on the back for being healthier than you were before.

We also recognize that many of you will find it difficult to identify with some of the traditional "balance" or personal care components that are often depicted in superficial magazine articles or by anyone not in touch with the realities of today's challenges. Vickie, who is a director of occupational services for a health-care cooperative and has three elementary-age children, commented on a mandatory three-day management seminar she attended at work. "When I got there, I was glad to see a component on work/life balance. But all the material was on relationships with spouse, time for hobbies, and time for friends. I found it interesting that those are the values they identified. My reality and values are getting the kids to school, what's for dinner, and do my kids have clean clothes for tomorrow."

Vickie's reality may also be your norm. Maybe you feel you don't have the luxury of adding in some of these activities. You probably don't have time for all of them — but we challenge you to adopt *one* positive habit and then evaluate the impact. Is that new habit really cutting into your ability to do your job, run the home, and look after your family? The answer most likely is no — and you can probably find a creative way to incorporate the new habit so that your employer and/or family doesn't feel the change adversely.

The bottom line is that there is no way you can happily meet all your obligations and look after everyone else if you don't take good care of yourself. Many people, women more so but not exclusively, feel guilty about taking time out for themselves. Living in a state of constant busyness, when they do finally get some time for themselves, they often don't know what to do or how to be!

Why Self-Care Needs a Place on Your To-Do List

If you are not getting enough self-care, consider the following three compelling reasons for taking better care of yourself.

You will get more done

If you are like many people, you say, "I know, I know — I would feel better if I exercised, ate better, and got more sleep." But for whatever reason, that doesn't always seem to be enough to get you moving in the right direction. What if you realized that your productivity would actually increase? Studies have shown that exercise can help improve your decision-making capabilities by up to 70 percent. Realizing this fact can help you overcome that typical feeling that you don't have time to exercise, read a book, or take nap. The fact is — you can't afford not to! Even by slowly adding one of these habits to your daily routine, you will start to notice the difference. If you are still struggling with feeling selfish, then remember that your productivity gains will help your family and your employer.

You will be around longer for your family

Often in our seminars people say that they don't have time to exercise, get enough sleep, or read a book because they are too busy doing things for their family. Well here's a wake-up call — you won't be able to do anything for your family if you drop dead! Regular exercise is proven to reduce your risk of cancer, heart disease, and diabetes. Reducing stress by taking some quiet time to read, meditate, or do some activity you enjoy will also strengthen your immune system and allow your body to better fight off everything from the common cold to more serious, life-threatening conditions. And most of you already know the link between good nutrition and disease prevention so making time to eat a healthy diet should be a goal for both you and your family.

It is important to remember that if your health falls apart, nothing else that is currently so important will really matter. You can't be the parent/spouse/son/daughter/employee/community supporter you want to be if your health is poor or you are six feet under.

You will be modeling life-enhancing behavior for your children

If you have children, you know that they will grow up with many of the same habits you have. It's a sobering thought that we are the most powerful influence in their lives and our actions speak louder than words.

Do you want your children to become adults who do nothing but rush from task to task? If you hope they will be able to sit down with a book to relax, then you need to model that behavior. If you want them to enjoy physical activities then they need to enjoy them with you and see you doing them alone. It's perfectly okay, and demonstrates good planning skills, when you deny them a request for your time because you have scheduled some exercise. That is a parenting success not a failure! Stop feeling guilty when you take time for yourself, and realize that you are teaching your children valuable skills.

Still wondering how it can be done? Here are some other people's creative ways of fitting in self-care:

- "I found I can squeeze in a 30-minute, no sweat workout at lunch. I change into exercise clothes and lift weights at the gym. I do a specific routine that definitely works my muscles but I don't work up a sweat. (I could never do this with a cardio workout). Then I can change back into my work clothes without taking the time to shower and redo my hair and make-up."

- "I take a power walk during my lunch time. Five trips around the block gives me time to zone out while getting some exercise."

- "By arriving 15 minutes early to pick up my son from school, I have time to read my book at least for that small segment every day."

- "After dinner, before starting on the dishes, homework supervision, and a huge list of tasks, I go into my room and shut the door for 20 minutes. Sometimes I read, other times I just putter around and make sure the room is tidied up so I can fully enjoy it when the kids are in bed."

- "My husband and I take turns having 24 hours in a hotel each month. I can't tell you how rejuvenating it is to have 24 hours completely to myself. I read, work out, take a bath, watch movies, and, of course, sleep. I come home totally refreshed and ready to face my responsibilities again."

- "I tape my favorite television shows and then watch them at 9:00 p.m. when my kids are in bed. I find that looking forward to 'my time' helps me get through the frustrating times."

- "I take really good care of myself during the workday. My sister teases me, but every year I buy a new Eddie Bauer lunch box and I use it to pack a great lunch and a bottle of water. I eat throughout the day in my car since my job keeps me on the road."

- "I travel for business a great deal and get my personal time on the airplane. I feel like I get my fill of reading and watching movies."

Now that you have heard a few ideas for fitting in self-care, was there one that triggered an idea for you? In Exercise 5, write down one idea that you will incorporate into your routine, and list when and how you can make the time to do it. If you want to list more than one idea, that is great, but don't try and start more than two new habits at a time. You want to experience success and if you try and make too many changes at once, you are more likely to fail. Choose something that you think you can sustain. Add one or two habits and keep at it for 30 days before attempting another.

EXERCISE 5
MY SELF-CARE HABIT

The self-care habit I will incorporate for 30 days is:

_____

_____

_____

When I will do it:

_____

_____

_____

How I can make time to do it:

_____

_____

_____

Incorporating just one new self-care habit into your routine will have an extraordinary impact on the other areas of your life. This is the inter-related concept in action and as you succeed in one habit, you will most likely be inspired to add more self-care habits.

Using Transitions to Create Pools of Calm Water

You can't live in Comfortable Chaos if you are rushing from activity to activity and experiencing stress in the process. Paying attention to the transitions in your day is another way to become more inter-related or holistic — and it can provide those much-needed pools of calm water we discussed in Chapter 1.

Think about your typical day and the number of transitions you go through. We're not talking about those major life transitions like changing jobs or having a baby. We are referring to all of those little transitions that occur each day, such as going from home to the office and starting your workday, switching between tasks during the day, and the myriad of evening transitions such as volunteer work and parenting responsibilities. These are all "anticipated transitions" since you can pretty much expect them every day as part of your routine. The grand total can be rather overwhelming when you count all the big and small ones!

Handling Anticipated Transitions

The morning is full of transitions, starting with getting yourself out of bed. Then you need to get yourself and your children ready and get everyone motivated to move to the kitchen and eat breakfast. This is followed by the always exciting and frequently frustrating experience of getting socks and shoes on and going out the door with all the necessary equipment for the day. Then everyone transitions again as they start their school, work, or work-from-home day. All this and it's still only morning!

Throughout the day, you will face many more of these anticipated transitions. If you work outside the home you will commute and then transition from your commute to being "on" at the office. You will then go from meeting to meeting, shifting your focus between individual thinking tasks and social or managerial tasks.

If you are a stay-at-home parent, your workday is full of transitions as you look after young children or babies and change hats throughout the day becoming caregiver, chef, financial planner, housecleaner, chauffer, and mediator to name just a few.

The end of the day has its own set of transitions. Each time a family member, you included, arrives home from work or school, a major transition occurs. Some people find it easy to shift gears into the home mode, while others really struggle. Getting ready for dinner is another tough transition time when everyone is tired and hungry. Later, the chores of homework, packing lunches, and getting ready for bed all present transition challenges.

The common thread through all of these transitions is that they can be anticipated and, therefore, you can improve how you handle them. Let's talk about some strategies for turning problem transitions into more enjoyable moments. In fact, this is how you create more pools of calm water in your day. Transitions are an excellent time to slow down and do something enjoyable that will help you move to the next phase of your day. The following are three steps to improving your transitions:

Envision the other side

Think about what you want to feel like when you are on the other side of the transition. For example, Bob enjoys arriving at work feeling like he has a jump-start on the day and will not face any surprises. So when he commutes to work, he checks his voicemail messages and makes a few calls on his cell phone. If he is unsure of his schedule, he also calls his administrative assistant to get an update. Then when he arrives at work he has a greater sense of control.

Ted likes to arrive at work feeling relaxed and refreshed. His strategy for commuting is to listen to books on tape. "Sometimes I sit in the parking lot for a few minutes after I have arrived since I just have to know what happens next!" For Ted, using his commute time to do something he enjoys is a different way of exerting control. Essentially, he manages his commute time and doesn't allow the outside world to intrude. This enables him to feel ready to face the day when he does arrive at work.

Both Bob and Ted arrived at their ideal commuting plan after thinking about what they wanted to feel like when they got to work. You can apply this same strategy to your commute or other transitions. Ask yourself, "What do I need?" Once you determine your goal, there are infinite ways to improve a transition. Some examples are found in step 3.

Be conscious of the "one more thing syndrome"

There is a major pitfall that can sabotage your good intentions for effective transitions. We call it the "one more thing syndrome." Even if your goal is to arrive somewhere on time feeling calm and organized, the "one more thing syndrome" can destroy your good intentions. What tends to happen is you look at the clock and realize you still have five minutes before you absolutely have to go out the door. So you decide you have time for one more thing — perhaps a telephone call or an e-mail, a dishwasher that needs emptying, or a bedroom that needs picking up. The possibilities are endless because there is always at least one more thing to do! Of course that five-minute task rarely goes as quickly as you think it will, or it leads to one other "must do." Then you are running late and realize you don't really have everything you need to go out the door when you thought you had an extra five minutes. The stress-o-meter spikes way up! Not to mention you haven't given yourself any time to focus on the transition at hand.

To improve your transitions, you need to become aware of the "one more thing syndrome" and consciously choose not to squeeze in any last tasks. Instead, gather everything you need to go out the door. Turn off the computer, put the dog outside, go to the bathroom, put on your lipstick — whatever those tasks are that you tend not to think of as part of getting ready. Then if you really do have five more minutes, consider leaving anyway and enjoy not having to hurry. Or, if you really can't stand not using the time to accomplish one of your tasks, bring the task with you and do it once you get to your destination. For example, bring the telephone number for the call you need to make and have the conversation when you are sitting in the parking lot of your destination and are early. Or grab a couple of pieces of mail that you have been meaning to read. This will feel so much better than rushing.

Eliminating the "one more thing syndrome" really does make your transitions become pools of calm water instead of rapids. Consider making the pool of calm water even more enjoyable by taking a mini-enjoyment break. Listen to some music, meditate, stretch (it can still be done while sitting in the car), or read a few pages from the novel you usually only get to at bedtime. This might even feed your self-care goals as well!

Design the improved transition

Now it's time to design your new and improved transition. Think about your toughest transition — the one that is causing you, and possibly other family members, the worst time. Generate some ideas for different ways to move through, and enjoy, this transition. To give you some ideas, we have collected some of the most creative transition plans from our seminar participants for a sampling of tough transition times.

Going out the door in the morning:

- "We have absolutely everything ready the night before. Lunches, backpacks, briefcases, and clothes are laid out. My daughter, who used to change her clothes three times in the morning, is now only allowed to change her mind in the evening — in the morning she has to go with what she laid out the night before."

- "I stopped nagging everyone and now simply announce that the van is leaving in ten minutes and then also give a five-minute warning. It works only because one day I left without my daughter when she wasn't ready. This made an enormous impression and no one has missed the van since that day!"

Transitioning between meetings at work:

- "When I call meetings they are scheduled to be only 50 minutes long, rather than the standard hour. This allows me time to physically get to my next meeting without having to rush and be late. The other meeting attendees seem to appreciate the 50-minute meetings and it helps everyone stay on track."

- "When possible, I try not to schedule back-to-back meetings. That way, I not only have some time to get organized for my next task after the meeting, but it also doesn't throw me completely off schedule if the meeting runs late."

Kids arriving home from school:

- "I have tea time with the kids. As soon as they get home, I get out their play tea set, serve juice or chocolate milk from the teapot and put snacks on the plates. The kids are always excited to have tea. It brings us all back together after a day apart, heads off the 'hungry grumpies,' and gives us a forum to share information about what happened when we were apart. It also signals that we are moving into the next phase of our day together."

- "We immediately head for the couch and just cuddle or read stories. I don't even try and unpack backpacks and remind them to hang up coats. We just drop everything and meet on the couch. After about 20 minutes of physically and mentally reconnecting with me they are ready to have a snack, clean up, and then play."

- "I found that my two children do best when they can immediately start playing with other kids. I schedule play dates for most after school days all year long."

What is your most difficult transition? By improving this challenging time you can dramatically improve the overall quality of your day. Exercise 6 gives you the chance to design a plan.

Handling Unanticipated Transitions

Now that we have looked at how to improve your anticipated transitions, it's time to talk about the ones that hit you out of the blue. You know the kind: You are in the middle of writing a report and are deep in thought when someone arrives at your desk and asks, "Do you have a minute?" Or you are at home trying to get dinner on the table while helping your child with his homework when you hear a loud crash and need to go investigate the cause.

EXERCISE 6
HANDLING YOUR WORST TRANSITION

My worst transition is:

_____

_____

_____

_____

_____

What the improvement will feel like (envisioning the other side):

_____

_____

_____

_____

My strategy for avoiding the "one more thing syndrome":

_____

_____

_____

_____

The improved transition:

_____

_____

_____

Either of these examples, plus the infinite other possibilities, pull you from the task at hand. That feeling of being interrupted can evoke all kinds of emotions. You may feel irritated, angry, annoyed, startled, or even confused. It takes a lot of energy to switch gears and deal with the new situation and often you are not prepared to be a good listener.

Because you can't plan for these types of transitions, the best you can do is develop awareness when they do happen. Instead of thinking to yourself, "I can't believe I am being interrupted again," try saying, "Oh, here comes another transition." The difference is subtle, yet powerful, because by calling it a transition, it feels like less of a personal invasion.

Once you have acknowledged the transition, then you can decide if you need to, or choose to, fully switch gears and focus on the new situation. Not every unanticipated transition must be dealt with right at that moment. In the case of the "Do you have a minute" coworker, you could say, "Actually I am right in the middle of something important. Can I come find you in 20 minutes when I am able to really listen?" Most people will appreciate your willingness to give them your full attention and will wait the 20 minutes. If their situation is critical and they can't wait, then you can rustle up the energy to shift your focus. Put down the report, turn away from your computer screen, and fully engage in the new situation.

In the case of the crash heard from the kitchen, you have no choice but to go investigate, but when you find the cause of the noise, you can then decide whether it can wait or must be dealt with immediately.

We have now covered two ideas for improving the interrelatedness of your life. The first is to add at least one self-care habit, and the second is to tackle your worst transition and turn it into a pool of calm water. Both of these will enhance your personal life, but you will also be setting an example as a Comfortable Chaos pioneer. And the world really needs your example!

Comfortable Chaos: A Noble and Pioneering Effort

Gayle starts her day in the office at 5:30 or 6:00 a.m. She reads and responds to every e-mail, often creating long responses and forwarding the note to the entire department. She takes on any task that needs doing or that she thinks needs doing. She manages four supervisors but isn't comfortable asking them to create new proposals or budgets. Instead, she does a first draft, collects their input, and then completes the final product herself. She attends every meeting she is invited to and then summarizes the meeting in an e-mail to her boss or the department. Her reputation is one of a hard worker and a kind and caring person. However, her staff wishes she would be less of a micromanager and some people find her style extremely irritating.

Her day is filled entirely with work — she snacks on sugary foods, drinks lots of coffee, eats lunch at her desk, and eventually leaves the office around 5:00 p.m. She has had several health scares in recent years and has returned to work from hospitalizations too soon because she felt needed at work.

Meet Gayles's work-style twin who is a stay-at-home mom. Connie is a parent to two kids ages nine and seven. She starts her day a little later than Gayle does — but only because she was up until after midnight making complicated decorations and favors for her daughter's upcoming birthday party. She's up at 7:30 a.m. and showered so she can get her kids off to school. Once back home she starts some laundry and does some cleaning. She spends three hours on two bathrooms — getting in all the corners with bleach and an old toothbrush. Looking at the clock she realizes she only has half an hour before she is due in her son's classroom. She eats a quick lunch of kid's leftover macaroni and cheese and dashes off to school. After her time in the classroom she works in the office making copies for the teacher. The PTA president approaches her and asks if she can help with planning the school's annual field day. She says yes and agrees to make telephone calls to recruit other volunteers. At this point school is over and she takes her children, and two of their friends, home for a play date. Then it's off to gymnastics and baseball with the kids and when she arrives home she is tired and frustrated and has to rely on a frozen dinner or pizza delivery once again. The homework and bedtime routine is handled by her husband and Connie uses this time to make cookies for teacher appreciation week at school. This leaves a mess to clean up at 10:00 p.m. and her husband gives up and goes to bed without her. Connie ends her day by sweeping the kitchen floor and corralling the kids' overflowing art supplies.

Do you know a Gayle or a Connie? Or perhaps you see some of their characteristics in yourself? There are certainly some admirable qualities about Gayle and Connie — they care deeply about their responsibilities. But the question to ask is, at what price? Is this really an enjoyable life? Are their work styles really the best examples for their employees and children?

We vote no. The Gayles in the corporate culture are actually modeling a style that is self-sacrificing and hinders the evolution of the world of work. Her behavior directly impacts her managers and everyone who works in her organization. They assume that to move ahead they need to behave like her. In reality, the Gayle types frequently don't get promoted because they may be viewed as unable to manage the big picture. Her direct reports also might feel pressured into modeling her behavior in order to receive favorable reviews. How do the parents who need to leave on time to pick up their children feel about her work style? Gayle may say she is supportive but her work hours speak louder than her words.

Even if Gayle doesn't have outside demands such as children or aging parents, she is doing herself a disservice. If she were to develop some outside interests and get some moderate exercise, she would probably discover that her productivity would vastly increase.

Gayle, and her team, would also benefit if she learned to delegate. She would have additional time to work on strategic issues, and her managers would increase their skills by starting and completing a project on their own. If she modeled a more balanced approach to work, Gayle would be playing a part in helping to shift the North American culture away from work at all cost.

Connie is also modeling a self-sacrificing style that is preventing her from quality personal time. She feels like she doesn't have time to exercise or go see a movie with a friend. The quality of all of her adult relationships has suffered and her life has become one-dimensional. Her children are of course learning from her actions and the message they are receiving is that children are the center of the universe and that kid-related activities have top priority. They are also not likely to keep up their good physical fitness activities such as baseball and gymnastics because when they are parents, they will be too busy taking their own children to activities!

We can all be role models who help to change this all-consuming work style that is so prevalent in our culture. At the office, if you create boundaries or make an alternative work schedule successful, you are one more example of how people can make a living and have a life at the same time. You prove to customers, coworkers, bosses, and subordinates that you can get the job done and still enjoy other interests. If you are a stay-at-home parent who continues to pursue personal interests and are conscious about managing your parenting and volunteer responsibilities, you are helping the next generation of children see how life can be multifaceted and enjoyable. So be a pioneer and be proud of getting a life!

Not All Pioneers Travel the Same Road

We want to end this chapter with our comments about working versus staying home with children. This continues to be such a point of comparison for parents and there has been much written about the topic.

Some books argue that staying at home when your children are young is the only right choice. Other books cite studies that indicate women are better mothers when they get the emotional and financial benefits of earning a paycheck. We believe that we shouldn't argue in the first place! There are many different choices when it comes to working outside the home, inside the home, or a combination of the two. We all struggle with the same issues — what differs are the solutions we choose. Respecting each other's decisions should be our goal instead of constantly comparing ourselves as a way to validate our choices.

This book also strives to strengthen the options for those who want to work outside of the home and still have a life, by showcasing the use of alternative work arrangements. This is just one of the many roads available and it should be a well-traveled road. When the number of people who are successfully working in part-time jobs, job sharing, or telecommuting increases, the opportunity has been expanded for everyone.

It should also be a well-known road. Today, it is very common to keep your alternative work schedule as secretive as possible. There is an entire underground world of people who are making nontraditional schedules work beautifully, yet feel compelled to act as if their hours fit the old school norm.

We are hopeful that alternative work arrangements will some day be just as common for men as they are for women. Rhona Mahony envisions in her book, *Kidding Ourselves — Breadwinning, Babies, and Bargaining Power* (Basic Books, 1995), a future world in which there are an equal number of stay-at-home dads as stay-at-home moms. We hope she is right, but disagree with her book's premise that the only way to have equal power at work is to give up the many responsibilities most women take on at home. Her vision of the future is that those in the work force, whether they are men or women, will be completely dedicated and not distracted by the responsibilities of home life.

Many of us don't want to give up the responsibilities and the joys of home life — and we shouldn't have to! For those who want to work outside the home there should be options between having all or nothing. For those who want to stay home with children full time, that choice should have just as much status along with the help and resources to make the job easier.

The next chapter addresses the critical issue of choice. Keep in mind what you have learned about *individual, imperfect,* and *inter-related.* You are ready to either revalidate your current choice or decide to make a change.

5

Chapter

Reclaiming, or Changing, Your Choice

Janice and Stacey are talking at the school entrance while waiting for their children to come charging out the door. Janice is secretly envying and feeling intimidated by Stacey's polished business-like appearance and her briefcase filled with interesting and important work. Janice dreams wistfully of elegant business lunches complete with stimulating adult conversation and savory, beautiful food. Stacey appears to have it all — a successful career and the flexibility to pick up her children after school. Janice feels strong pangs of loss and longing and wonders once again if she should start planning to go back to work.

At the same time, Stacey is looking at Janice and wishing she too were dressed in comfortable jeans and a tee shirt. Janice looks so relaxed; she didn't have to rush out of a meeting to get to school because her nanny was sick. Stacey is already dreading the fact that she will have to try and make a couple of calls once she gets home and will probably have to lock herself in the bathroom to get some peace and quiet. Then she will shift into Mommy mode but knows that once the kids are in bed she will need to catch up on some work. She envies Janice's freedom to focus on the kids without distractions and imagines Janice peacefully reading a book in bed when her kids are asleep. Stacey, on the other hand, feels like she is rarely fully present when she is at home because work is occupying such a big space in her brain. She wonders for the third time that week whether she should quit her job and stay home.

How ironic is that? Both women feel envious of the other's lifestyle. These feelings are huge warning signs that neither is entirely at peace with their current choice.

It could be that Janice and Stacey need to adjust elements of their current life without drastically altering their work/life choice. Janice could add something to her stay-at-home life to provide what is missing, and Stacey could subtract something or change her approach so that she can be more present when she is at home. They also need to explore their feelings of envy to determine if they signify that a radical change is needed.

So how do you know what to make of your envy? A little envy is a completely normal human emotion, but if you are like Janice or Stacey who frequently question their choices and only seem to see the glamorous side of other people's lives, then take this envy as a wake-up call that you need to either revalidate or change your choice. This chapter will help you to decode your envy and use other exercises to decide on your work/life style. You may easily decide to revalidate your lifestyle choice or to make a change. Or you may find that an obvious decision does not emerge right away. There is no right or wrong way of getting to a decision. We have three exercises to help you decide what's right for you.

Determining What's Working and What Isn't

Exercise 7 is a simple list-making exercise that will help you see what is working about your current lifestyle choice, and what's not working. Let's start with an example. Jennifer is a self-employed financial planner with a very successful practice. She struggles with having enough personal time to exercise and pursue other passions, while still maintaining quality time with her husband and two children. It has been her stated goal for a long time to take Fridays off. Here is her "what's working/what's not working" chart:

What *is* working	What is *not* working
The business is well established	Hard to say no due to service-oriented nature of business
Love the work	Able to accomplish Fridays off only 50 percent of the time
Blocking out time for specific work and leaving room for the important things	Am the master scheduler at home as well as at work
Training new assistant	Assistant is still learning – can't fully delegate
Have established a client minimum	
Have great clients	

This exercise helped Jennifer to see how much she really enjoys her work and some of the strong attributes of her current situation. Before doing the exercise, she found herself wondering if she should try and reduce her full-time schedule. But after listing what is working, she felt a strong connection to the business she had built and realized she was not willing to downsize her operation. She also recognized that she was operating in a more intense period than usual until her assistant was fully trained. She used this information to stick with her plan and make minor modifications to her daily schedule to fit in exercise during her workday.

Now list what is working and not working about your current situation.

EXERCISE 7
DETERMINING WHAT'S WORKING
AND WHAT ISN'T

What *is* working	What is *not* working

The Envy Decoder

As we discussed at the beginning of the chapter, envy is a signal that you are not entirely at peace about your own choice of lifestyle. The envy decoding process will help you bring to light the root of your feelings.

Let's use the example of Janice and Stacey from earlier in the chapter. Janice is the stay-at-home mom who was envying Stacey who works outside the home. For this exercise, Janice will list the envy she feels, what it represents, and how she could add this element to her current life, and then assess whether that addition truly meets her needs.

The envy	How could I add it to my life?	Does this truly satisfy the need?	What is the underlying need?
Polished business-like appearance	Dress up more – wear jeans less	No	Sense of accomplishment Feeling competent
Briefcase with work	Put my volunteer materials in a briefcase	Not really	Autonomy

By doing this exercise, Janice has unearthed some interesting information. She came up with some good ideas for how she could add what was missing in her life. For someone else, these ideas might have been exciting and implementing them would squash the envy because the stay-at-home choice now incorporates some missing ingredients. But in Janice's case, she did some additional soul searching. She was conscious of the fact that business clothes and a nice briefcase are the 2 percent visible accouterments of working outside the home, but do not represent the 98 percent realities of going back to work. For Janice, starting with these envies as a trigger helped her to realize that dressing up and putting her volunteer work in a briefcase wasn't really enough to meet her underlying needs, which are autonomy, a sense of accomplishment, and feeling competent. Janice is currently exploring a return to the paid workforce.

Let's do the same exercise for Stacey's situation (see page 71).

Even though Stacey's ideas for adding what is missing turned out to be a dead-end, the exercise did lead her to new ideas. She realized that she didn't really want to wear jeans to work or wear them every day. She just valued the sense of freedom they represent, along with a relaxed attitude. Stacey decided to focus on getting more freedom and relaxation in her life and did things

The envy	How could I add it to my life?	Does this truly satisfy the need?	What is the underlying need?
Comfortable clothes	Work from home Wear jeans to work sometimes	No	Sense of freedom Feeling relaxed
Focused time with kids	Quit work Reduce hours	No	Feeling like a good mom

like making spontaneous trips to the park instead of planning for every second once she was away from the office.

She also discovered that her envy of Janice's ability to spend focused time with her kids didn't necessarily mean she wanted to quit her job. She recognized that seeing Janice at school had created a picture in her head of blissful days at home with the kids. Once she separated her envy from the fantasy life she was envisioning, she realized that there are different ways to get what she needed. In her case, what she really wanted was to feel like she was doing a good job as a parent. Stacey revalidated her decision to work but she negotiated with her manager to make some changes in her responsibilities and schedule so that when she got home she still had the energy she wanted for her children.

Now it's time to list your envies and decode them.

EXERCISE 8
DECODING YOUR ENVY

The envy	How could I add it to my life?	Does this truly satisfy the need?	What is the underlying need?

Which Direction Are You Moving In?

The following exercise works best if you are considering making a major change in your lifestyle. If you have been ruminating over this for a while, ask yourself, "Am I running away from something, or running toward something?"

If you are running away from a choice instead of moving toward something new, this is a valuable piece of information. For example, if you are working full time outside the home and are contemplating starting your own business, check to see what is driving your desire for change. Are you running away from fear of failure or even fear of success? If so, exiting under these circumstances will not feel very good and could hurt your confidence in the long run.

If the problem at work isn't your fear, but is a specific situation such as a difficult new boss, budget pressures, an increased requirement to travel, or some other factor, this may not mean that the work itself is a problem. The situation at work, however miserable it is, doesn't mean that the entire package is bad. This is a classic situation where you don't want to throw the baby out with the bath water. Instead of fantasizing about quitting work entirely, figure out if you can change the work-related problem or your method of handling the problem. Running away from work without really being drawn by the merits of the new situation can lead to much disappointment and regret.

On the other hand, if you truly are running towards something, that is a great sign of your authentic connection with the new lifestyle. Assume again that you are fantasizing about quitting work to start your own business. If you can realistically imagine your new daily schedule, are aware of the pros and cons, yet remain excited about the change, then you are likely to be successful. You could even be leaving a great situation at work but it doesn't matter to you because you are emotionally drawn to your new situation.

Take a look at Exercise 9 to help determine which direction you're heading.

EXERCISE 9
DETERMINING YOUR DIRECTION

Am I running away from something or toward something?

_____

_____

_____

_____

Where to Next?

If you have revalidated your current choice:

- Use the tools and ideas from Part I to make some improvements to your current situation. Perhaps you like your work but want to make your anticipated transitions more enjoyable. Or perhaps your stay-at-home parent role is definitely the right choice for you, but you need to create some new boundaries to prevent exhaustion and burnout.

- Read the chapters in Parts II and III that match or are closely related to your current situation. For example, if you work part time, read Chapter 10 because you will get lots of ideas from other part-timers about how they make the choice work for them. Not only will you relate to their stories and challenges, but you can assess your own part-time situation to see if you have all the key elements in place or could make improvements. You can also get ideas from the related chapters such as the chapter on job sharing (see Chapter 11) and the one on staying home full time (see Chapter 9).

If you decided to change your choice:

- Read the chapters in Parts II and III on your possible new choices. For example, if you are contemplating staying home full time, read Chapter 9. This will give you a clear picture of the realities of the choice, plus introduce you to others who are living the ups and downs of this situation. You want to have a solid understanding of the pros and cons before you plan your lifestyle change. You will also get lots of tips and ideas that will speed your learning curve and adaptation time.

- Read the applicable chapters in Part IV. This is the section that gives you à la carte help. There is help on everything from finances, child care, strategies for entering the work force after a break, and creating an alternative work schedule.

- Plan how you will incorporate the tools and ideas from Part I. Think about how you can apply the three "I"s to your new situation in order to make this new life as enjoyable as possible.

If you are on the fence:

- Temporarily suspend your need to make a decision. Read everything. Start with the chapters in Parts II and III that sound the most appealing to you, but be sure to read all of the options. You may discover that a choice you thought was out of the question is not as unrealistic as you thought. It's also possible that you will get ideas where you least expect them. Each chapter contains stories of real people and situations. You never know when one of those stories may be the spark that gives you an idea for your own life, or suddenly makes an idea you were considering feel like the right choice.

- Go back to Chapter 1 and do the priorities exercise again. Then, for each priority, ask yourself which work/life option best supports that priority.

Congratulations on successfully completing Part I: Shifting to Comfortable Chaos. Armed with the tools of the three "I"s, *individual, imperfect,* and *inter-related,* you are well on your way to enjoying the rapids and paddling to some pools of calm water. The rest of the book will give you stories, examples, and tools for the specific challenges in your life.

Part II

Thriving on Full-Time Work While Still Having a Life

6

Chapter

Fulfilled by Full Time: How to Make It Manageable and Protect Your Priorities

Kathleen is the director of client services for a large corporate law firm. She thrives on the breakneck pace, the high-level responsibilities, and the variety of the work. But she also has a very full life at home with a husband, two children, and a large house to look after. With all of these responsibilities, you might think that she doesn't get any time to herself. Think again. She works out three days a week, hikes once a week with friends, and serves on two nonprofit boards. She might sound like superwoman, and she is — but not for the reasons you might think. Kathleen evaluated what was important to her and then made some major changes in order to create time for each of the roles she wants to play at this point in her life. You will learn how Kathleen accomplished this later in the chapter, as well as hear from other full-time workers who use different strategies to create what they want out of life.

Working a traditional full-time job does not mean you can't create a satisfying life. (We define a traditional full-time job as one where you work at least 40 hours per week, are employed by someone other than yourself, and typically adhere to the traditional office hours of 8:00 a.m. to 5:00 p.m.) If you have decided that this lifestyle is the best fit for you, or you have some type of restraint that prevents you from dramatically changing the way you work at this point in time, there are still numerous strategies you can use to ensure that you stay true to your priorities.

In fact, creating room for your priorities outside of work can actually make you a better employee.

Take a Dual-Centric Approach

The dual-centric concept was coined by the authors of a fascinating study called "Leaders in a Global Economy." In the study, the participants, who were all executives, were asked the following two questions:

- "In the past year, how often have you put your job before your personal or family life?"

- "In the past year, how often have you put your personal or family life before your job?"

Because this was a study of executives, it is not surprising that most participants (61 percent) were what the researchers called work-centric. These are the executives who consistently put more priority on their work life than on their personal or family life.

But it is also rather exciting that 32 percent were what the researchers called dual-centric. Dual-centric means that they consistently put the same value on their personal and family life as they did on their work life. The study also noted that the dual-centric participants were not comprised entirely of women — men were just as likely to be dual-centric as women.

Even though 32 percent is definitely the minority of executives, it is still a significant number. It's encouraging to know that the traditional "kill yourself for the company" mentality of the executive ranks appears to be changing. This is great news for Comfortable Chaos readers who are dual-centric and still want to hold positions of responsibility.

But there is even more good news about being dual-centric. In the same study, dual-centric people had the highest ratings for feeling successful at work. They also felt much less stressed, with 26 percent of dual-centric people experiencing moderate or high levels of stress, compared with 42 percent of those who are not dual-centric. Experiencing less stress directly translates into better health. Isn't it great to know that focusing equal time on your personal life is actually good for you?

As well as considering participants' feelings about success and stress, the study also looked at objective measures. They reviewed metrics such as reporting level, compensation, and size of staff, and found no real difference between the work-centric and dual-centric people. This means that the work-centric executives who spent more time working (on average five extra hours per week) and experienced added stress and fewer successful feelings did not come out ahead in any of the tangible measures.

The implication for you, someone who wants a life beyond work, is that you are not missing out on the traditional measures of success. Even though the study included only executives, the results can be extrapolated to nonexecutives. You can probably think of someone at work who completely sacrifices everything for the job, only to be passed over for recognition or promotion by the charismatic and effective performer who also happens to have a life outside of work. Truly effective people also have winning personalities and people skills. Once again there is a connection to being dual-centric.

In another study, researchers at the Ford Foundation concluded that the skills used in family life carry over and provide a positive benefit to the workplace. Skills learned from family and private life include collaboration, information sharing, nurturing, and multitasking. These are extremely valuable traits in a team-based environment or leadership position. These skills are also applied in the form of problem *prevention* — a highly underrated and often invisible talent that should receive much more glory than the fire-fighting type of problem *solving* that normally prevails in today's work environment.

So rejoice in your dual-centric nature! It's the essence of the second I, *inter-related*, or viewing your life in terms of the big picture and recognizing that each piece contributes to the whole.

Now it's time to apply some strategies that bring the dual-centric, or inter-related, vision to reality. There are three main approaches to making full-time employment workable and for creating room for your other priorities. We'll start with the most visible change.

Change Your Assignment

Your specific assignment, or job, is often the biggest factor in whether or not you can accomplish your work responsibilities while still having a life. Basically, the specific work you do plays a big part in your ability to make your chaos comfortable. Before considering your specific assignment, you may want to take a step back and first think about your particular profession and industry.

For some people, the profession they chose has been a lifesaver when it comes to combining work and family. Wendy is a national account manager for a company that sells outdoor advertising. She is married and has two school-aged children who are very active in sports. "I always knew I wanted to be in sales as it gives me flexibility. If my son has a baseball game, I can go. There is kind of an unspoken rule that as long as you meet your numbers, your work schedule is your own business." This doesn't mean that Wendy takes it easy. She works very hard and is able to say, "My numbers speak for themselves."

Wendy's situation isn't the case for everyone. You may not have given much thought to flexibility when you chose a career in your twenties. Or maybe the industry changed in a direction that no longer inspires you. Either way, you should think about whether the nature of the work itself allows you to lead the life you desire. If not, you may need to consider a different profession or industry.

But it's also possible that your profession and industry are not the issue — instead it's your particular assignment (or the exact duties in your current job). One way to assess your assignment is to determine if it is a good fit for your coefficient for chaos (see Chapter 2). If your assignment does not mesh with your personal style and ability to tolerate chaos, you will feel like you are constantly paddling upstream. Coping with the chaos levels in your assignment takes too much energy and prevents you from feeling successful, which is a key part of Comfortable Chaos.

This was the case for Matt, a sales support person assigned to 15 high-energy, mega-achieving salespeople who were always pushing to include him in customer meetings. In his previous assignment he had provided behind-the-scenes sales support and was awesome at his job. When he moved to his current position, the duties were essentially the same but he also had a great deal of interaction with the customers in order to understand their needs. He had a very low threshold for chaos but was surrounded by salespeople who fed on it, multitasking to the extreme. It drove him nuts — and he fell on his face. Finally, when he was thinking back to a parallel job situation he had in college, Matt had a realization of what was wrong. At the time in college, he was working in a restaurant as a cook and receiving lots of praise from management. They suggested he become a waiter and Matt jumped at the chance because it was viewed as a step up. But when he became a waiter he hated it. He didn't like dealing with the customers and preferred working behind the scenes, even if it did get busy. "I'm a cook, not a waiter," he realized. Soon after having this realization, Matt left the position where he interfaced with salespeople and customers and found one that was a better fit for him.

Ask yourself, "Am I a cook or a waiter?" This information, along with your CFC, can be telling. Maybe you are a waiter with a high CFC. If you are stuck in a cook-type position where you are bound to a routine, you may end up feeling exhausted and depressed. Just because you are highly qualified for a job does not mean that you will enjoy it. Believe it or not, self-knowledge is more important when it comes to your happiness than your actual job skills.

So let's say you have assessed your profession, industry, and job and everything is a good fit, but there is some element of your particular assignment that is a problem in terms of work/life balance. For example, if your assignment requires heavy travel or long and demanding hours, it may be impossible to consistently spend time on the priorities in your personal life.

That was the situation for Sharon who had a high-powered career in the financial industry. When her daughter was born she made her first assignment change. "I left my position for another that I believed would be fewer hours. In reality, there were still time demands such as late evenings, weekends on call, some travel, and an annual management retreat. Things were better than in my previous assignment, but when my second child was born, even some overtime was more than I felt happy working." Sharon was debating what to do when she got a call from an old client. "He had a position available and asked if I was interested in it. The decision to accept the new position was a difficult one because it was a step down in terms of my career. But I knew from my earlier interactions with the company that the job would be a relatively easy one with flexible hours and little to no overtime."

Sharon took the job, which was chief financial officer for a small lending company and typically works a 40-hour week. During the school year she adjusts her hours and starts at 7:00 a.m. (her husband handles the morning child-care responsibilities), so she can leave by 4:00 p.m. to pick up her kids from school and daycare. She likes this arrangement because her school-aged daughter is only in after-school care for one hour, plus she can schedule the activities her children enjoy.

This purposeful downshift in responsibility has been the right choice for Sharon. "If I knew then what I know now, I would have taken an immediate and significant step back when our first child was born. If I had done that, those years would have been richer and more fulfilling for me."

Sharon's choices may appear drastic but it's all in how you look at the move. Downshifting your work responsibilities can certainly be a temporary situation; maybe you are shifting out of high gear for a period of time. Depending on how you describe it on your résumé, no one would necessarily know that you took what you perceived to be a step back.

You may find that Sharon's situation really resonates with you. Or, you may have a very different reaction. If the thought of giving up your hard-earned position and status makes you cringe, then look for a way to maintain what is important to you. You don't necessarily have to sacrifice your career path or status level. Look for another position at the same level that requires less travel and has a slower pace. The assignment might be less exciting, but better suited to your requirements at this time in your life. In the process, you could gain valuable new experience.

We need to get rid of the old image of the career ladder and think of it more as a jungle gym. The traditional image of a career ladder suggests preset steps that are sequential and inflexible. While the ladder is a route to the often aspired to "top," it is rigid and usually tenuous. We have all seen people who were clearly on their way up the ladder when a rung broke and they are left disappointed and frustrated after having followed the rules for so long.

The concept of the career jungle gym is definitely a paradigm shift; however, it can be much more creative, adventurous, and fun than a ladder. Freeing yourself from the career ladder allows you to take advantage of horizontal moves that offer growth, challenge, and a schedule that allows for family priorities. You move around the jungle gym based on your needs and desires, and may even end up in the same destination as the career ladder. It may take more time to get there, but you will be in better shape because the workout challenged more muscles. And if at any time you change your mind about life on the jungle gym, there is no reason why you can't jump back on the career ladder.

The key is to understand your priorities for this point in your life. Changing assignments, whether it is within your company or outside of your company, is a great solution for many people. You can still do the work you enjoy but in a capacity that better meets your needs.

Jennifer, a school counselor, has two young daughters, aged two-and-a-half years and six months. She needs to work full time for financial reasons and found the transition back to work after maternity leave to be particularly difficult. Her assignment at the time was as a community mental health provider for the schools and she worked four ten-hour days. Although she enjoyed her day off, the ten-hour days didn't work well with her husband's swing shift schedule. He would have to go through the laborious process of packing up both kids, often waking them from their naps, and getting them to daycare when they only needed to be there for one hour before Jennifer could pick them up.

So Jennifer changed assignments and became a school counselor. She shortened her days and now works from 7:45 a.m. until 3:15 p.m. so she is home before her husband needs to leave for work. Jennifer also gets all the school holidays off, including the summers. Her two-and-a-half-year-old doesn't really understand the loss of "Mommy day," but Jennifer feels she has made a good choice for her current situation and for down the road when her children will attend the school where she works. The new assignment has also helped her feel better about her need to work. "Now I am used to working with two kids and really enjoy what I do. At work I can use the bathroom in peace and have some time to myself at lunch. It's a good balance."

Changing assignments can make all the difference to your lifestyle. Whether it is a major change involving new work, new people, and a new company, or a minor change within a familiar environment, the key is finding the one that allows you to use your skills, be true to your CFC, and apply the boundaries that allow you to live your life outside of work.

Change Your Alignment

The second way to make a change in the traditional full-time world of work is to modify how you approach your current assignment. It's all in how you align, or adjust, the way you go about accomplishing your work. In any job, there are infinite ways to get the work done and this gives you an enormous amount of freedom.

By creating a better alignment with your work, you enjoy the process so much more and increase your overall satisfaction with the job. This has a carryover effect to your personal life because you can arrive home with much more energy and feel ready to tackle your home responsibilities, as well as enjoy your family and get some personal time.

In deciding whether a change in alignment would help you meet your nonwork commitments, it's important to think once again about your coefficient for chaos. For example, if you are a high CFC, you tend to enjoy heavy multitasking and prefer to jump between projects and tasks all day in order to keep yourself interested and energized. What do you do if you are faced with one major project that precludes you from your normal bouncing around approach? You can take the big project and break it into a series of small tasks. Then move rapidly between those smaller tasks, ensuring that you are alternating between interactive tasks such as telephone calls and meetings, and "alone" tasks such as drafting a presentation. You might even find that you do better on the "alone" tasks if you sit somewhere outside your office so that you won't face the temptation of your e-mail or telephone.

If you are a low CFC, then you value the ability to work on one project at a time. If the nature of your assignment brings interruptions and rapid-fire decision making, then you are going to frequently feel frustrated. Look for ways that you can create structure in your workday. Consider scheduling a specific chunk of time to work on each project. Clear your desk of other assignments and forward your telephone to voicemail during that time. If that's not possible, look for a coworker you can swap "on duty" time with. He or she can answer your calls while you are working for a set period of time and then you can switch.

Sometimes you can make an alignment change by adjusting the physical environment in which you work. This was the case for Eric, who worked as a sales representative from his home. His company believed in a complete virtual office environment but Eric found it too isolating to make calls from home all day. So he talked with one of his main customers who gladly loaned him a desk in their office. They felt like they had direct access to him, and he enjoyed working amongst the noise of the busy office.

Whatever your CFC, by making some simple adjustments, you may be able align your assignment to your CFC and can work more efficiently and enjoyably. This will carry over to your personal life because you are getting more done and are less likely to have to stay late or take work home. You will also arrive home in a much better frame of mind and be more effective in your personal life because your workday complemented your individual style.

So look for creative ways you can make your assignment more your own. Just because you have always done something a particular way or you have concerns that doing it differently would rock the boat, doesn't mean it's not worth trying. What do you have to lose? In today's results-oriented culture, you may find that getting to the finish line is all that matters.

Change Your Abutment

Okay, we realize that abutment is a rather strange word to use in the context of making changes in your work life. "Abut" means to lie adjacent or to touch at one end or side of something. Since your personal life certainly touches your work life (in fact, they often ram into one another), "abutment" is the perfect descriptive word. We spend our days "abutting" all over the place.

However, in terms of moving toward Comfortable Chaos, you are looking for ways to make work abut with home in a more productive and enjoyable fashion. So far we have talked about changing something at work — either your assignment or alignment. Maybe the answer for you lies in changing something at home — something that abuts with your work life. Instead of looking at your work and home lives as straight pieces of wood lying side by side, look at them as planks of wood that fit together like a finger joint.

Kathleen is someone who has used an abutment strategy. She is the "superwoman" from the beginning of the chapter who works full time and has a husband and two children but still finds time to work out, hike, and serve on two nonprofit boards. Unlike Sharon, who "downsized" her career, Kathleen didn't want to give up the responsibility and status of her position. But she found that her work hours continued to creep upward and she had a 45- to 50-minute commute that caused her to miss seeing her children in the morning and arrive home too late to get them to their activities.

She and her husband made a major decision to move into the city and dramatically reduce Kathleen's commute. "Now that I am only eight miles from work, I can take the children to school and still get to work by 8:00 a.m. This also allows my husband to pick up one of the children for sports and I pick up the other."

Changing her commute isn't Kathleen's only abutment strategy. Her school-aged children have chores and are held accountable. She believes that each family member should do what he or she is best at. "I do almost all the cooking but my husband doesn't mind cleaning up the dishes. One of my children loves to help cook and the other would rather set the table."

Kathleen also hires lots of household help. "Get a cleaning service and a yard service, have your groceries delivered, your car washed, and your dry cleaning picked up — anything that takes less time for someone else to do versus you doing it. I used to spend the whole weekend doing laundry and cleaning. Now I go hiking or to the kids' sporting events."

Naturally all of this does come with a price tag. "Living in the city meant very high house payments to be in a nice secure area where the children would have a lot of room to play. It also meant private schools for both children. Our house payments tripled and private school tuition for both children is over $15,000 versus being free in the public schools. It will be over $20,000 when they are in high school not including books, the cost of riding the bus, and activities." For Kathleen, these financial costs are worth it because her salary supports the expenses and it allows her to keep the job she loves along with a very satisfying personal life.

Kathleen also stresses the importance of having a great support structure — especially a supportive partner. She has a husband who is 100 percent behind her career and is a true partner at home. Wendy, another person we interviewed, also noted the importance of teamwork with her husband. "My husband and I alternate on who leaves early. If it's your day to leave early, you can go in as early as you want. Then the other person gets the kids off to school."

Other couples create an abutment strategy by opting for one partner to stay home full time with the children. This obviously provides a great deal of flexibility for the working partner. Ericka is an executive vice president of a public relations firm. For many years both she and her husband worked, but when she was pregnant with her second child, her husband proposed that he stay at home. Ericka says, "My husband John is an integral part of how I can do what I do. I can call up and work late and it doesn't impact our family. In some ways, I have the best of both worlds. I get to enjoy the kids but check out when it gets rough."

Ericka also commented on handling the emotional side of reversing the traditional roles. "John has had to create inroads in the stay-at-home community. The PEPS (Program for Early Parent Support) group has accommodated it pretty well. The sacrifice on my side is I am not as tuned in to the children as John is. Just this morning he coached me on how to make my little guy happy. It's awesome that he knows but I also felt insecure."

Whether your abutment strategy is to shorten your commute, hire a nanny, team up with your partner, or decide to have one parent stay at home, it can make a world of difference in lowering your chaos level. Like any change, there are often some trade offs, but if the benefits are strong, you can congratulate yourself on finding a solution that works for you.

Moving Your CFC Along the Continuum

Changing your assignment, alignment, or abutment can take some time. Assignment changes, in particular, take a well thought-out plan and even then you may have to wait for the right opportunity to come along. So what can you do in the meantime? You may need to temporarily move your CFC along the continuum.

Let's say you are in a stressful job that is more ideally suited for a high CFC. The problem is you are a medium CFC and the alignment changes you have put in place have not made your chaos more comfortable. You may need to temporarily move your CFC higher up the scale. Even though it's not your true nature to be a high CFC, you can operate like one for a period of time. Just recognize that you are making this shift, and keep working on your assignment change plans. Knowing that the situation is temporary should help your sanity as you continue in a role that is not your ideal.

Another technique you can use while you are waiting to make a change is to consciously control your activities and environment outside of work. If, like in the example above, you need to operate at a high CFC level at work when it is not your preference, then be sure to be true to your lower CFC when you are at home. One engineering manager told us, "I get my fill of stress and excitement at work. When I am home I enjoy quiet activities and peaceful surroundings."

Maintain Your Boundaries

Whatever changes you make, the need for boundaries does not go away. They are critical when you are working full time because your days are so jam-packed.

One of the toughest boundary struggles for full-timers is leaving the office on time. It's so easy to get pulled into one more meeting or realize you need more time to finish a project that is due the next day. This means that you have to be ultra-efficient during your time in the office so that at the end of the day you have accomplished the most important priorities. (See the ten tips for getting it all done later in the chapter.) But in the end it takes discipline or another commitment to get out the door on time.

For Sharon, the chief financial officer of a small lending company, she needs to leave work so that she can pick up her children from after-school care and from daycare. Jennifer, the school counselor, needs to be home in time to assume child-care responsibility so her husband can get to work on time. Having to leave by a certain time to make another commitment, whether or not it is child related, is actually a good strategy. You have no choice but to leave on time. Of course you do have a choice on how close you want to cut it, but then you are also choosing more stress!

On the flip side, having these commitments can also bring frustration during those times when a half hour more at work would have made all the difference to completing a project. When this happens, Kathleen brings work home that she can do later in the evening. Others, like Jennifer, have a strict rule about not bringing work home. Your situation will be dependent on your assignment, the way you choose to get your work done, and the boundaries you set for yourself. If you need a reminder on the six steps for creating a beautiful boundary, go back to Chapter 3 and plan on implementing a new boundary.

Ten Tips for Getting It All Done

As a full-time worker you want to accomplish your many work priorities as quickly and efficiently as possible so that work doesn't consume all of your time. Use the following tips at work to help you boost your productivity.

Decide on your top priority projects

Your projects should be carefully selected so that you are solving key problems for your organization or company. Any project you select should get a "yes" to one or more of the following questions:

- Is this a critical problem causing significant cost, excess flow time, and valuable staff resources?

- Is this a difficult problem that everyone wants solved?

- Is this a priority for my boss or upper management?

- Would solving the problem be highly visible to upper management?

- Can I measure the success of the project in cost or time saved?

After answering these questions, you should have a good sense of whether or not you have chosen critical projects to work on.

Use the 80/20 rule and plan

Apply basic time management techniques. Make to-do lists for your various projects and other tasks, and then schedule when they will occur. If you use an online scheduling program, be sure to block out time to work and not just to keep track of your meetings. Then make sure that 80 percent of your time is spent working on your critical projects — remembering that not all items on your to-do list carry the same weight.

This is based on the 80/20 rule coined by Wilfredo Pareto, a nineteenth century Italian economist. Pareto's principle can be applied in several ways. For example, his theory suggests that 80 percent of your results will come from 20 percent of your efforts. To take your success even further, strive to spend 80 percent of your time on the really important projects, and allow only 20 percent of your day for the smaller, less consequential stuff. This can only happen with careful planning and by avoiding constant telephone calls and e-mail interruptions. If you are working on a key project, put your telephone on "forward all" and then schedule a half hour for returning all calls.

Use the "project of the week" concept

Depending on your job, you may have six to ten key projects that are your focus. The common approach is to try and work a little on all six each week. The problem with this idea is that it is difficult to get momentum and make a real surge of progress. And it's the surge of progress that is so rewarding and motivates you to keep going. So every week, decide which project is your "project of the week" and block out chucks of time to accomplish specific tasks that will propel that project to its next phase.

Get over the guilt of e-mail

Trust us, no one is keeping score on how many unanswered e-mails you have. Although you certainly can't ignore e-mail, there are ways to manage it — but first it takes a mental adjustment.

For those of us who have been in the workforce for more than ten years, we can remember when the only work that could "pile up" was memos in the "in" tray and little pink telephone messages. Even then, no one expected an instant answer. Memos and pink messages could be pondered over and delayed. But now, with the explosion of e-mail, we feel overwhelmed and obligated to instantly reply. On top of that, anybody can e-mail you without your permission. Gone are the days of a secretary who screened your calls and prevented low importance callers from getting to you.

Here's one strategy for e-mail. Check it a couple of times a day for urgent or important messages. Scan for anything from your boss or further up the chain of command. On other e-mails, take a quick look at the subject line and the sender to get a clue as to whether the message is critical. Depending on your e-mail system, messages can even be sorted automatically as they come into your inbox. It's important to understand the technology you have available so you can leverage it as much as possible.

Another way to make the technology work for you is to set a standard protocol with key coworkers regarding the subject line of e-mails. For example, if you and a team are all working on a project, you could agree to name all e-mails related to the project the same way. Then you can quickly see these e-mails or have them sent to a special folder. You could go a step further and agree with your team members on some type of urgency code in the subject line. It could be as simple as using the word "hot" — as long as everyone agrees on the definition.

When working on your critical projects (which is most of your day), do not look at your e-mail. Turn off any annoying beeps that signal a new incoming message. Once every couple of days, do an e-mail clean up or "purge" as we like to call it. Delete notes you don't need to read. Quickly scan informational notes and move them to a folder so they don't sit in your inbox. Then answer notes or forward them to others for answering. And most important, ignore some messages, especially the ones where you were copied and the sender is inviting everyone to comment. Unless it's critical to your key projects, get out of the online chain of discussion that is likely to follow. Also ask your coworkers to avoid using "reply to all" unless it is necessary.

For a helpful book on how to disconnect from the constant barrage of electronic messages, see *Turn It Off* by Gil Gordon (Three Rivers Press, 2001).

Develop the need for speed

Get used to the idea of working quickly and not wasting time on other activities. Think of it as working hard and playing hard. The working hard is not so bad. You get a great sense of accomplishment by checking off the items on your to-do list. Whether you choose to have a quick lunch so you can leave the office at an earlier time, or use your lunch as personal time for a workout or some other way to replenish yourself, the key is to work quickly during your defined work hours so that you can get on to other things.

Avoid any meeting that doesn't help you with one of your critical projects

How many times have you spent one or two hours in a meeting and left with only a few tidbits of useful information? And then there are those thrilling all-day events where you lose an entire day of productivity and precious time to work on your key projects. If we could measure the total amount of lost productivity in each company or organization in North America due to meetings, we would all be shocked.

As someone dedicated to Comfortable Chaos, you need to be aware of the impact of meetings on your productivity and know that every hour is critical. Pay attention to that feeling you get when you are squirming in your chair, knowing that the meeting is preventing you from completing your to-do list for the day.

Obviously, the meetings you call or ones that directly affect a key project are a priority. The difficulty is with all the other meetings you are asked to attend. Make it a habit to question the person who called the meeting; what is the purpose, why are you needed, and how long will it take? You can do this diplomatically but you need these answers to determine if you really need to attend. If you feel you don't need to be at the meeting, explain why without being overly apologetic. Sometimes you can't tell for sure if you are truly needed so you might suggest attending via teleconference or offering to attend for the first half hour.

Another strategy is to establish a time limit and say, "I can only attend for an hour." Of course there will always be a few meetings you can't negotiate on for political reasons. The key is to try and strategically pick your meetings to ensure that they don't eat up too much of your precious work time. You may even find that after you have been doing this for a while, you will develop a reputation for scrutinizing meeting requests. This will cause many people to limit the number of times they request your attendance in the first place. How wonderful — when you value your time, others will too.

Learn the tools that are pertinent for your job

If you have one of those fantastic support people who knows what you are thinking even before you tell them, and they make your projects top priority, then it probably doesn't pay to do things like create your own charts and materials yourself. But if you don't have a support person, you of course need to learn how to create your own documents and charts. You may still want to learn how to use the relevant tools if you share a support person with other people, because you may have to wait in line. It can also be much more efficient to do your draft directly on the computer using the appropriate software. That way, you can update the material whenever you need to and are not reliant on whether someone else is available. You can teach yourself most of the common office applications (such as word processing, presentations, spreadsheets, and databases) with a tutorial. But you may find that signing up for a short class will make you create the time. Be sure to put your new skills to use right away after taking the class. Otherwise, you are likely to forget some, or all, of what you learned.

Depending on the culture in your organization, there may be an additional bonus to creating your own materials: it adds to your credibility. In many companies, the people who are technically savvy with their own computers are seen as competent and modern thinkers. If that's the case where you work, it could be a wonderful image booster for you to acquire these skills. However, in other company cultures, respect is given to those who can command an assistant to type as they talk. Watch for how the leaders in your company handle this issue and then take that into consideration as you decide what to delegate versus do yourself.

Be highly organized and work "lean"

It is very time consuming to be disorganized because you spend a lot of time looking for things. Obviously, this is time that you can't afford so you need to keep your physical environment organized. If getting organized isn't your forte, ask someone else to help you set up a system that you can maintain. If you don't have an assistant, you could involve your team in getting everyone organized. The people who love to do this will typically volunteer, and then as a group you can set up some common systems so you can find each other's work when needed. If that doesn't work, it may even be worth it for you to hire someone and pay for it out of your own pocket.

Some basics that typically help are to keep a minimum amount of "stuff" on your desk. Keep your files purged by spending five minutes a day tossing old material. (Plus this makes for a good break from the high-speed work pace you typically maintain.) It also pays to be organized electronically. Have a system for online filing that lets you find things easily. You may want to store the majority of your documents on a server that is accessible to other people on your team. That way, team members can find what they need even if you are out of the office.

Think before you say "yes"

Too many people are quick to say "yes" whenever there is a new task or when someone asks them to do something. This is the kiss of death for anyone who wants to live in Comfortable Chaos. Resist the automatic "yes" at all costs. Instead, look at your schedule, or mentally check it, and determine when you could work on the new task without jeopardizing key projects. Or, if it would benefit you to take on the new task, decide how your schedule could be rearranged or if other tasks could be delegated or eliminated.

It's also perfectly acceptable to stall. If you are put on the spot, an effective answer is, "I'd love to be able to take that on — let me see if I can rearrange other commitments and I'll get back to you."

Surround yourself with capable and positive people

Work is much more fun and productive when you are with upbeat and talented people. You may have experienced the opposite, which is an atmosphere filled with tension and poor teamwork. These toxic situations are bad for anyone, but particularly detrimental when you need to make every hour count. Spending time on politics or venting with unhappy coworkers is just not an option. So don't spend your precious minutes with these people, and look for healthy work environments with people who are open minded to how, and where, work gets accomplished.

Whether you choose to work in a traditional full-time position or need to for financial reasons, you do not have to count yourself out when it comes to Comfortable Chaos. Use the power of a dual-centric approach, and then modify your assignment, alignment, or abutment. Add in some efficiency gains and you will be out the office door feeling proud of your accomplishments and looking forward to what awaits you at home.

f o m C
o r t
a l b e
C h
a o
s

Chapter 7

Flextime, Compressed Workweeks, and Telecommuting: Three Wonderful Ways to Distribute Full-Time Work

Kelli is a data specialist in the employee relations department of a Fortune 100 company. She wakes up at 3:30 a.m. to get ready for work and soak up the silence in the house. As she drives to work shortly after 4:00 a.m., there is almost no traffic. Arriving at the office, she finds it satisfying to be the one to turn on the lights on her floor of the building and loves the feeling of having accomplished a big chunk of work by the time her coworkers arrive at their desks. Kelli works a compressed workweek by working 40 hours in four days (a 4/10 schedule), with flex hours of 4:30 a.m. to 3:00 p.m., Tuesday through Friday.

At this point you are probably either thinking "this woman is crazy!" or "that's an interesting schedule." While this routine would certainly not be ideal for everyone, it works for Kelli. It has become so ingrained in her that she says, "On my days off, I actually get frustrated when I am interrupted while showering in the mornings. I am so used to having my coffee and getting ready for work in peace because I leave before anyone else in the house is awake."

Kelli's schedule is just one of many options and combinations of three different strategies for maintaining a full-time schedule. If you want to keep your full-time job, or the prospects of reducing your working hours are insurmountable, there are some creative ways that may make full-time work more palatable and move you to a more Comfortable Chaos. These three schedules are flextime, compressed workweeks, and telecommuting.

Flextime is the ability to change when you start and end your workday. It could mean that you abandon the traditional 8:00 a.m. to 5:00 p.m. for a different, yet regular, schedule such as 7:00 a.m. to 4:00 p.m. Or it can mean that you have the flexibility to adjust your hours depending on your personal and professional needs for the day. Both of these options are pretty common, and depending on your company and position, may not take much negotiation to implement. In fact, in certain fields such as sales, flextime is pretty much the norm.

When you work a *compressed workweek* you're squeezing 40 hours into fewer days than the traditional five-day workweek. One of the most common options is to work 4/10s like Kelli does — with or without the ultra-early start time. Another variation is the 9/80 schedule or nine-day fortnight. This is when you work nine-hour days for nine workdays in a row, with one day off every other week. In some companies this schedule is so common that you almost expect people to be gone on Fridays — the coveted 9/80 day off. Like flextime, a compressed workweek is often an easier "sell" to management since it adds no extra cost.

Telecommuting is working from a remote site — normally from home. Typically you need a computer or laptop and high-speed connection to your office. It is often combined with one or both of the other two full-time options. Depending on the nature of the work, it may not matter exactly what time the work gets done.

All three arrangements are creative solutions that have worked successfully for many people. The key to making one of them, or a combination of them, work for you is understanding exactly how they will work in your situation and anticipating the full ramifications to you and those around you. Since they are all still full-time options, many people underestimate the importance of thinking through the details and fully evaluating their job requirements and their personality type. In most cases, just as much planning is necessary with these options as with part time or job sharing. In the case of telecommuting, it may need even more planning. Let's take a look at each of these options in more detail.

Flextime: Working When It Works for You

Flextime has actually been around in the workplace for decades. It may not have had a name early on, but it existed nonetheless.

In 1982, Ian was a supervisor at the State of New Mexico Health Laboratory that tested babies for phenylketonuria (PKU) and other inborn metabolic diseases. He had a child from a previous marriage who lived 2,000 miles away with her mother.

When he and his second wife had two sons, he decided that this time he would spend more time with his children. So he approached his director with the idea of going in to work very early in the morning and leaving in the early afternoon so that he could minimize the time his children were in daycare. His work entailed performing and supervising diagnostic tests. There was no compelling reason for him to have to work a standard schedule, as long as he had some overlap time with his employees. It was an easy plan to implement with his managers. He worked that schedule, going in at 6:00 a.m. and leaving at 2:00 p.m., for seven years before moving to another job. Even though his second son just graduated from high school and Ian now has his own business, he still makes flextime a priority in what he considers his balanced life.

Today, there are even more positions like Ian's, where the functions are performed fairly independently and can be done during different hours. If you work as a computer programmer, writer, graphic designer, or any of the hundreds of other creative-type professions, it may not matter when the work is performed. In fact, even when cross-functional cooperation is needed, it may not be a big deal to work a schedule that is different by just a few hours from your coworkers. By shifting your schedule to starting earlier or later, you can often shorten your commute due to less traffic, increase the amount of time you spend with your family, and get some quiet thinking time in the office.

That is certainly the case for Kelli, although she does miss the early mornings with her children. But the payoff is being there when they get home from school and being able to get them to their sporting events and other extracurricular activities. This is somewhat of an idyllic picture, but clearly the downside is having to get up at 3:30 in the morning four days a week. Kelli says she is used to it, and it is now no big deal. However, she did mention that most nights she tries to get to bed by 8:30 p.m. — a choice that would not work for everyone. She also says that many mornings when she doesn't have to get up, she naturally wakes up early anyway. This could be a blessing or a curse depending on how you personally view it.

If you are thinking about proposing flextime to your employer, ask yourself the following three questions.

How much of my time is spent in cross-functional collaboration?

Cross-functional collaboration is the time spent in meetings and face-to-face communication with people outside your department. If cross-functional collaboration takes up 80 percent or more of your time, flextime may not work well unless your schedule only varies an hour or two from the company norm. If the answer is around 50 percent, flextime may be a great option. The exact percentage will influence how far you "flex." In other words, knowing the number of hours per day you overlap with coworkers gives you an indication of how much time you need to be in the office at the same time.

Also factor in the urgency of the cross-functional collaboration. If your answer about how much cross-functional time you spend was 50 percent, but the issues you are working on are almost always very time sensitive, then your coworkers may not be able to do their jobs when you are not in the office.

How will I accommodate communication among my direct reporting relationships?

You already know how important it is to meet the expectations of your boss. In particular, you will need to think about his or her communication requirements and work-style preferences before you propose a change to your schedule. For example, if your boss expects a face-to-face tie-in each morning and is not open to doing it over the telephone, that is a major obstacle. But it doesn't mean you can't flex your schedule in some other way. Instead of coming in later as you originally planned, consider starting earlier in the morning and going home earlier in the afternoon.

If you have subordinates, think about how you can continue to be available to them. Depending on their work schedules, you may have to make yourself accessible at different times or be reachable by telephone. You could also schedule more official one-on-one meetings so everyone knows when they have an opportunity to bring up issues and concerns.

Can I honestly sustain the schedule I am proposing?

If you propose going into the office at 6:00 a.m., you need to be sure to be there at 6:00 every morning! Are you a morning person? Will you need to get to bed earlier — and can you? If you are just not a morning person and already feel stretched to get to work by 9:00 a.m., saying you'll start earlier may not be realistic. Don't forget the importance of the first I, *individual,* and knowing yourself.

If you do decide to go in early or start later, do you have the support you need from family and/or your child-care providers to consistently meet your new schedule needs? Make sure there are also some benefits for them or your plan is at risk for failure.

Compressed Workweeks: How to Not Shove Ten Pounds in a Five-Pound Sack

"During the wee hours of the morning I sometimes wonder why I'm working so hard. But on Fridays when I am skiing with friends in new powder while everyone else is working, it seems like it ought to be against the law to feel so good!" This is a quote from Jim, who works a compressed workweek. The typical way to do that, as we said earlier, is the 4/10 schedule. However, because of the demands of his high-tech job, he works 12-hour days, four days per week. But with a 30-minute commute in the morning that stretches to 45 minutes in the afternoon, his total time away from home is almost 14 hours. Jim admits that the schedule can often be tiring, but his Fridays off give him time to pursue his passions and spend time with his children, and he considers it to be a good trade-off.

Katie is a human resources manager who, during her 25-year career at the same company, has moved to a 9/80 schedule whenever her current position would accommodate it. She would work 80 hours in nine workdays instead of the normal ten, and would take every other Friday off. "That day was just for me," says Katie. If I felt like staying in bed, sipping tea by the fireplace, or shopping, I did just that. I often had to work to get over the guilt of having so much time to myself, but when I did I was happy to do household chores and work on home remodeling with my husband on the weekend."

On the surface, a compressed workweek sounds like a schedule that everyone would want, but it's actually not that simple. You need to really think about what it will feel like to work a nine- or ten-hour day, plus commute, when you are used to an eight-hour day. One or two more hours a day doesn't sound like much, but depending on the nature of your work, it could really make the difference between coming home feeling good about your day or arriving home physically and emotionally spent.

Jim's schedule works very well for him, but that is partially due to the support he has at home. His wife is a stay-at-home mom who fully supports his alternative schedule. Jim stated that his 4/12 schedule "requires you to be an early riser, have a committed partner at home to cover for you during Monday through Thursday, and have the self-discipline to stick to a schedule. I don't think most people could do this unless they really enjoyed the job. Financial motivation would likely not be enough."

Beth was once tempted by the appeal of having Fridays off but then recognized that the payoff wouldn't outweigh the sacrifice. It was when she was a sales manager with 15 high-energy salespeople reporting to her in a very hectic environment and she was looking for an alternative work schedule that would give her more time at home with her children. The company proposed the idea of working 4/10s. It was initially quite tempting. She thought,

"I can maintain my current income and work four days per week!" She was already working long hours, so what would the big deal be? Then reality set in. She thought, "Let's see, if I'm currently working about nine or ten hours per day, five days per week just to keep my head above water, then would a compressed work week be 4/12s or 4/15s? Also, as a mother of young children, she was not willing to spend so many hours away from her children for the four days she worked. She knew she would miss the morning hours with them and dinners only to be a grouchy tired mommy when she was home on Fridays trying to recuperate.

This leads to the first of a number of questions you need to ask yourself before considering a compressed workweek.

Do I have the physical and mental stamina for a longer day?

Start by thinking about it just as Beth did. How long will your day really be, including the commute? If it seems realistic, a good way to test it is to work the new schedule for two or three days in a row. You should also experiment with different ways of breaking up the day. When working a longer than eight-hour day, lunchtime becomes even more important than before — you really need the physical and mental break. But with such a long day, you might want to save part of your lunch hour for later in the afternoon. Do something physical if you have been sitting all day and consider getting out of the office even for a short period of time.

Does my job realistically lend itself to my absence one day per week or every other week?

This was the second thing Beth had to ponder when she was considering condensing her workweek into four days. Not only was it unappealing in terms of how long she would be working and gone from home, but who would handle all the issues that arose on Fridays with her salespeople? Well of course she knew the answer to that. She would end up being on the telephone and the computer from home on "days off" because issues that came up were often time sensitive. A compressed workweek in this case would clearly be a recipe for increased stress, anger, and frustration rather than a more balanced life.

If you also have a large team of people or a demanding group of customers who need a great deal of interaction with you, is it realistic to think you could actually work a compressed workweek? There would be one day per week, or every other week, where they wouldn't have access to you. You must be realistic about this. Some jobs just do not lend themselves very well to these arrangements.

For example, are there issues that regularly come up that are time sensitive and only you can, or should, handle them? If this happens frequently, even one day out of the office may not allow you to meet the requirements of your job. If this occurs only occasionally, it may not bother you to take a telephone call on your day off knowing that it is rare.

How will the work be covered on the days I am not in the office?

Even though you will be working the same number of hours, there are bound to be issues that come up on your day off. And of course the telephone doesn't stop ringing or the e-mail cease just because you are not in the office. Is there a coworker who could act as a back-up for you? This person could handle the emergency or "hot" issues that can't wait until your return. Be sure to check that you both have the same definition of emergency so the coworker doesn't handle less, or more, than you think is necessary.

How will I communicate my schedule to others in order to reduce any possible resentment?

This will take good planning along with some finesse and tact. Just as we talked about in Chapter 3 when implementing a boundary, you want to make sure to take the emotion out of protecting your day off. Be careful how you decline a meeting for that day. Your manager and coworkers will quickly pick up any tone of voice that suggests it is your absolute right to have the day off. Instead, propose a different meeting day or occasionally participate by telephone. Firm boundaries implemented with diplomacy and a little flexibility will go a long way in preventing resentment.

Also, don't leave people guessing about your schedule. In your voicemail, be sure to change your greeting for the day to say you are out of the office, but so and so can be reached if there is an urgent situation. The tact comes in by not saying something like "it's my 9/80 day off." The same goes for e-mail — people need to know you are not reading your messages that day. We provide more tips on this topic in Chapter 10.

Telecommuting: Getting Beyond the Image of Working in Your Pajamas

A great deal has already been written on the subject of telecommuting. The reason we are including it here is because it can be such a valuable part of your Comfortable Chaos toolkit. Whether you telecommute full time or part time or combine it with an alternative work schedule, it can be a beautiful path to a more peaceful existence.

Imagine not having to sit in traffic for an hour and a half every day, being able to take a lunch break or a short nap, or being able to walk out of your home office during a break and read a book to your child who has been playing upstairs with his nanny. Mary is living a similar dream. She is a regional manager for a software company and has a three-year-old son who she takes to preschool by 8:00 a.m. and picks up by 4:00 p.m. every day. To get a full day's work, she regularly checks e-mails around 7:00 a.m. before getting her son ready, and then catches up on administrative tasks in the evenings and on weekends when needed.

Many managers also recognize the beauty of allowing their employees to telecommute. Joyce, an associate IT director for a wireless communications company, had a key employee who was moving from Seattle to Phoenix and was going to quit. "Instead of letting this valuable employee leave the company, I suggested the idea of her working from Phoenix," said Joyce. "The timing was good because the company had started to work on a standard policy for telecommuting and had some good ideas documented."

The employee was able to work out of a satellite sales office for two or three days per week. This allowed her to have access to the company's computer network, interoffice mail, and some administrative support. She worked the remaining days from her home and managed her workload so that when she was at home, she didn't need the support of the satellite office.

Clearly not every manager understands the importance of retaining valued employees and is willing to be creative like Joyce. However, in this case, the telecommuting worked very well. It was a win-win situation for the employee and the company because they all were willing to be flexible and creative. Joyce also had another employee who worked from his parents' home in Pennsylvania for two months. He had a professional voicemail greeting, set a clock to Pacific Standard Time, and worked the same hours as he did when he was located on the West Coast. Joyce said, "Since many of his business contacts were in other offices and meetings often took place by telephone, most people didn't even know he was in Pennsylvania."

To get the success experienced by Joyce and her employees, a great deal of planning needs to occur. In fact, telecommuting requires the most planning of all three options in this section because there are logistical, technical, and communication issues to address. From an employer's point of view, telecommuting is the most challenging and scariest to manage since the employee is not visible. To be blunt, how will your manager be sure that you are working when you're not there? There is an obvious need to have very specific, concrete deliverables. Some jobs inherently have very measurable outputs, which make it easy to prove you are working hard. But there also needs to be a high level of trust and communication between the employer and employee.

To help make the arrangement more successful, many companies have detailed guidelines in place for telecommuting. If your company does not have any guidelines, your manager may have some specific requirements. If telecommuting is unfamiliar territory to your manager, be sure to cover all the relevant details in your proposal (see Chapter 15). It benefits both the employee and the employer to be very clear on how the arrangement will work. But before you are ready to design a proposal, ask yourself the following questions.

How will my manager and I measure my deliverables?

You need to have some tangible way to show your accomplishments. With some jobs this is built right in because you have a sales quota to meet, code to write, or pages to edit. But if your work isn't easily measured, you will need to communicate your progress differently. Maybe you could write a short weekly activity report for your boss or provide status against a project plan.

Telecommuting can pose some other challenges. There may be political ramifications of not having enough "face time" at the office. The old adage of "out of sight, out of mind" does sometimes still come in to play. For example, Bill was a manager who was judging people by how long their cars were in the parking lot rather than by the quality of their work. Once, after he made this type of remark, one of his salaried managers challenged him to check what time of the day she had responded to his voicemails to prove that she often worked later than he did. She helped to change the perception that work only occurs when in the office.

What if you handed your boss a framed snapshot of yourself sitting at your desk at home the day before you began telecommuting? That would be a humorous yet effective way to get across the point that "out of sight" doesn't have to be "out of mind."

How, and how often, will I communicate?

It is paramount to have a proactive communication plan when you are not on site. Don't wait for people to call you. Instead, consider a daily routine of calling into the office when you start your workday to see if there is anything you need to be tied in on. Or send an e-mail to your team or manager, letting them know your plan and schedule for the day, along with good times to reach you.

What equipment is needed and who will purchase it?

This is an area that may need some negotiation. You may not be able to expect your employer to pay for all of the equipment that you need at home to telecommute if it is redundant to what you already have in the office. In other words, if you have everything you need at the office and you are the one who is proposing to telecommute, it seams unreasonable to require your employer to buy you a second computer and fax machine.

If you already have a computer at home or a laptop at work that you can bring home with you, it is probably realistic to ask for help with any additional software you may need and help with getting networked. If you don't have the necessary equipment at home, you may offer to purchase some or all of it, since you are initiating the proposal. Creativity comes in handy here. Sometimes there are unused machines at work that can be taken home or maybe you buy the equipment but your company allows you to use its purchasing power to obtain significant discounts.

Does my work have confidentiality or security issues?

This isn't necessarily a roadblock but you will need to demonstrate how you will protect confidentiality and maintain security standards.

Am I clear on professional standards for telephone and e-mail etiquette?

As Joyce stated, "When someone calls the telecommuter there should be no *Wheel of Fortune* television or children yelling in the background. In addition, your office telephone should be forwarded to your home office telephone which should have a professional voicemail greeting, not the one made by the cute five-year-old."

What will I do to keep feeling like "part of the team"?

Make it easy for those in the office to reach you. For instance, program your boss and coworkers' telephones so your remote office telephone is on their speed dial. You should also make sure that when you are in the office you are attending team meetings and networking with peers.

Will I feel isolated if I am working at home by myself?

If you are a person who thrives on constantly being with other people, working alone may not be for you. Think about your co-efficient for chaos and the physical environment at home to determine if you will feel energized and productive. You may find that telecommuting a few days a week provides the right mix between working alone and interacting with others.

Am I the type of person who procrastinates?

Many telecommuters have failed because they had to clean up their kitchens, tidy their desks, or give the dog a bath before they could concentrate on getting their work done. Veteran telecommuters and their managers warn that there are many distractions at home. It is imperative that you have the drive, motivation, and maturity to stay focused on your work, and avoid the procrastination trap.

Do I have a workable child-care plan?

It's important to correct the occasional uneducated manager who believes that telecommuting is a secret plan to cuddle your children while working. One time, the same manager who counted cars in the parking lot, made a comment about an employee. He said that he didn't want to allow her to telecommute because there were other women in the office who had child-care issues and that wouldn't be fair! That is old thinking and by the way, telecommuting should never be used as a substitute for securing appropriate child care. You will need to find child care just like any other work arrangement.

Also, talk to your manager about how to handle a day that you need to care for a sick child. You may request to telecommute that day with the agreement that you will make up the time later or claim half of the day as sick time if you are not able to put in a full days' work. This depends largely on the policies and working norms of your company.

Telecommuting Light

If, after answering the above questions about telecommuting, you find that you are not an ideal candidate for telecommuting full time, you may still be able to use this strategy a few days a week or on an intermittent basis. Telecommuting does not have to be an all-or-nothing proposition. Many people telecommute a few days per week and then come in to the office on the other days. Just the simple luxury of avoiding getting dressed up and sitting in your car during rush hour for one or two days per week can do wonders to lower your stress level.

Lorraine, who is a sales manager, occasionally telecommutes for one day, or part of the day, when she has a lot of work to do that requires uninterrupted concentration, such as writing proposals for customers, preparing employee evaluations, and reviewing budgets. She can get much more work accomplished than if she were at work with a steady flow of people coming in and out of her office. She has an agreement with her boss about this arrangement. She simply leaves him a message informing him of her plans to telecommute the following day.

You could also try telecommuting part time if you experience resistance to the idea of a full-time telecommuting schedule. There may be some remnants of old thinking at your company, and by demonstrating success one or two days per week you may be able to break through the resistance. Be sure to also show your willingness to change your telecommuting plans to come in for an important meeting or team-building session.

For more information on how to set up a telecommuting office, take a look at *Telecommuting*, another book in the Self-Counsel Series.

The Common Elements of Three Wonderful Ways to Distribute Full-Time Work

The three work arrangements we have talked about in this chapter — flextime, compressed workweeks, and telecommuting — have quite a few attributes in common. For example, they all require good communication between you and your coworkers, manager, and employees. You must also have integrity about your hours and be motivated. If you are the lone ranger coming in to work at 5:00 a.m., four days per week, you never want to feel that your coworkers or manager doubt whether you actually make it in on time.

These three wonderful ways of working also require clear agreement between you and your manager as to when it may be necessary to come in on a regularly scheduled "day off" or stay late. Or how many days per week, if any, telecommuters need to physically be in the office. Then, you must have good common sense and excellent boundaries to know when and how to stick to your guns, and when you need to be flexible.

In terms of the long-term career implications of working one of these schedules, there is mostly good news. No one interviewed for this chapter felt that their long-term career goals had been negatively impacted as a result of working flextime, a compressed workweek, or telecommuting. We do believe that some short-term ramifications are possible. When you are out of the office, key decisions could be made or important projects doled out, but the chances of that can certainly be minimized. Being flexible when necessary, handling your schedule with tact and diplomacy, and staying connected with your work group will go a long way toward preventing any potential negative ramifications.

Your Schedule As Part of the Bigger Picture

It is becoming more common for entire work groups to participate in alternative work schedules. This can be a great strategy for getting your own Comfortable Chaos needs met. You could propose that your group look for productivity improvements and also assess individual work schedules. The two often go hand in hand because work process (the how) and work time (the when) are often directly connected. It may turn out that productivity gains could be achieved by having people work different or overlapping shifts.

It could also be the case that productivity gains are achieved because of happier and less stressed employees. Janelle has a team of operations specialists and she is the product control manager. All four people in her group work a 9/80 schedule. They have a rotating schedule that allows for two people out each week, one on Wednesday and one on Friday. Everyone knows the schedule ahead of time and if someone needs to change his or her day off, the team is flexible and adjusts the schedule to accommodate. Janelle says her work group feels far more relaxed than before and each person is better able to meet his or her personal priorities because of the schedule. Their company benefited in yet another way because employees use their days off to schedule medical appointments and other personal appointments that are often the cause of extended lunch hours or missed work.

Having said this, it does not mean that your management needs to break out in hives thinking that if they allow one person to try an alternative work schedule "everyone will want to." We frequently hear this from our corporate clients but they really don't need to worry. Lots of people, whether for financial reasons, fear of slowed advancement, old paradigms, or personality types, do not want to implement alternative work arrangements.

There is another way the "three wonderful ways" goes beyond the individual. In our research, it appears that men are making inroads into alternative work schedules through flextime, compressed workweeks, and telecommuting. Since they are not sacrificing any income and these schedules are becoming so much more common, both men and their employers seem to be much more comfortable with these work arrangements than before. Back in 1982 when Ian was working a flex schedule, it was very unusual for a man to be altering his schedule to accommodate children. But today, this is not seen as being out of the norm!

Although women are at least equal participants in the three alternative schedules we have just discussed, at this point, they are also more likely to be pioneers in other creative work arrangements. There are a variety of reasons behind this, not the least of which is motherhood, which presents a common and compelling reason. We certainly hope that this exclusiveness will change and more men will become willing to try the other alternative work arrangements.

For both men and women, the separation between home and work continue to blend, which is a positive step toward looking at life holistically. This does require a huge paradigm shift for many, but is so worth the effort. There is beauty in seeing the interconnectedness of all the parts of your life, using those interdependencies to feel more authentic, whole, and fulfilled while still having clearly articulated and self-enforced boundaries. This is our goal in the third I, *inter-related.*

Imagine that your new schedule allows you to spend more productive time working without the stressful time in traffic. Maybe you are able to take a walk or a nap during your lunch break. Or you go in early so you can be home when your adolescent shuffles in the door with a problem from school that can't wait. Whether it's flextime, a compressed workweek, telecommuting, or some hybrid or combination, doesn't this seem like a natural and wonderful way to work? It could be your path to Comfortable Chaos.

8 Chapter

Working Independently: How Freelancing or Consulting Could Be Right for You

Lou Ann snuggles deeper into her comforter and cozies up against her husband Ian. "Isn't it great that we are here on a rainy morning while everyone else is in rush hour traffic?" says Ian. Lou Ann couldn't agree more. Since they both started working independently out of their home, they get more sleep, can linger in bed, and still get to work sooner than during their commuting days.

Extra sleep is one benefit enjoyed by Lou Ann and Ian, but there are other advantages to working independently — as well as some challenges. This chapter will help you understand the many options for independent workers and assess whether it's the right choice for you.

The terms freelancer, consultant, and contractor are often used to describe an independent worker, but what do all of these terms mean? After checking the dictionary and online sources, we have concluded that the differences are very subtle, if they exist at all. The *American Heritage Dictionary* defines a freelancer as "a person who sells services to employers without a long-term commitment." The same dictionary defines a consultant as "one who gives expert or professional advice."

In reality, people call themselves whatever term they like best. Companies that hire independent workers also develop their own sets of definitions — which of course are not consistent even within a specific industry. It's interesting that the term "consultant" seems to carry some prestige and is widely used by people in the field of information technology. The term "freelancer" is often associated with writers, artists, and other creative types and carries its own image as a free-spirited type. The one term that has some shred of continuity is "contractor." It tends to refer to someone who is working through a staffing agency or consulting company, but even this isn't a hard and fast rule. For now, let's not worry about the terminology — let's explore why more and more people are striking out on their own as independent workers.

Carol has been working as a consultant managing technology and computer-related projects since 1998. She has very specific goals in her personal life, including researching her family's history, being a leader in her church, traveling, and improving her fluency in German. When asked about the positives of her work arrangement, she replied "Everything! Let me count the ways. I like having the flexibility to set my own hours — although this is of course also influenced by my clients' needs. But if it's a sunny day and I don't have a pressing deadline, no one cares that I take off early because they only pay me for the hours I work. There is also a lot more flexibility to travel. When I took six weeks off last summer to go to Europe, it wasn't really an issue since I had negotiated it as part of my contract arrangement."

Mary Ann provides management expertise to a variety of clients with a focus on the telecom sector. She thrives on the variety of work and the opportunity to share her expertise. "I have great clients and interesting and varied work assignments. I like working with a team of younger or less experienced staff so I can provide mentoring in addition to my project duties for the client."

As a graphic designer, Jan creates logos, wedding invitations, maps, and brochures for a variety of clients. After working as a traditional employee at several companies, she loves the flexibility of being a freelancer and being able to make her own schedule. She adds, "I work when I want to and take the jobs I want to take. If I decide a client isn't working or that we aren't meshing, I can simply drop the client and not have to answer to anyone on why I did that." Jan is expecting her first baby and plans to continue her average of 25 to 30 hours per week when the baby sleeps. But she's smart enough to have also arranged for child care two days a week!

Carol, Mary Ann, and Jan all enjoy the flexibility and variety of their work. And they have another thing in common — they all took a hard look at their own styles and preferences and embraced the first I of Comfortable Chaos, *individual*. Some of them intentionally chose to make the switch from corporate to independent work as their lives became too chaotic, while others found themselves trying it out of necessity after a layoff. Either way, by ending the traditional employee/employer relationship and becoming a consultant, freelancer, or contractor, they were able to exert more control over their schedule and work life. By setting their own personal boundaries about how much work to take on and when to perform that work, they are free from the confines of the traditional corporate work schedule.

Another great benefit of going independent is the ability to distance yourself from an unhealthy corporate climate if it's impacting your overall mental and physical health. Carol found this to be a huge relief. "As a consultant, everything is cut and dried. I go in and do the very best job I can, but I don't need to get so involved in the politics. I can just focus on exactly what I'm being paid to do. When I leave the office, work is mostly off my mind. When you're trying to get a job done well, you can't help mulling these things over outside of work sometimes." But she notes that the mulling is focused on the work itself — she doesn't have to expend any extra energy on workplace dramas.

Work Schedules and Boundaries

Independent workers don't care less than their employed counterparts do about the quality of their work. Instead, they want the freedom to establish a highly individual schedule that allows them to accomplish their work so that it is consistent with their priorities and goals. For those independents who are seeking to spend more time with their families, the freedom to move back and forth between work and home is a comfortable way to integrate their lives instead of juggling their various responsibilities.

This is the case for Darcel, who works as a contractor in the operations department of her former company. As a full-time regular employee at a high-paced software company, she was expected to put in 40 or more hours a week and do whatever it took to get the job done. When she had her daughter three years ago, she resigned as an employee but maintained her relationships, knowing she could work as a contractor. Now, she only works when she needs the income and selects assignments that she can complete from home. Darcel fits in work through the day as she can and typically works when her daughter naps and for an hour or so during the day while her daughter plays. The rest of her work is completed in the evenings when her husband is home.

Jan, the graphic designer also moves back and forth between work and other activities because it fits the nature of her business. "I typically fit in work throughout the day and into the evening depending on my current projects and deadlines. And I sometimes have to meet with clients on the weekends or evenings, since that is when they are available. At first, that made me feel like I was working all the time. Now I feel like it balances out. If I meet with someone on the weekend, then it may be slower during the week. Or I may take a day during the week and declare it a relaxing day and not work at all."

Others create more formal boundaries between their work and personal life because they prefer the various pieces of their day to be cleanly compartmentalized. This is the case for Carol who designates Wednesday mornings off limits for work so she can lead a Bible-study group at her church.

Still others use their physical spaces as a way to illustrate their availability to their families. Paul, who works from home as a business consultant providing strategy for software and telecom companies, is often working when his wife and nine-year-old son are at home. Paul said, "It took me a while to get used to working at home. When I'm behind the closed door, I'm working. My son knows that when Dad's serious he shuts the door. I mostly leave the door open and my family respects my time when I'm working. Sometimes my son will peek in and I may wave him in. Sometimes he just comes in to sit on my lap."

Where Is Your Chair? Working from Home, the Client's Office, or the Coffee Shop

When you think of a consultant or freelancer, you often picture someone working from home and enjoying the freedom to stay in his or her bathrobe and slippers. Although many people fit this description, there is no typical work location, or dress code, for an independent worker.

For many independent workers, such as Mary Ann, their work location depends on the needs of their customers. "The schedule depends on the client and where the client is located. Sometimes I work at home, other times at client sites." This is also true for Paul who mostly works from his home office but attends meetings at the client's site or other locations such as coffee shops. There are also times when he works at the client's site on a more regular basis. But for Paul, it is important to always maintain his mindset as an independent worker, and he thinks that if he spends every day in the client's office he runs the risk of feeling like an employee. "I try not to do 8:00 a.m. to 5:00 p.m. at their office because then it feels too much as if I will continue there. I need to be thinking about my next engagement and don't want to be involved in their politics." During these onsite client engagements, Paul tries to schedule three or four days a week in his home office. "But I never talk about working from home — I say I'm working from my office."

Other independent workers typically work from their client's site. This is true for Carol and it's something she discusses with the client upfront. Often she needs to be onsite to work with other team members but she informs them of any personal commitments and determines if some of the work can be done from home.

For Darcel, the whole point of being an independent worker was to be able to work from home and minimize the time her child was in the care of others. She is careful when selecting assignments to make sure the projects can be done away from the client's office. Darcel has even found a niche that works well: she discovered that work that needs to happen in the evening is very valuable to her client. "The ideal projects are the ones they need to hand off at the end of the day and then I can have the projects back to them in the morning." Darcel provides them with a difficult to fill service, and at the same time maintains her goal of working at home.

Assessing If This Lifestyle Is a Good Fit for You

Just like the other alternative work schedules we have discussed, there are some potential drawbacks if your personality is not suited to some of the realities of working independently. Following are some questions to answer to determine if this choice is for you.

Are you willing to find work by networking, marketing, and selling?

This is probably one of the biggest challenges for independent workers. Later in the chapter we'll explore using a staffing agency to find assignments. However, even if you do opt to use an agency, it's important to develop the mentality of continually networking for work.

First, you will need to clearly identify and articulate what services you can provide and how the client will benefit. If you are a freelance writer for example, list all of the types of writing products you can produce and what types of clients may need those products. Try a brainstorming exercise to help you expand the possibilities or enlist the help of a few friends. Then create a document such as a résumé or summary of past projects that you can send or e-mail to perspective clients. You may need to create several versions that are specifically targeted for different types of clients.

Many independent workers find it easiest to first call upon their former employers and coworkers. It's not nearly as difficult to approach someone who knows you and the quality of your work as it is to approach a stranger. The next step is to network with everyone else. You could start with former employers and friends who know your work. But eventually you will need to have the guts to start putting the word out that you are looking for work. That means talking with more than your family and friends. You need to think through the various groups of people you know, think about what work they do and whether they could refer you to anyone else. This is where some independent workers feel awkward, but it's something you need to learn in order to maximize your success.

Jan, the graphic designer, agrees that the ability to find work is an important skill. "To get the work you have to be a go-getter and actively pursue clients. I think most designers kind of fail at that — they like to create their art and having to do sales and marketing is a struggle." But designers, artists, and writers take heed. Selling is a necessary step for getting your creations out into the world. You may need to take a class on marketing your work, but the investment will pay off.

For Jan, the marketing and sales hasn't been very difficult. She has an outgoing personality and isn't afraid to talk about her work. To find new clients she does a mixture of formal and informal networking. She attends local women in business meetings and has found them to be very helpful. At one meeting, she started talking with some naturopathic physicians who were excited to meet a graphic designer and by the end of the evening, people were coming up to her to ask questions. Jan also networks informally wherever she goes. "Most jobs come from people I meet. Even shopping, I'll meet someone and mention I'm a graphic designer, and they'll say I need some work done or they know someone who is looking for a graphic designer."

Other independent workers find the marketing piece a real challenge. Andrea is a consultant who provides strategy, information architecture, and content development for websites and information systems. She has been an independent consultant for 15 years and normally work is easy to find. But with a tougher economy, Andrea has felt the impact and has to really push herself to avoid a feast or famine cycle. "I'm not great at going out to market myself. When you are a one-person shop it's hard to stop and market yourself when you have commitments to a client." Andrea does look for work by contacting former clients, but it's definitely not her favorite part of the job. She sums it up well by saying, "I don't have a problem balancing work and home — it's more difficult to balance work and looking for work."

Paul, the strategist for software and telecom companies, is another consultant who has been affected by the downturn of the economy. "I have to network harder now and have become more clear on defining the project for the customer. Before, the clients would almost think of it themselves. Now, I have to give them a proposal around what their issues are." Paul networks with former coworkers and clients to find work and also uses staffing agencies. He even takes it a step further. "It's helpful to talk to them about their business challenges and try and turn the staffing agency into a client. The recruiters don't often have a clear understanding of what their clients need so I offer to go with them to their client meeting for free and help define requirements."

Paul's creative approach is critical for survival in a tough market. If regular word of mouth techniques aren't working, look for new ways to introduce your services — even if it's indirectly. The more contacts you make, especially when you meet face to face, the greater the opportunities for work.

Are you able to establish boundaries that fit your working style and support your goals?

If you are considering becoming an independent worker, you probably have some goals in mind. Whether it's to spend more time with your children, enjoy more personal time, or reduce your stress, make sure you create the boundaries that will allow you to meet your goals. Boundaries are also critical for controlling the independent worker's version of the corporate beast and to tame the *imperfect* nature of Comfortable Chaos.

When you become an independent worker, you are also a business owner and it's very easy to fall into a pattern of constantly working. Even successful business owners such as Jennifer, the financial planner, say that a slow week can bring on worries of the demise of the business. Because the business is "your baby" you will likely feel pride and an overwhelming desire to succeed and may find yourself sneaking in work at all hours of the day or night.

If you left corporate life in the first place so that you could "get a life" you may not find this style of independent work entirely fulfilling. Think about your work style and what type of boundaries you could establish for yourself. Maybe you will create a "work free zone" in your home that is devoted to your other interests. Or perhaps you will have scheduled office hours in order to contain and limit your working time. Also, pay attention to your personality type and coefficient for chaos. Do you prefer constantly moving between work and home duties, or do you thrive when there is some structure to your workday? Giving some thought to this question now will help you avoid frustrations later.

This becomes even more important if you have a partner and/or children at home. You need to clearly articulate your work strategy and office hours to your family members so they can respect your work time.

Are you able to accurately assess potential clients and avoid potential problem clients?

At first you may think that there is no bad clients as long as they are paying clients; but this can lead you into trouble. First of all, some clients are slow to pay or completely disappear when the invoice arrives. This is the independent worker's worst nightmare so you will need to assess whether you can learn to spot potential problem clients and turn the bad eggs away. You can also do some research and learn the appropriate tricks for your industry, such as having the client sign a contract, collecting a deposit or retainer, and withholding delivery of the completed project until payment is received.

But there are other types of clients to avoid besides those who don't pay. A just plain difficult client will eat up lots of your time and prevent you from working on other projects. You need to hone your intuition so it is sharp during that first meeting with a client. Clients who seem difficult during the first meeting, when they are likely to be on their best behavior, will only get more challenging as the work progresses.

Jan, the graphic designer, has a story that is the ultimate example. She felt some concerns when meeting with a particular client for the first time. The client requested a logo but wanted to use the one from his previous business and just change the name. Jan explained that for copyright reasons she couldn't do that but would be glad to create a new logo. The client mentioned that he had PageMaker, a graphics software program, on his computer. This raised a few flags for Jan. She went ahead and sent him some preliminary logo designs she had prepared but didn't hear back from him. She followed up with e-mails and telephone calls but still no response. Then one day she was driving by his building and there, up on a sign, was her logo with only a few minor modifications! Since taking legal action would be too costly, Jan chalked it up as a learning experience.

Are you able to build positive relationships and develop client-specific networks?

In the first question, you had to decide if you could be a go-getter and network to find new clients. Well, once you have clients, then you need to be able to work effectively with them, and that's an entirely different skill set.

As the "expert" who has been hired to provide some product or service, you walk a fine line between directly telling the client what needs to be done and working with his or her ideas and input. Most clients have given quite a bit of thought to their project so it would be a mistake in building a relationship with them to dismiss their suggestions. As Jan put it, "You don't want to tell them exactly how to do it — you need to work with their ideas and diplomatically suggest alternatives." One of the most successful strategies is to take one of their ideas and build on it or modify it in such a way that the client still has ownership. Then the client feels valued as a person, yet can congratulate himself or herself on having had the good sense to hire you.

Another strategy is to clearly communicate what you plan to deliver and to get the client's agreement. You can do this via a contract or, at a minimum, document it in an e-mail or letter. Then be sure to continue to communicate and clarify any agreed-upon changes. Clients want to know that you are working on the right thing and appreciate the reassurance.

There is another aspect to relationship building that extends beyond your immediate client. You want to be able to quickly establish positive relationships with anyone else you may need to work with to complete the project. Sometimes the client will want you to interface with a number of different people, or you may need to find new resources on your own to produce the desired result. For example, if you are an interior designer hired as part of a team creating a new house, you will need to coordinate with the architect, builder, and all the suppliers. In addition to your regular suppliers, the client may insist on ones you haven't worked with before. This is where you must be able to work collaboratively. This often requires a great deal of assertiveness and diplomacy! If you decided to become an independent worker because you like to be an individual contributor, you will still need people skills because no one gets to work in a complete vacuum.

Working in the client's office poses another set of challenges. One of the things many people take for granted if they have worked for a company for several years or longer is the advantage of knowing whom to call to get things done. In every company there are policies and procedures, but in reality, most of us pick up the telephone or send an e-mail to someone we know can help. Once we have built good relationships with key experts, we become accustomed to timely and accurate answers.

As an independent worker, you arrive cold into a client's work group and often know very little about the organizational structure, let alone who the key people are who get things done. There is nothing worse than a consultant who arrives and acts as if he or she knows more about the client's business than the people working there! Be respectful and approachable. A little humility goes a long way and you will need the help of others to be successful.

If you are working at the client's office, even the mechanics of getting telephone or computer connections can take an outsider precious hours to coordinate. However, if you can learn to quickly create a network, this will not be an obstacle to your success. The key is being willing to ask some questions. A great place to start is when you are negotiating with your client on the specifics of the assignment. Ask, "Who will be my key contacts for questions on logistics and on the project?" Be sure to gather several names and their telephone numbers, and ask for back-ups when they are not available. Request a high-level understanding of the organizational structure and where your key contacts reside in the hierarchy.

It's also a great idea to find the savvy administrative person who knows everyone. As any good salesperson will tell you, be extremely polite and respectful to these people. They can often make or break your project.

Can you work independently and manage to a deadline?

Even though you will still work with other people and may even sit in a cubicle or office just like the employees of the company, the nature of your relationship is different — and so are the expectations. You will either be paid by the hour or by the project, and this makes the value and cost effectiveness of your work very visible to the client. You will definitely want to ensure that your clients feel like they are getting their money's worth — or more. Your future work is dependent on the reputation you build so it's critical that you can deliver on your commitments.

For some people, having such concrete deadlines and specific expectations can be intimidating. They prefer having the responsibility rest with the team and its leader. If you are not comfortable with the spotlight or don't have basic project planning skills, the decision to be an independent worker may not be for you. However, lots of people really thrive on this role. It can be very motivating and empowering to know that the client is depending on you, and your income is directly related to your ability to get the job done!

Can you give up the traditional rewards of working in a corporate setting?

By traditional rewards, we are not just talking about a thank-you coffee mug or a 20-years-of-service watch. There are some unique intangible rewards in many corporate-type jobs and you need to think about your own motivations before becoming an independent worker.

One of the intangible rewards for many people is having a reputation for being competent and knowledgeable. When you develop a level of expertise in a certain subject or you have nurtured relationships with other departments in order to get tasks accomplished, people in the company tend to come to you, and are often appreciative of your expertise and ability to solve their problems. For some people, that feeling of being needed becomes a large part of their identity and they even feel threatened if someone invades their turf. There is nothing wrong with deriving satisfaction from the level of competence you have developed, but if you are considering becoming an independent worker, you will need to be able to decide if you can exchange this type of satisfaction for a different one. According to Paul, "When you leave a traditional job, you ask, who the hell am I? You have to get past that and redefine your identity. As a consultant you have to build your expertise and change the client's thinking in a respectful way. It feels good that you have helped and you take that as the win."

Not only must you derive your satisfaction differently, but you also have to be willing to build trust with every new client. Even if you have a solid reputation based on past consulting jobs, each new client lacks significant experience with you. This means you will have to build your reputation every time you start a new project.

Can you cope financially and emotionally during the times you don't have work?

The financial and emotional implications of not having work can be very different so let's discuss them one at a time. Financially, you need to be disciplined and organized so that you plan for periods when you will have no income. It's interesting that all of the people interviewed for this chapter were financially organized or became financially organized once they started working independently. They realized that they needed to be the captain of their own ships and, at a minimum, had gathered all the elements of their complete financial picture and had a good understanding of each piece.

They also recognized that the income from a particular job might need to sustain them through a dry period so they became good at saving. Carol made this transition when she became a consultant. "You can't just spend everything you make. You're on your own to save for retirement and finance your down time." In Chapter 12 you will learn the many ways to develop financial savvy — and we recommend this for anyone who is considering an alternative work schedule. But as an independent worker, this is imperative. It's not cause for panic but you must plan for how you will weather any income gaps.

On the emotional side, not having a project can be a blessing or a curse. You may treasure these pockets of personal time and pursue other interests until you find more work. But it's also possible that the feeling of not having paid work can leave you feeling anxious. Even if you have planned for the down times financially, it can be hard on your ego and your psyche to not be engaged in a project. You can have good intentions and spend your time marketing and selling your skills but this can start to feel very draining after a while. Remind yourself that this is only temporary and that you will find work. Do continue your marketing and networking efforts but also remember to have some fun. Your corporate counterparts still have to show up to the office even when the work is slow and then they may have to worry about layoffs. You, on the other hand, can go out for a walk, spend time with your children, or clean out a closet. Celebrate your freedom and consider this one bend in the river of your white-water raft trip.

Staffing Agencies: Friend or Foe?

The world of staffing agencies is a rapidly changing industry. What was once a venue primarily for clerical workers, typically women, is now a diverse marketplace for a variety of skills. We are calling these companies "staffing agencies" for the purpose of simplicity, but many of them refer to themselves as consulting firms or other names. Their survival is very much tied to the state of the economy. When companies are hiring, new staffing agencies sprout up like dandelions, and when the economy takes a downturn, many agencies are mowed over.

So what exactly does a staffing agency do? They make their money by establishing clients and then providing those clients with workers. Some agencies do both permanent placement and temporary placement, while others specialize in one or the other. For permanent placements, also called direct hires, the staffing agency works to find a "permanent" employee and then charges the company a fee — often a percentage of the employee's first year's salary. For temporary placements, the agency provides the company with temporary workers who are employees of the staffing agency. The use of temporary workers has become quite popular since it allows the client company to have a fluctuating work force that can easily be expanded or reduced depending on the workload and/or available budget. The client company also avoids having to carry the cost of benefits, bonuses, and other non-salary types of compensation.

There are some very good reasons for you to work through a staffing agency. If you hate searching for assignments, this may be the solution for you since the agency does all the legwork. Or you may want to work for a particular company, and that company only wants to bring you in through a staffing agency. Either way, if you decide to work through a staffing agency as a temporary worker, it is helpful to know the two pricing models used to bill companies.

How staffing agencies bill

The first pricing model is called a mark-up rate. In this case, the client company knows what your direct hourly rate will be and often is involved in negotiating that rate with the staffing agency. The client company will also pay a percentage mark-up to the staffing agency on top of your direct rate. So if your direct rate is $75/hour and the mark-up is 30 percent, then the client company is billed $97.50/hour. Now, don't get too outraged just yet. The staffing agency has to cover the fixed costs of carrying you as an employee (things like social security and taxes), plus they have to cover their recruiting and administrative costs. They call these fixed costs, statutory costs.

When you are considering an assignment under this arrangement, be proactive and ask what the mark-up rate will be to the client company. It's unlikely that you will be offered this information so it pays to ask. You can also ask to know the staffing company's fixed costs. Then do some quick math — the mark-up includes the fixed costs plus their profit. We can't tell you exactly what the profit should be, but two to three percent profits are not unreasonable. Higher profits may be justified for specific, highly sought-after skills.

The other type of pricing model is called a bill rate. In this case, the client company does not know your direct rate. Instead, the hourly bill rate includes the amount you make plus the fee to the staffing agency. Again, ask what the bill rate is to the client company and ask about their fixed costs. Most staffing agencies prefer the bill rate model since they can work directly with you on your hourly rate and offer flexible benefit packages. This model provides some advantages to client companies as well since they can control costs by establishing the bill rate ranges. Some people also believe that the bill rate model supports a strategy of mitigating a co-employment perception.

Co-employment and length of assignment

Co-employment is a term that became more common after the *Vizcaino versus Microsoft Corporation* case. In this case, temporary workers at Microsoft sued the company claiming they were "defacto employees" and were entitled to the same benefits as regular employees, including stock options, which were very lucrative at the time. The temporary workers successfully argued that they were no different than regular employees — they worked on the same assignments and many had been with Microsoft for years. The court agreed and the overall cost to Microsoft was $97 million.

Since that case, many companies have taken measures to ensure that their temporary workers could not be deemed "defacto employees." Strategies include clearly spelling out that employee benefits are only for employees and creating different practices for temporary workers that clearly separate them from traditional performance reviews, progressive discipline procedure, and employee reward programs. One of the most common strategies is to limit the length of time a temporary worker can be on assignment, and in some cases, to also specify a required "break" between assignments. At Microsoft, temporary workers can work no longer than 12 months and then cannot return on another assignment for 100 days.

If you decide to work with a staffing agency, find out whether the client company has any limitations on the length of assignment — this may affect whether or not you want to take a position. Also recognize that because of legal concerns, some companies insist on bringing on their temporary workers through a staffing agency. By using a third-party employer (the staffing agency), the client company has less work to do to ensure they are in compliance with tax laws. Some also believe they mitigate their risk of perceived co-employment by bringing temporary workers in through staffing companies.

Choosing a staffing agency

So what if the use of staffing agencies is appealing to you, or the only route to your desired client company is through a staffing agency? In addition to asking how their billing structure works, what their mark-up versus bill rate is, and about any length of assignment limitations, you should do some other digging before signing on. You may want to copy the list of questions in Checklist 1 at the end of this section and use them when you are evaluating staffing agencies.

If you are interested in working at a particular client company, like your former company, for example, find out which staffing agencies the company uses. Most companies have a list of staffing agencies that they work with and have contracts with. Don't make the mistake of thinking that you can pick your staffing agency and then talk the company into doing business with them. It costs time and money to negotiate a new contract with a staffing agency and most client companies like to use a small number of staffing companies to improve their negotiating ability and to simplify their communication and maintenance processes. If you don't have a particular client company in mind, ask the staffing agencies which companies they have contracts with. The quality of their list is an important consideration.

Once you are ready to investigate a particular staffing agency, start with the history of the company. Check their website to see how long they have been in business. A brand new company isn't necessarily an automatic no — but the owners should be experienced in the industry. It's not uncommon for managers or recruiters from experienced firms to leave and start their own companies or join with new start-up efforts.

The next major item to check is the agency's benefits package. You may be able to find this information on their website, or often you can get a more detailed description by requesting a benefits booklet or brochure. The benefits can vary greatly between staffing agencies. Some offer a very bare bones package but that may be okay with you if you have benefits through a spouse or partner. If the benefits are sparse, the staffing agency will have reduced expenses, which should maximize your hourly rate. Other agencies offer a very robust benefits package and allow you to pick and choose the pieces that you need. If you opt for the costly benefits like medical and dental and 401K contributions, then you need to expect that your hourly rate will reflect those choices. The benefits research you do goes hand-in-hand with the bill rate versus mark-up question. You need to understand all these dynamics in order to find the agency that best meets your needs.

The next item to check is employment contracts and non-compete clauses. Almost all staffing agencies will ask you to sign some type of employment contract. It is usually for the duration of the client assignment and basically states that you can't leave a current assignment for another agency. This protects the agency from losing the money they invested in finding you the position and paying the statutory costs if you decide to quit. The agreement may also say that the client company can't hire you away during the assignment. This too is probably okay because if you want to become an employee of the client company, you can either wait for the end of the assignment or the client company will negotiate with the staffing company to hire you.

Noncompete clauses are entirely different and somewhat controversial. Their intent is to prevent you from working for a competitor during the assignment and often after the assignment. The noncompete clause may require that you not work for the client company and/or other companies in the same industry for a specific period such as a year. Be wary of signing one of these agreements. Unless the staffing company has poured a lot of training dollars into you, the request seems unwarranted. Check with an attorney before signing one of these agreements.

There is one last detail worth checking and that has to do with the agency's sign-up process and follow-on commitments. Darcel, the independent worker, who exclusively takes assignments with her former employer, always checks to see if they have an orientation requirement. "Some agencies have a four-hour orientation which is very difficult for me to attend due to child-care issues." So Darcel avoids these agencies or asks if she can get the orientation information in some other manner. She also recommends finding out if the agency will require you to attend any regular meetings. Some agencies have a quarterly information session where you can ask questions. Just ask if they consider these meetings "required."

The three phases of an assignment

The best way to get a realistic picture of the staffing agency is to ask for references from their current employees. There is nothing more enlightening than talking to someone who is living the experience. Ask the current employees or associates about the three phases of an assignment.

The first phase is when the staffing agency is searching for positions and matching candidates to the positions. How did the associate feel about the communication process during the search? How well were they screened to ensure the position was a good fit? Their answers will probably depend on their relationship with a recruiter at the agency. Steve, a manager at an international staffing agency, says, "Recruiter relationship is really the most important factor. You want people who are going to work for you — people who will help further your career and not just look for an assignment. A good recruiter helps with career planning and provides training and guidance, as well as access to other clients." Steve says that good recruiters also "reverse sell." This means that they don't just rely on the positions coming in from the client companies, they call companies when you are available and pitch your skills.

The second phase is the "on board" time when the associate is performing the work. Could they turn to the staffing agency to resolve any problems? Were they paid in a timely manner? Was there any confusion or misrepresentation of benefits? At some agencies you will continue to work with the recruiter when you are performing the work. At other agencies a human resources generalist will take over. You can get good service either way but find out whom you should call with questions or concerns while you are on the assignment.

The third phase is the termination of the assignment. In this phase the staffing agency may not always have much control. Often times, the manager at the client company will tell the associate that the assignment is ending instead of contacting the staffing agency. But you can ask the associate if the staffing agency became involved in the end of assignment process once they were notified. Did they help the associate through the mechanics of the exit process and answer questions? Did the agency start communicating about possible new assignments?

It really pays to thoroughly research the staffing agency you will be working for. Consider shopping around again once you have completed an assignment with a particular agency. Even if you had a positive experience, there may be an even better choice for your next assignment.

CHECKLIST 1
EVALUATING A STAFFING COMPANY

1. Pricing Model

   a. Mark-up or bill rate?

   b. What are the fixed or statutory costs?

   c. What is the mark-up or bill rate the client company will pay?

2. Are there any length of assignment limitations from the client companies?

3. Does the company have contracts with your targeted client companies?

4. History of the staffing company — check their website.

5. What benefit packages do they offer, if any?

6. Employment contracts or noncompete clauses?

7. Sign-up procedures. Are there orientations or meetings?

8. Check references — current contractors

   a. The finding an assignment phase including recruiter relationship

   b. The onboard phase

   c. The end of assignment phase

A New Model: Using a Mixture of Different Employment Arrangements

Staffing agencies can be a useful way to find assignments as an independent worker. But some independent workers are taking a new approach and use agencies only in certain circumstances. Paul, the business consultant, is modeling what we believe is an innovative twist on independent work. He has mastered the mechanics of the three different ways to be "engaged" in an assignment.

The first is the pure independent consultant model. This is where he works directly for the client and bills them the agreed-upon amount. This work naturally pays the best since there isn't a percentage that is going to a staffing agency. Paul calls this "the high-margin, gravy work." He understands the market well, networks continually in order to maximize his chances of this work, and knows what to charge. He is also proficient in the mechanics of independent work. Paul has set himself up as a limited liability corporation. Other people start as a sole proprietorship. Be sure to research which is appropriate for you and consider consulting with an attorney.

When Paul can't get independent work, which has been an issue only after the slowing of the dot.com economy, he leverages some of the staffing agencies. "I have made contacts and check with them weekly." Paul also maintains his corporation status when he takes an assignment through a staffing agency. He works with agencies that are comfortable with what's called a "corp. to corp." arrangement. The agencies pay him as one of their suppliers and Paul maintains his tax advantages.

The third strategy is really ingenious. On the surface, it would appear to be the traditional employer/employee relationship. But in this case, the "employee" doesn't view himself or herself in the traditional way. As Paul explains, "Lots of companies want an employee not a consultant. So I agree but don't focus on that typical relationship. I maintain my objectivity and think of it as a six-month engagement." Paul calls it "W2" work to reflect the fact that he is paid as an employee of the company and receives a W2 form. The key is, that in his mind, he remains a consultant and sees the arrangement as only short term. He still gives his all to the employer, just as he would in the other two strategies, but he views the W2 situation only as the mechanics of the engagement. For whatever reason, the client company believes in hiring people, so he adjusts to their preference and then goes about the business of providing his services — always keeping an eye toward his next engagement.

The challenge in following Paul's model is becoming adept at the details of all three arrangements. Paul agrees that it can be confusing at first, but once you have set up a system and have some practice it gets easier. He also cautions that you need to make sure you have enough engagements to legitimately claim business expenses. Again, consult with an attorney to be sure you understand all the details.

Getting Started As an Independent Worker

So how do you get started if you want to become an independent worker? It doesn't have to be as difficult and overwhelming as you might imagine. If you are currently working for a company, there are several ways you can ease into independent work.

One way is to explore converting from a regular employee to a contractor or consultant at your company. This is a good solution if the many dimensions of being an employee are preventing you from achieving the Comfortable Chaos you desire. By becoming an independent worker, you may be able to distance yourself from the politics and certain meetings and obligations, and focus more on the specific tasks.

Another way to explore the independent life is to continue working at your corporate job, but do some research about the market for your services. Then try lining up projects on the side. That way you get a taste of how easy or difficult it will be to get work, and you have the opportunity to practice the new skills you will need to develop.

Many successful independent workers did not test the waters, but instead dove in head first after a layoff. They were able to network through their former employers or friends to find that first freelance or consulting job. Of course the ease in which they found that first job depends on the economy, the market demand for their particular services, as well as their individual networks and reputations. The point is that people have successfully made the transition under what could be considered difficult circumstances. This may give you the courage to at least try out your dream of being an independent worker.

Whether you try it out slowly, or commit to this new way of working, you will need to do some research on the mechanics of setting up your business. Check your library or bookstore and you will find a wealth of titles on the details of business licenses, taxes, and corporation status, as well as books on how to sell and market. Other resources are the Small Business Administration and SCORE (Service Corps of Retired Executives). They can assist you with writing a business plan, which is a critical first step. You may also want to consult with a tax accountant upfront so you know which records to keep. You can also learn a great deal by talking with people who are already working independently. Offer to take them to lunch to find out how they got started.

Lastly, we want to offer a few thoughts on home offices. You need to first decide what type of work style will best meet your needs. For example, do you envision yourself working in uninterrupted blocks of time? In that case you need a space that is somewhat separate from the rest of your household. Ideally, you would have an office with a door. This is what Andrea has done. She has an office off her bedroom and can shut the door. "I can go in right away in the morning, then stop and take a shower at noon. This way I'm not interfering with my family's morning routine." Andrea and her husband both work at home and employ a nanny. Andrea enjoys her lunch break with the kids but finds that she needs the morning to be an uninterrupted stretch of time for work.

Others prefer, or accept, a more dynamic working arrangement. Darcel purposely sets up her laptop downstairs in her family's playroom. That way her daughter can play, use the family computer, or watch a video. This works well for the two or three hours Darcel works during the day, but keep in mind that this is a tough road and takes a great deal of discipline and patience. For Darcel, it does present challenges in the evening when it would be much easier to be away from the house while her husband is on child-care duty.

You may want to experiment with different setups until you find the formula that works best for you. As you are setting up your desk, computer, and files, don't forget about good ergonomics — you don't want to sideline yourself by developing a sore back or a repetitive motion injury.

Independent Workers: The Future of White-Collar Work?

If you have been in the workforce during the last five to ten years, you know how much corporate life has changed. You probably now see yourself as much more in charge of your own destiny — the days of a company looking after you are pretty much gone.

It is quite possible that traditional white-collar jobs may soon be gone as well. As a way to reduce costs, we predict that companies will continue to reduce their numbers of "core" employees, and instead rely more on project-based work. This means that instead of spending money on the complexities of managing employees, they will match the right people to the project. More and more independent workers will be needed and only time will tell if a certain preference develops about how those people are engaged. Will staffing companies become more popular and provide a method for companies to outsource the hassle of payroll and benefits administration? Or will laws change to make it easier to directly bring on independent workers? Either way, you are not making a mistake to learn to see yourself as your own company.

This is the focus of Tom Peter's book *The Brand You 50: Fifty Ways to Transform Yourself from an "Employee" into a Brand That Shouts Distinction, Commitment, and Passion!* (Knopft, 1999). Tom believes that more than 90 percent of white-collar jobs will be reinvented or reconceived in the next decade. We aren't sure we agree with 90 percent, but we definitely concur that there will be a major shift away from the traditional employer/employee relationship.

All of this doesn't have to be scary. In fact, it's encouraging that the independent workers we interviewed for this book all felt very positive about their futures. We asked if their vision of their future career path had changed, and if so, what did they now dream of? Everyone said that they wanted to continue working independently, and their joy about the way they spent their time came through loud and clear.

Carol commented, "My dreams these days are completely 'un-career' related. I've changed the focus of my life from my job and career, to my 'real life.' Don't get me wrong, I do focus on my projects and clients, and do an excellent job — but for me now, it's just a reasonably interesting way to work and pay the bills."

Paul had another fascinating perspective. "My dreams before had destinations on them. I would achieve this level at the company, have this number of clients, and generate this amount of revenue. Now, I don't have an ultimate goal. I want to continue to do things that are challenging and fun, and yes, I do have objectives around revenues. But I'm getting more satisfaction out of seeing it all come together." Paul gave an example of talking with a friend he hadn't been in connection with for two years. It turns out that he had been on a path of getting exactly the experience that this friend now needs. He likens it to following circles versus a linear career path. "You just don't know where the circles will go," says Paul. "Now I wait for the unexpected opportunity. Those are the ones I gravitate toward."

So what will you gravitate toward? If your future is as an independent worker, we wish you a wonderful journey and the ability to continually adjust and move toward Comfortable Chaos.

Part III

Loving Life at Home Full Time or Part Time

f o m C
f o r t
a l b e
C h
a o
s

Chapter 9

Staying Home Full Time: Embracing the Nebulous Nature of It All

"Before I left my job, I had visions of spending blissful days with my children, taking up new hobbies, cleaning out closets, and just basically getting everything done with no stress." Ann, a six-year veteran of staying home full time, laughs when reminded of that statement she once made. She is certainly not alone in her perception that staying home is all fun and relaxation. Unless you have walked in the socks of a stay-at-home parent, it's hard to really understand the day-to-day realities.

This chapter will give you a realistic glimpse into what it's like to stay at home full time with children. Whether you have already transitioned to a full-time role at home or are just considering this option, you'll learn the pros and cons of this very misunderstood lifestyle. Numerous tips and solutions are also given on how to overcome various challenges.

Let's start with the positives of staying at home full time — and there are many. One of the obvious benefits is that you will be the primary caregiver for your children and will be there for all their milestones, achievements, and challenges. When asked why she left a successful career and a flexible work schedule,

Mimi gave the same answer as many stay-at-home moms, "I wanted to be at home with my children." That statement speaks volumes, and if your heart really wants to be at home full time then this is an important signal. Your gut feeling is very meaningful, but you may still want to read the rest of the chapter to make sure you have an accurate picture of life at home.

There are other wonderful benefits of staying home full time. You have a great deal of flexibility when it comes to scheduling and planning your time. No more complicated coordination with your calendar at work. You set the pace and the schedule for the entire household. This leads to another benefit — your overall stress level will diminish. Ellen describes this well. "When I was working, I would often go to bed with my brain churning on work issues and problems and I had a hard time relaxing. Between remembering all of my work and my family obligations my brain literally felt full. Now that I am at home full time, I am still busy but it's much less complicated. I don't feel pulled in so many directions."

Being at home is also much less stressful when your children get sick. Instead of frantically trying to get your mother to come over or trade off care with your spouse so you can at least get to your critical meetings, you can more easily let go of your plans for the day and really nurture your child. Your children may also benefit on those days when they are a little under the weather because you can let them stay home instead of dosing them up with a pain reliever and hoping they make it through child care or school that day.

Another benefit is that you can often reduce the overall pressure on your partner and the entire family. If your spouse or partner is working, he or she will feel some relief at no longer having to drop off or pick up kids from child care. Be careful though, not to commit to taking on every household task as the stay-at-home parent. Put some thought and time into making the routines of the household run more efficiently and smoothly, and the entire family will feel the benefits.

Lastly, with some ingenuity and effective planning you should be able to take good care of the caregiver — you.

Stay-at-home parents typically get more sleep than parents who work outside the home and there are many creative options when it comes to fitting in some exercise and personal pursuits. We'll talk about how to make sure this happens later in the chapter.

Now that we have covered some of the benefits of staying at home full time, let's start to delve into the daily realities of living this lifestyle. The best way to do this is through the framework of the three "I"s we discussed in Chapter 1.

Staying at Home Is Highly Individual

Life as a stay-at-home parent is a very individual endeavor because everyone has such a unique and different experience when they stay home to raise children. That's because your coefficient for chaos, parenting style, lifestyle choice, and financial resources can all shape your stay-at-home experience.

Even two spouses parenting the same children can approach the stay-at-home role differently. Ruth and Dave are somewhat of an unusual case. Thanks to company mergers and good fortune with stock options, they both left their jobs three months before their first child was born and stayed at home together for two years. During that time they also had another child, Dave remodeled their house, and Ruth occasionally did some independent consulting. They both felt strongly about dispelling stereotypical gender roles and leading thoughtful, purposeful lives instead of blindly following along with what everyone else was doing. That having been said, they still had vastly different experiences while staying home together.

Ruth is a high CFC person who likes to set goals and see tasks completed. While she values being in control of her own time, she does need a fairly high degree of structure. She found the stay-at-home role to be a real challenge. At times she felt restless and unfocused. She also worried about finances and was acutely aware of not bringing in any money.

Dave has a much lower CFC and required much less structure than Ruth did. However, he tended to focus on one task at a time in a methodical approach. Unlike Ruth, he had a much more pleasurable and fulfilling experience as a stay-at-home parent. In fact, when it came time for one of them to return to work, they jointly decided that Ruth would return to work 30 hours per week. Dave is very happy continuing to be at home with the children.

Dave and Ruth are just two examples of the many possible experiences as a stay-at-home parent. Both were successful at the role, yet they handled the duties differently, and one of them found it easier to enjoy the process than the other. You will have your own unique experience as a stay-at-home parent. The better you know yourself, the more likely you are to know if this choice is right for you. You will also be able to customize your approach to the many duties of a stay-at-home parent, and by working with your personal preferences you increase your chances of a positive experience.

It also helps to fully embrace the fact that staying at home and shaping a life that is right for you and your family is a highly individual choice. Throw out society's preconceived notions and judgments, and create a situation that works for you and those around you.

Staying at Home Is Definitely Imperfect

If there is one thing that parenting teaches us, it's that life is messy and imperfect. Staying home full time will give you lots of opportunities to give up perfectionism. One time, Ellen decided that she had time to do an exercise tape before getting showered and out the door with the kids. But she didn't factor in her three-year-old daughter having an "accident" on a chair in the family room. This required cleaning up the stain on the chair and convincing her daughter that the other pink outfit would be just as nice. When she finally succeeded, her older child started having a total meltdown about a toy breaking. That is life at home with kids! Some days it seems to be like this all day long. The positive side is that we realize the need to be more flexible and to live more in the moment if we want to keep our sanity.

Staying at Home Is Intensely Inter-Related

At first it may seem like the choice to stay at home full time is rather one dimensional and therefore not holistic. But nothing could be further from the truth. Just because you no longer have paid work as part of your world, doesn't mean that the remaining pieces of your life are not connected. For example, one aspect of your stay-at-home role is parenting, and another is running the house. Your success in one area will contribute to your self-esteem and carry over to the other. The reverse is also true. Let's say you are in the midst of remodeling the house and there is constant mess and a makeshift kitchen. It is quite likely that you will feel less patient with your children and not be able to live up to your normal standard of parenting.

There is another aspect of inter-related that is unique to the stay-at-home parent. Of all the work/life choices, this role provides you with the greatest impact on the overall happiness and health of your family. Your actions have a huge effect on your children because they interact with you all day long. The entire family is typically at your mercy when it comes to what they eat, what they wear, what social activities they will attend, and the overall atmosphere of their home. The tone you set is contagious, and your mood and happiness will also have a direct impact on their lives. This can be a rather daunting realization but you do have to cut yourself some slack. Your life as a stay-at-home parent will have many ups and downs and there will definitely be times when your patience will run thin.

Now that you have had a glimpse of the stay-at-home world from the perspective of the three "I"s, it's time to move on to the specific challenges of this choice.

Handling the Nebulous Nature of the Job

The word *nebulous* kept presenting itself, whether spoken or implied, in our interviews with stay-at-home parents. Most of us, like it or not, spend much of our school and work lives abiding by the structure that has been imposed on us by someone else. We push against it and are often irritated by it, but it does, in a way, offer us shelter from too much chaos. When you become a stay-at-home parent of young children, the only structure that exists is in things like doctors' appointments, naps, feedings, and preschool, but even those are somewhat flexible. When the kids get older, there is some structure provided by their school schedules, but the rest you have to create yourself.

So how do you handle the nebulous nature of being a stay-at-home parent? Here are some strategies to help you cope.

Design and create your own structure

The first thing you have to do is decide how much structure is right for you.

If you are a high CFC, you may have a great need for structure, although it probably needs to be the structure of your choosing. If you are a low CFC, you may innately avoid scheduling too many things because you know it will feel overwhelming.

Gretchen is a mid-range CFC who stays at home with her two young boys and has created a routine for her day. In the morning she runs errands or exercises with her preschool-aged son. Later in the morning, she picks up her other son who is in half-day kindergarten and they all go home for lunch. She reserves the afternoons to do something fun with the kids, allowing plenty of time to get home and start dinner without a rush. She likes having a mix between high activity times and planned quiet times. For some high CFC people, Gretchen's routine would feel too constricted; they would prefer winging the day in search of excitement and high activity. However, this approach is not the case for all high CFCs. Some really thrive when they have a tight schedule and lots of activities on the calendar. We know some stay-at-home moms who carry a PDA with a schedule that could rival that of any corporate executive.

Dave, the stay-at-home dad from earlier in the chapter is a low CFC. "If structure isn't needed, why create it?" he asks. He has a loose plan for his days that includes getting out and doing something in the morning. Whether it is errands or the zoo, he likes to get away from home a portion of the day in the morning. Then in the afternoon he does projects and chores.

As you can see, there are different approaches to adding some structure to reduce the nebulous nature of staying at home. Think about your preferences and experiment with different levels of structure until it feels right. Then try these other tips to further reign in the nebulous nature of life at home with kids.

Surrender to the fact that the work is never done and set boundaries

Remember the corporate beast? This is a useful perspective whether you are at the office or at home. It's impossible to be completely caught up with all your work! And as a stay-at-home parent, you live amongst your "to dos" and can never escape them. Instead of driving yourself crazy and your health into the ground, shift your paradigm to set some boundaries about when to stop. This helps with the nebulous nature because boundaries are another way to put more definition in your days.

In terms of housework, this may mean breaking down tasks into very small pieces such as "I will clean this room today and another room tomorrow." It can also be a time boundary such as straightening up the house for ten minutes every morning after the kids leave for school, or limiting the time you read to your child to half an hour every night instead of allowing it to go on and on and ultimately eat up any adult time you may have before going to bed yourself.

Recognize and embrace your many daily transitions in new ways

We covered transitions in Chapter 4 but they are worth a review when thinking about the stay-at-home role. Not only can transitions help you create some pools of calm water, they also add milestones to your day and provide a comforting sense of routine and structure.

The number of small transitions that occur each day as a stay-at-home parent are staggering. Recognizing and marking these transitions can help you to harness the nebulous oozing mass of your day and become more focused and satisfied. What are some common transitions that you have in your days? Some typical ones include getting your kids up and ready in the morning, sending them off to preschool or school, preparing lunch for yourself and any children that are at home, and then welcoming home older children from school and beginning the dinnertime preparations.

If your children are very young and don't go to school or preschool, then you have an even larger reason to punctuate the many small transitions that occur naturally or by your own self-imposed structure. Gretchen's daily routine that we talked about in the first strategy also helps her by creating definite markers in the day. By insuring that everyone transitions well from their morning activities to afternoon, she generally has enjoyable afternoons. The kids do well with the structure because they know what is expected and when they will be shifting activities.

One of the key things to remember about creating a transition is to allow plenty of time so that the transition isn't stressful because you are running late. The other trick is to do something to make it enjoyable. Check the transition ideas again in Chapter 4 to get some ideas on how to improve your difficult transitions and turn them into comfortable pieces of structure in your day.

Creating a Sense of Accomplishment and Positive Feedback

When you have just done the fourth load of laundry and your son arrives home with his filthy soccer uniform and a collection of dirty socks in his gym bag, it's hard to feel like you are getting anywhere. The nature of stay-at-home work prevents you from ever feeling truly "done" because your family never stops dirtying their clothes and wanting to eat.

To top it all off, you also don't get much positive feedback on the work you do. Parenting can be a thankless job — and all the effort you put into creating happy, secure, and well-mannered children may not be evident for several years. On top of that, nobody comes over to admire your newly organized linen closet and tells you what a fabulous job you did. Nope — you are on you own when it comes to creating a sense of accomplishment and providing feedback. Here are some tips for making sure you end your day feeling appreciated and with a sense of accomplishment.

Start viewing your home as your workplace

Making this subtle shift can make a huge difference to how you feel. You probably won't view the entire house as your workplace, but think of a few important zones. The kitchen is certainly a workplace, as is the laundry room, your desk, and possibly some other areas of the house. You should set yourself up for success just like you would in an office. This means having the right tools, organizational systems, and processes that make your job easier.

Judi, who recently left her job of 12 years, said, "I explained to my son that I no longer left the house in the morning when they went to school. Therefore, he had to now think of the house as my place of work." She came to the conclusion that a messy house equated to mental chaos and agitation for her. Now she holds the kids more accountable for a higher level of organization within the house and she tidies up her "office" every morning after the kids leave so she is ready for her day. This also allows her to manage the chaos to her personal tolerance level.

Put small, trivial-seeming tasks on your to-do list and check them off

Cindy is a stay-at-home mom who lists getting up, getting the kids' lunches made, and getting them off to school as separate line items on her to-do list. She said this made all the difference to her and we believe it! If you don't count those things, it can feel like you didn't get anything done all day, and of course that is not the case.

Dave also uses this strategy. He says, "I like to break things down into 10- to 20-minute time frames." He commented that he is good at constantly breaking projects into bite-sized pieces interspersed with small blocks of fun with the kids. His to-do list has things on it like "weed garden bed #1, weed garden bed #2, play with kids."

If you are goal and task oriented, you can benefit immensely from this simple, yet powerful tool: the detailed to-do list. Congratulate yourself at the end of the day on a job well done.

Delegate even though you don't have employees

Most stay-at-home parents don't have a housecleaner or other staff person to delegate to, but that doesn't mean that tactful, thoughtful delegation can't happen. Any time you are feeling overwhelmed or something has been on your to-do list for several days without getting checked off, carefully consider to whom you might delegate.

Most children older than four years old can help at least a little with laundry, food preparation, and cleaning. Supportive significant others will, when asked, also assist with tasks or switch tasks. Get creative; you may even be able to trade tasks with a friend. One group of women decided that they would all work together to clean each other's homes since they all disliked the solitary drudgery. Each day, they all went to a different person's house. In the end, they had all spent the same amount of time cleaning that they had previously, but it was more fun and they had actually done better work.

If you have the money, consider hiring someone to do something that you previously did yourself. Try it for a few months and see if it makes a difference. Many people leave our seminars vowing to cut something from their budget so they can hire a house cleaning service after seeing how much of their time goes to general household maintenance.

Give yourself a performance evaluation

Unlike those tedious forms you used to have to complete at work, you can make your evaluation simple and effective. It sounds a little silly at first but think about all the goals you had when you decided to stay home. Some of them may have been unrealistic, but others, such as the ones connected with parenting, are probably very important to you.

Your performance evaluation could have different categories — with parenting being your biggest responsibility. List the various aspects of parenting that are critical to you, such as teaching manners, helping with homework, or dealing with a behavior problem. Then evaluate your strategies and skills for each area. Are you making progress? Are there other things you want to add to your parenting plan? Maybe you can take a class or read a book on the parenting issue that needs more of your attention. Be sure to include this on your to-do list so that it gets done and you can reap the sense of accomplishment. Reading the parenting book is an accomplishment even if you don't see immediate improvements in your child.

Dealing with the 24/7 Experience

In no other profession are you on the job all day, every day. You arise to your responsibilities and your "office," and you go to bed hoping you will get to sleep all night and not have to wake up with your charges. Certainly, all parents face the 24/7 responsibilities of raising children, but it's the focus on the role and the fact that your home is also your workplace that can prevent you from feeling like you ever get a break.

Even going on a family vacation isn't really a true break. You actually have more work because you typically plan the trip, buy the necessary gear and food, and coordinate the packing. Once on vacation, you are still on duty as a parent, and then when you get home there is the enormous task of unpacking, doing the laundry, and catching up on the chores you left behind.

We aren't intending to paint an entirely depressing picture. The pluses of staying home are still very rich, and a family vacation is still a change of scene from the four walls of home. But to counter the 24/7 realities of your role, consider employing some of the following strategies.

Look at what you're trying to control and why

This is a reminder about your "want and can" area from Chapter 3. It can be so easy to micromanage when you stay at home and this contributes enormously to the feeling that you never get a break. To prevent this, look for the things that are in your "WaC" area but are not worth the effort.

Every time we do a seminar for a parent group, this subject inevitably comes up. One of the most common areas of control where parents run into stress and problems is what their children wear. Now, we are not advocating that you allow your child to go to school in summer clothes in the winter or in dirty, torn clothes. The advice we give to parents is to think about why they are trying to control things and whether they really need to take it to the far end of the spectrum of control. Could you organize the clothes your child has to choose from to insure that they are appropriate for the season and the occasion and that they are all in good repair and clean? Then allow them to select from the choices that you have provided with the stipulation that any changes in their decision are made the night before school instead of in the morning. Many of our parent group participants have adopted this method of relaxing some of their controls to improve their overall stress and energy levels and smooth out relationships with their children.

Plan when to sit down and when to get out

In your role as a stay-at-home parent, you spend a great deal of time on your feet. When you do sit down to eat or pay some bills, you frequently have to pop back up to help a child or deal with a crisis. The only way to really sit and rest is to plan it as part of your day. Look for opportunities to create 15 minutes to sit and put your feet up, read a magazine, or enjoy a cup of coffee. You might schedule it as part of a transition. For example, as you are approaching the time when you need to prepare dinner, give yourself a much-needed break before you start. If that seems too difficult, try for the 15 minutes after dinner. Explain to your family that you are taking a short break and then stick with it so they get used to the new routine. Physical and mental breaks are essential to any worker's productivity and well-being. Don't short yourself just because your workplace is in the home.

The other part of taking a break is making sure you do get out of the house. This can be particularly difficult if your child is a newborn, but even a short walk up the street will do wonders for your mental health. As your children get older, plan outings that are not too tiring for them or for you. Many stay-at-home parents enjoy a balance between going out and staying at home. Lastly, "mom's night out" is popular for a reason. Meeting your friends in the evening is great therapy and lots of fun. Don't skip this important ritual.

Create that Friday feeling

For people who work a Monday through Friday job, there is a wonderful sense of completion and impending right to relax that comes with Friday afternoon. You can almost sense it in the air at the office as people start to slow down and become more casual and friendly. The after-work plan may mean going out for a beer or leaving early for a weekend getaway.

For the stay-at-home parent, Friday afternoons often just blur into all the other days. So why not create a Friday afternoon ritual that works for your current situation? It could be something as simple as changing to your "weekend" clothes. Or it could be declaring that Friday is take-out night for dinner or that it is family game and pizza night. It could also be the night that you get a babysitter and go out for a date with your significant other or good friends.

And then when it's Sunday night, and everyone who has to gear up for work on Monday is complaining of their upcoming schedule, you can smile and tell them how much you look forward to Monday and the return of your normal routine!

Overcoming the Isolation

Even if you have other people in your neighborhood who are staying home full time, it doesn't prevent you from feeling like you are stranded on your own little island. When it's just you and the kids, you may feel very alone and really miss interacting with other adults and the civilized world in general. Follow these tips to overcome the isolation.

Hang out with "your people"

The term "your people" is our code word for others in a similar situation who speak your language. When you get together with other like-minded stay-at-home parents, you have found "your people." It is such a relief to hear that they face the same struggles and it can be so helpful to get new ideas for coping with the challenges.

You can find a group through many different organizations such as PEPS (Program for Early Parent Support) and Mothers and

More. Both organizations have chapters or programs in most cities. You can also create your own support group by introducing yourself to neighbors and other parents you run into at the park or the library. Be bold and strike up a conversation. They probably need the support as much as you do.

Make yourself do something stimulating or out of the box

Another strategy is to challenge yourself to use the intellectual side of your brain. Let's face it, some of the tasks of running the home are rather mind numbing. You might join a book club or a political discussion group. You could also plan a trip to a part of your town you want to explore or visit a museum or art gallery.

If the intellectual stimulation isn't enough, go for a physical challenge. Maybe there is a new sport or workout you have always wanted to try. Recruit a friend to go with you or trade him or her for child-care time so he or she can also pursue a passion.

Adjusting to the Lack of Pay and the Drop in Status

One of the most tangible differences between being in the paid workforce and staying at home is not receiving a paycheck. You are also not contributing to social security or a pension plan, which can have long-term financial impacts when you retire. This can bring with it a myriad of emotional and relationship issues such as lower feelings of "worth" as defined by society.

Sadly, full-time parenting is not truly valued by society and the government. In fact, there is sometimes a feeling that you can't even complain about your role. Katherine, a stay-at-home mother of two says, "Not being allowed to express ambivalence about being a parent is hard. We are supposed to love it wholeheartedly, you know, unless we want to be classified as a bad mother. The only thing we are allowed to complain about is the housework and our spouse's failure to pitch in enough."

Whether or not Katherine's perception seems accurate to you, there is no arguing that the stay-at-home role has a financial and social impact. To counter those realities, there are several things you can do.

Work on your sense of intrinsic value and create your own rewards

Right now, you are probably thinking, "Sure, easier said than done!" Certainly, having a sense of our own intrinsic value is something that most of us have always strived for to some degree. Let's face it, even in the paid workforce, it is rare these days to actually get the rewards and recognition that you feel are due.

With this in mind, developing a robust reserve of your own intrinsic value, motivation, and rewards is key to being a happy stay-at-home parent. One friend used to view Mother's Day as her at-home "performance review" — a time to hear about what a great job she had done over the past year and receive a sizable token as a reward. Of course, she was invariably disappointed. Once she discovered how to believe in her own value and build in small rewards for herself, she was much more content.

Sometimes you have to recognize the small victories. Ellen receives a great sense of personal satisfaction when she is able to send her children off to school with lunches that are not only tasty and appealing but also packed with healthy and nutritious foods. Just knowing that her children will be putting several key nutrients in their bodies during the mid-day meal makes her feel like she has accomplished something that is important in the big picture.

Manage the money

You may not be earning the paycheck, but it doesn't mean you can't take on, or assist with, managing and investing your household finances. Bringing in the money is really only part of good financial management. A strategic spending plan and sound investment strategy is what has made many ordinary wage earners millionaires in their retirement.

Start with something small like tracking the family spending to get a sense of control. You'll be amazed at how empowering this can feel. Depending on your partner's preferences and your own interest in the topic, you may stop at that point or go as far as taking on the tax preparation or signing up for an investors club. So get out those calculators and take control!

Do some advocating

You don't have to become a full-time activist, but as a stay-at-home parent, your voice and opinion need to be heard. You can call or e-mail your legislators on issues that are important to you. Another idea to consider is working to make the stay-at-home parent role more visible, appreciated, and compensated. Mothers and More <www.mothersandmore.com> is an organization devoted to supporting women who have altered their career paths in some way to care for their children. They have a list of political goals they are working towards and you could join their effort, or join a similar group.

Allowing Time for the Transition

If you have recently made the move from working outside the home to staying home full time, or you are about to make the change, it's important to have realistic expectations about adjusting to your new role. It really does take more time than you think. You are letting go of your old role and learning a new one. It takes practice to develop the skills, patience, and techniques that work best for your stay-at-home experience. Learning to stand tall and state your occupation also takes time. Expect the full emotional transition to take a good, solid year. One woman we interviewed said that it took her a full year to stop telling people at cocktail parties what she "used to do." At that point, she knew her transition was complete.

Whether you are a veteran of staying at home, new to the action, or just considering this choice, there is much to celebrate about the role of the stay-at-home parent. You are making a difference in the world by raising the next generation. To do that takes flexibility, strength, and stamina. Laurel says it well, "For me, a balanced life is a daily course correction based on the outside influences, my emotional state of being, and my family as well. As an 'at home mom,' that may be one of my biggest responsibilities."

o m C
f o r t
a b e
l h
C a o
s

10

Chapter

Part Time:
Not Just for Retail Anymore

Amy makes $40 an hour, supervises a staff of eight, makes strategy decisions as a management team member, and is responsible for a $60 million-a-year budget. She must work 40 to 60 hours a week, right? Think again. Amy is one of the growing number of professionals who work part time.

Part-time work is evolving beyond retail and service positions (where unfortunately the pay is still low and the benefits often nonexistent) to an economically viable and life-enhancing choice for many types of professionals. For health-care technicians, flight attendants, police officers, and others whose work can be highly independent, negotiating for a part-time schedule is often relatively simple. Their employers can use part-time professionals to cover a variety of shifts and thus retain some of their most valuable and skilled employees.

The real excitement in recent years is the expansion of part-time work to professions that once were thought to be completely off limits. Occupations such as law, medicine, management, and consulting now have part-time professionals among their ranks. These people work fewer hours per week but have developed strategies to handle the interdependent nature of their work.

In addition to these part-time trailblazers in the traditional professions, other people are creating their own version of working utopia by going out on their own. They start businesses, become freelancers, or act as independent contractors in order to control their own schedules and work fewer hours. And as more and more people find part-time positions or reshape their jobs to be part time, the opportunity for others is strengthened. Part-time work is a very real and desirable option, and this chapter will help you determine if it's right for you.

Naturally, a major question for anyone considering part-time work is "can I afford it?" Chapter 12 gives you the structure and resources you need to determine if you can reduce your hours. But in case you feel obligated to dismiss part-time work because of the reduced income, give yourself the chance to envision what part-time work might mean to your quality of life. You may find yourself so excited about the possibility that you will get very creative about finances.

Meet Some Part-Timers

So who are these people who are managing to do meaningful work on a part-time schedule? Their professions and personal needs vary, but they all have chosen the part-time lifestyle and created schedules and support structures that work.

Debbie works three days a week as a pharmaceutical sales representative for a major pharmaceutical company. "Working part time has reduced my stress levels by 100 percent," says Debbie. She works Mondays, Tuesdays, and Thursdays, which gives her two days a week to spend with her two-year-old son and to do errands and tasks that used to take up too much weekend time.

After Karen's first child was born, she put into motion a long-anticipated plan to work fewer hours in her job as assistant attorney general. She now works three days in the office, telecommutes one day, and has one day off. She thrives on completing her work in a compressed time frame so that she has time to meet the obligations of running her home and still has energy for her husband and baby. "Working part time has been a lifesaver for our marriage. The stress in our home if both of us worked full time in high-stress professional jobs, along with a baby, would ruin our marriage."

Vickie has children in elementary school and her priority is being able to see her children off in the morning, and to be at the bus stop to meet them in the afternoon. She works 9:00 a.m. to 3:00 p.m., five days per week. As a director of occupational health at a health cooperative, she is the only person at her level working a part-time schedule. "I enjoy working," says Vickie. "I was married at 30 and 33 when we had our first child, so working is more a part of who I am than I would probably like to face. I love my kids. They truly make me feel complete. However, I also know myself. I am a far better mother for being able to have outside interests than I could ever be staying home all day with them."

Bente is a single mother of a five-year old and works four days a week at a health and fitness company she started with three other partners. Monday through Thursday she takes her daughter to her parents' house, gets to the office by 9:00 a.m., and then leaves by 4:00 p.m. On Fridays she is home with her daughter but handles any customer service issues. "I started the company because of a passion for the topic and the flexibility — I wanted more control over my schedule."

Nancy is a mid-life working professional who still finds the importance of balance critical. "Just being in the middle of four generations is a full-time job." Nancy is active in assisting her aging parents and is also called upon to babysit her grandchildren on occasion. She is self-employed as an investment manager and carefully manages the number of clients she works with in order to maintain a 30-hour per week schedule. Nancy is living proof that having young children is not the only time that Comfortable Chaos is needed.

Nice Work If You Can Get It

So how do people create or find part-time work? There are three approaches to finding part-time work.

Use your current employer

Staying with your current company never looked so good. That's because it's often the easiest way to move from full-time work to a part-time schedule. You can use your reputation to either alter your current job or seek another job within your company. The key to the part-time kingdom really is your reputation. It also helps to have a skill or area of expertise that is valued and in demand.

For Carolyn, approaching her current employer was certainly the strategy that worked for her. When she requested a part-time schedule after her second child was born, she had been with the company for 11 years and had a strong reputation for quality work. The fact that she had history and knowledge in a specialized area of human resources made her pretty confident that the need for her skills would allow for flexibility. It certainly didn't hurt that she was well liked and supported by her manager.

Karen, the assistant attorney general, was even more strategic in planning for eventual part-time work. "I purposely chose to work in the public sector coming out of law school. When I interviewed at the big law firms, I found out how many partners were women, but also looked into how many of those women were married and had children. What I found was that very few women in big law firms had young children. Women either did not have kids or, once they did, they stayed home full time. I chose public sector legal work so that one day, hopefully, I would be married, have kids, and be able to balance the two."

In both Carolyn's case and Karen's, their employers had policies that allowed part-time work. However, our research and experience suggest that the existence of a formal policy is not a good indicator of whether part-time work is actually occurring. In fact, according to the American Bar Association, 95 percent of law firms have a policy allowing part-time employment, but only 3 percent of lawyers are taking advantage of it.

Even if you do decide to take advantage of your company's policy, what seems to matter most is the opinion of your immediate manager and your ability to put together a compelling case. That's because most companies that have polices make implementation of the schedule discretionary. This means that it is really up to your supervisor to approve the request on a case-by-case basis. Your reputation, skills, and abilities are far more important than whether your company has a policy. Many managers will fight the corporate red tape necessary to keep someone they feel is a key player.

Some companies actually roll out the red carpet for part-timers — although these companies are not as common as we would like. Debbie's pharmaceutical employer created an entire division for part-time sales representatives. The division began several years ago when a few senior sales representatives went to their vice president and explained the business case for retaining experienced sales people they might otherwise lose. This forward-thinking VP saw the wisdom in their plan and helped create the new division. The part-time sales reps in this division work on carefully selected accounts and are exempt from after-hour duties such as hosting client dinners. Partnering with full-time reps ensures that those client dinners do occur as needed. Getting into this division is far from automatic. You must be a sales representative with a good track record and have a minimum of two years with the company. There is also a formal application process. Debbie agrees that a person's past results and reputation are key factors in being accepted into the part-time division.

So whether you modify your current position like Carolyn and Karen did, or apply for part-time work within your company like Debbie did, you can use your past success as the oars to row yourself to a place that has a few more pools of calm, enjoyable water.

Create your own part-time work

For some people, working with their current company isn't an option, or they have a desire to create something new on their own.

Nancy, the investment manager, carefully chose her current profession to include the ability to work fewer than 40 hours per week. When she was ready to move on from teaching, a profession she had selected so that she could maintain the same schedule as her children, she interviewed people about their work. "I wanted to find work that I could manage. I have a tendency to get consumed by work, and I needed something that I could manage and control." So after numerous interviews and research, she decided on the financial planner/investment manager field and started a business with a partner.

Today, she very deliberately maintains 25 clients and knows them extremely well. Part of what she enjoys about the work is the challenge of developing an ongoing understanding of her clients and their needs. Sometimes she feels that she ends up understanding them better than they understand themselves and, therefore, is able to anticipate their financial worries and concerns. She knows that for her, maintaining any more than 25 clients at her high standard would require more hours than she wants to dedicate.

Mary Jo is another person who has created her ideal part-time work situation. She is a former nurse who started a business as a trainer and professional speaker on health and wellness topics. "I like being in front of people," says Mary Jo, "but it can get draining after a while." So she mixes her very public work with the solitary work of freelance writing. "I love the balance of training with more solitary creative work like writing. And freelance writing also includes telephone interviews, which can be done from my home office, in my pajamas if the mood strikes." Her two part-time jobs can, at times, add up to more than full-time work, but the important thing is that she controls the hours. She and her husband traveled for pleasure 110 days out of last year! She often takes her laptop on trips and writes, but she still has the luxury of traveling far more than anyone who works full time.

For more specific information on working independently, see Chapter 8.

Job hunt for part-time work

Although this strategy can be more difficult, it certainly can work. Depending on your profession, you may be able to find job postings for part-time positions. By using the key word "part time" in an online search, you can quickly find the few that meet your schedule requirements.

However, if you come up blank or it's not likely that your ideal job would be offered part time, then you need to get more creative. Your reputation and skills will once again play an important role. If you, or your skills, are viewed as "in demand," you may be able to convince a potential employer to allow you to work part time to fill their full-time position.

This was the case for Bente, the single mom, before she started the fitness company. As a director of worldwide operations at a successful software company, she was in high demand when she went job hunting after the company was bought out. It certainly helped that this was during the boom of the dot-com industry, but her skills and reputation were also a major factor.

The strategy she used was to investigate companies where part-time hours would be workable. "I turned down ones that wouldn't work due to the company's culture or the responsibility of the particular job." But when she did find an opportunity that looked promising, she would interview for the full-time job and diplomatically let them know of her schedule requirements. "On two different occasions I successfully negotiated a four-day-a-week schedule."

The other tactic is to agree to work full time when you first take a job, but with the understanding that you would like the option to go part time after you have proven yourself for six months or a year. Vickie used this strategy to get her part-time position at the health-care cooperative. She was new to the city and realized that starting out full time was the best approach for eventually securing the schedule she desired.

So far in this chapter we have met some part-timers and found out how they created their positions. But before we go further into discussing how to make a part-time assignment successful, it's time to stop and do some serious soul searching. This work schedule choice is not for everyone.

Do You Have the Right Personality for Part-Time Work?

One of the first things to assess before deciding to work part time is your personality style. If you are a hard-driving, high CFC person, you may find that this work schedule increases your stress instead of reducing it because you are forced to do less. This doesn't mean that everyone will fail or be frustrated by part-time work. No matter what choice you make — full time at home, full time at the office, or something in between — you will always have those bad days where you wonder "what if," and you imagine yourself being happier in one of the other choices.

The key is being able to separate normal "what if" regrets from a daily struggle of telling yourself you are doing the right thing. Some people really feel a lot of anxiety while working part time. There are a couple of issues about part-time work that make these people a little nuts.

The first is the extreme discipline it takes to manage your boundaries. Some part-timers really have a hard time saying no. If you can't say no, you will find yourself stressed and working far beyond your scheduled hours.

Mary Jo, for example, once agreed to work part time for a consulting company. She had previously been doing some project work as an independent consultant, but they wanted her "on the payroll" for financial reasons. When she hired on, they wanted full time, but she negotiated part time. Although her employer agreed, the workload was not reduced commensurately. She continued with her project work and was also asked to supervise the call center employees. She saw some red flags in this situation but agreed to give it a try. It didn't take long before Mary Jo was feeling stressed by this arrangement. She had always been an extremely conscientious hard worker who wanted to please everyone. "They weren't used to working with part-timers, and I wasn't used to setting limits. So I ended up quitting before they could fire me. I could practically see my boss's sigh of relief."

Even though there were several problems with Mary Jo's part-time arrangement, she recognized that a key issue for her was not being able to set limits. It was against her very nature to say no — she's just one of those people who needs to exceed expectations in order to feel a sense of accomplishment. Mary Jo knows this about herself and used an example of a situation she had years ago in a full-time job to describe this trait in herself. "I had invented this particular job and the work was only limited by my own stamina. I was always tempted to do more." When she left that position, utterly exhausted and not in the best of health, her company hired two people to replace her.

There are a couple of other drawbacks related to setting limits that can be very frustrating for some people. One of these is the frustration of not being able to dive into exciting new projects and even feeling jealous of others who get to do the work. Michelle is a labor relations specialist who says, "Working part time drives me crazy. I see what others are working on or new opportunities arise and I have to say no." Michelle works three ten-hour days in the office and three hours from home one day a week. Even though she puts in a total of 33 hours a week, she feels like "not being there" and the restrictions of being unable to schedule meetings every day of the week, prevent her from working on some of the more coveted projects.

The other drawback is the frustration of not feeling totally "in the know." For some personality types this may be a nonissue, for some it may be subtle, but for others it can be huge. In most companies knowledge equates to power. At the end of the day, being "in the know" probably makes no difference to anyone but you. Make sure that you can give up that feeling of always being in the "inner circle." Otherwise it will be nearly impossible to set appropriate boundaries for any alternative work schedule.

It also takes tremendous self-discipline to limit clients if you are in business for yourself. Jennifer, the financial planner with her own business, says that working with new clients is the most fulfilling part of her job. Because she does not want to give up the thrill of getting to know new clients and figuring out how to meet their needs, she has opted to continue working full time. If you face a similar issue, be sure to give careful thought to your limits when it comes to new clients or new projects, and how you will turn them down.

Selecting the Right Ingredients for Success

There are a number of important ingredients to look for when creating or seeking a part-time position. The greater the number of these ingredients you can integrate in your search, the more successful you will be.

Selecting the right type of assignment

The assignment is a very important ingredient — you couldn't make your meal, or your part-time situation, very palatable without it. There are three factors to think about when it comes to assignment.

The first thing to check is whether the work can truly be accomplished in a reduced workweek. This is probably the most difficult challenge faced by part-timers. In your zeal to sell your employer on a part-time schedule, be sure to avoid agreeing to accomplish everything that you have been doing on a full-time schedule. As we saw with Mary Jo, this is clearly a recipe for disaster! You need to carefully map out your duties and plan your schedule to determine if it is realistic. Part time is not merely a label for shoving full-time amounts of work into less time and for less pay. This is not the time for "the little engine that could." Don't tell yourself, "I think I can, I think I can." You have to know how you will complete the agreed-upon work in the reduced number of hours. This same caution applies if you are starting your own company; you need to clearly define how much work you plan to do and understand the reduced profit that is associated with that choice.

Now this doesn't mean you can't accomplish what is really essential and important to your boss — or really do well in your own business. As you get farther into part time, you will definitely learn to get more done in less time. But you also need to clearly identify which tasks absolutely have to be accomplished by you and which ones can be delegated or eliminated from your to-do list. If you are part time, something definitely has to give.

The second factor to evaluate regarding the assignment is whether you will have control over the scope of work and the boundaries. In Carolyn's assignment as the manager of contract labor administration, this was a key part of her success. However, she can't claim that she orchestrated this aspect of her part-time plan. It actually happened when her beloved boss retired, and she knew that she couldn't really hold on to her senior manager position as a part-timer due to massive reorganization and change. She also wasn't too enthralled with the particular assignment anymore.

Carolyn got lucky. Her new boss was familiar with her skills and asked her to take the contract labor administration position knowing that she wanted to continue working part time. Carolyn had some reservations since it's a very specialized area of human resources and she was concerned that she would be out of the political loop and lose visibility to the "real world" of line managers and employees.

Well, thank goodness she didn't dwell on that perceived negative. She inherited a job that was essentially its own little kingdom and she got to be queen. Unlike the politics that drove her crazy in previous assignments, she got to develop and implement the plan along with very capable staff and a few key stakeholders. This is huge news when you are used to working months, even years, on a plan, only to have it squashed by some new chieftain or changing political climate.

Another issue related to controlling the scope and boundaries of the work, is assessing whether you will be expected to look just like a full-timer in some aspects of the job. An example of this is teaching. Jeanette is a teacher who used to work part time but decided that it just wasn't worth it since she was expected to come in for all staff meetings and other types of meetings. This meant she was at school five days a week, plus she found that the planning time for part-time teaching wasn't significantly less. She now substitutes exclusively and loves it since there are no additional expectations once she has completed the day.

So be sure to assess whether you have enough autonomy to manage what gets done and when — and check whether there will be any expectations you can't control. You can then go into the part-time position knowing you can satisfy yourself and any critics, and that you can indeed get the job done.

The final factor to think about is whether you have a "real job." This may seem like a strange question but it's an important one. In a "real job" you own a piece of something, are a true contributor, and are held accountable. You have the ability to implement plans and quantify success. It's a tough thing to define — but you'll know if it's missing.

Carolyn knew a part-time human resources staff member at her company who did not have a "real job." Colleen was a capable and well thought of staff member, but her part-time schedule of choice had limited her ability to hold a "real job." She worked two ten-hour days per week (somehow she managed to convince her supervisor that this would be successful). Twenty hours sounds like a viable part-time position, but in reality, being in the office for only two days a week makes it difficult to execute a project from start to finish or to collaborate with others. The result was that Colleen got some of the less desirable and piecemeal type work. Her mangers found it hard to save up projects that could be done in two days. Unfortunately for Colleen, she was laid off and it's hard not to speculate what would have happened if she had been more flexible with her hours and worked to create a meaningful job.

Selecting the right type of boss

Unfortunately, you can't go online and order the ideal boss over the Internet. But knowing the characteristics of the perfect boss for a part-time position is a huge help. Understanding the characteristics of an ideal boss may cause you to realize that your current boss could jeopardize your success. This may mean finding a different position with a more idyllic boss, waiting to make your part-time proposal when the chain of command has changed, or searching for an opening in a different department.

So what do these ideal bosses look like for a part-timer? First, they have a mostly hands-off style. They are not the type to require excessive status reports or hold an excessive number of meetings. They know you are competent and they only expect to hear from you when you want their advice or need to share some information.

Second, they respect your part-time choice and value you as much as a their full-time employees. That means they support your choice and defend your schedule if questioned by co-workers, customers, or managers higher up the food chain. They say wonderful things like "she's not available today but I'm sure that will be her first priority tomorrow." If these types of supportive responses don't come naturally, but your boss is open to them, you can do a lot of positive coaching.

Third, they tend to be balanced individuals themselves. They don't necessarily need to be parents, which is what you might hope for if you are working part time in order to spend more time with your children. But they do have outside interests and realize that pure face time at the office is not the measure for productivity and success. (Surprisingly, many of the people we interviewed commented that male, childless bosses were often the most supportive.) Be sure to assess if they just talk about having work/life balance or if they really live it. If they themselves have poor boundaries, consider this a red flag even if they say they will support your part-time status.

Selecting the right work environment

Work environment can include a whole host of factors. For example, company culture, and specifically the culture in your particular department, is critical. In some companies, there is an attitude that everyone should work 12 hours a day. Obviously, this type of culture is not even a candidate for a part-timer. But there are lots of companies where the culture is more subtle and you will need to evaluate whether it will tolerate, accept, or embrace your part-time schedule. Do they measure your performance by how much you get done and the quality of your work or by how late your car is in the parking lot? The farther on the scale your company is toward embracing part-timers, the more you will enjoy and thrive in your work.

Another key work environment factor to consider is whether you will have supportive coworkers and staff members. We have all probably had work experiences with toxic coworkers and you know how damaging they can be to the group. As a part-timer, you will need the support and understanding of your coworkers, so avoid any groups that already have tension, backbiting, and general pettiness.

This doesn't mean you should expect all coworkers, staff, bosses, and customers to be instant supporters of your new schedule. The next section will give you tips and ideas on how to manage your key relationships so that your part-time status really becomes a nonissue.

Successfully Managing Relationships

One of the best ways to establish credibility with a part-time schedule is to carefully manage the times you are not in the office.

Vickie is very proactive with her relationships at work. "My subordinates know that I am always available to them. I check my voicemail frequently. E-mails usually wait until I am at a company computer because remote access is too difficult at my home. I was very upfront with my explanations as to why I am doing this, and I continue to poll staff members every three or four months to make sure they are not suffering due to my hours. Truthfully, most of them forget that I am working part time. I don't ever let customers know that my hours are not convenient to their needs."

Nancy's strategy is to establish trust with her clients so that they don't have any concerns about her being unavailable. "I manage my clients by servicing them very thoroughly so they know that they are special. They know when I'm not available. I build the trust relationship first, and then they give me the freedom I want. When I send them an e-mail telling them I will be gone for two weeks, there won't be a single message when I get back. But to earn that privilege I am proactive. When I am working I call them, go to lunch, and get to know them extremely well. People appreciate that."

Like most part-timers, Karen makes sure that key people can reach her when she is not in the office. "I give my home and cellular telephone numbers to my legal assistant and clients so they can reach me when I'm out of the office. I also check my work voicemail several times a day when I'm at home." Karen says that in reality, most clients will not call on her out-of-the-office days. They tend to respect her schedule, and she believes it's because she has made sure that they have what they need and she doesn't leave them hanging. Karen is able to strictly manage her boundaries and therefore giving out her home telephone number is not overly risky in her situation. Not everyone can, or chooses, to manage their boundaries the same way.

Karen also makes a point to be flexible on coming in for key meetings on her day off. She pays for full-time daycare partly so she can come in for important meetings, and she says that showing this commitment really pays off. Karen is fortunate to have full-time child care, but even if you don't, it's a good idea to create a daycare situation that allows for some flexibility. (See Chapter 13 for ideas on creative and flexible child-care solutions.) Karen also recommends making sure people know that you will make an effort to accommodate their schedule. A common approach for Karen is to say, "that's typically my scheduled day off but I'd be glad to rearrange my schedule."

Michelle uses part of her days off to maintain key relationships. "I have an informal list of people I need to keep in touch with and I call them on my days at home while my kids are napping. Sometimes it means putting in a video for the kids and making the call from the farthest part of the house, but it works. I feel connected, and they feel like I'm at work every day."

Effectively managing the time you will be away from the office is definitely critical to how you will be perceived by others. But you also need to spend time building relationships while you are in the office. It's a fact of life in our collaborative working world that you can't do it alone. Having the best skills on the planet is rarely enough for success — you need the support and help of other people.

So brush up on your basic people skills. You don't need to suck up or be patronizing, but you do need to have good communication skills and pay attention to nonverbal clues. It's also a good idea to occasionally volunteer for unpopular tasks. You will be seen as a team player if you take a turn being safety coordinator or the holiday party organizer. Some of these duties really have a strong payoff — you could end up enhancing your network or earning your boss's gratitude for taking on a task he or she was eager to delegate.

Naturally you have to be selective about these extra duties and not take on too many — but the investment in building relationships, team spirit, and trust are invaluable. Also keep in mind that there is no complete insurance against the occasional jealous coworker. Carolyn thought that her part-time schedule was a complete nonissue until one day a subordinate told her that a peer liked to make a big point of stopping by her office on one of her days off and announcing, "Where's Carolyn? Oh, that's right she's not here today. It must be nice to have those banker's hours." At first Carolyn was angry and plotted her revenge. But then she realized that this reaction was pretty rare and wasn't really damaging. She decided to look for opportunities to win over this manager instead of making him her enemy. By becoming a supporter of his pet projects and offering to loan staff members when he was in a pinch, she turned him into an ally instead of an enemy.

Now that we have covered relationship building, it's time to get to the core of a part-timer's existence: getting more done in less time.

Productivity Power: You May Actually Get More Done in Less Time

By working part time and leading a life of more Comfortable Chaos, you may benefit by a certain amount of gained productivity. Depending on your personality and approach, it's possible that you will get more done in less time. This section is also particularly relevant for job sharers (see Chapter 11).

One of the obvious reasons for an increase in productivity is that you can work at a higher level of intensity. On Carolyn's part-time schedule for example, she worked Mondays and Tuesdays and both of these days were extremely focused and productive. By Wednesday morning she could feel her tiredness. But since she was home that day, she let the kids wake her up instead of the alarm clock, and then started her day at home. Even though a day with the kids is far from relaxing, it's a different type of work. By the time Thursday came along and Carolyn was back in office, she was geared up again for a super productive workday.

When Carolyn was working full time, she did not very often have five high-intensity days in a row. Somewhere during the week, tiredness or frustration would set in and her pace would slow down. And getting up at the crack of dawn, nursing the baby, finding something to wear, and then commuting in traffic five days in a row felt just plain brutal! For many people, our bodies, minds, and spirits don't work optimally with the North American model of five days of work and then two days of rest.

Fatigue is not the only factor that can make full-time people less productive. They can also suffer from what we call a lack of contrast. If you have to concentrate on the same set of problems and tasks for 40 or more hours compressed between Monday and Friday, your brain doesn't get the advantage of working on a different task. It's like only allowing yourself to eat protein between Monday and Friday, and then having your fruits and vegetables on Saturday and Sunday. Like your body, your brain craves variety. So if you stop your normal work routine and do something else, whether that something else is artwork, exercise, reading, playing with a child, or cleaning your house, your brain gets refreshed for your work tasks. Subconsciously it may even continue to be working since you may get an "aha" moment about a work problem while you are digging in your garden.

One more "easy" way to boost your productivity is to find time to exercise. Fitting in exercise isn't a piece of cake for anyone no matter what his or her work schedule. But as a part-timer you need every possible advantage, so find a way to squeeze in some sweat time.

Clearly, working fewer hours helps your brain and your body to be naturally more productive. But there are also more tangible things you can do to increase your productivity and get more done in less time. (See the tips at the end of Chapter 6.) As a part-timer, the last thing you want is to find yourself working more hours for less pay. But let's move on to talking about the whole point of working part time — your days off!

Managing Your Time Off: How to Avoid "Full Time Creep"

This is one of the biggest struggles of the part-time worker. It is so incredibly easy to let work bleed into your scheduled time off. When you find yourself working from home without pay, we call this "full time creep."

This definitely happened to Carolyn in her position. It tended to occur when there was a key project requiring lots of meetings or there was a specific hot issue that she was in the middle of coordinating. There is nothing worse than trying to talk to a senior manager or key customer when your three-year-old is yelling "I need to go poopie — come help me!"

Carolyn also found herself feeling incredibly stressed when she tried to get lunch for her kids while sending a critical e-mail from the laptop on the kitchen counter. Add a service person arriving to do something at the house and a spilled glass of milk and she was ready to go over the edge! That doesn't feel like Comfortable Chaos — it feels like way too much white water in the rapids. Luckily, this scenario was not the norm for Carolyn so she chalked up these occasional stressful periods as part of the cost of working part time. But she did work hard to avoid these types of days by being proactive at work and constantly re-evaluating which projects need her attention and which ones could slide or be delegated.

Vickie has the same struggle. "When I went part time, the work didn't. There will always be more work than I can handle, even full time. This position, along with most other directors at my office, works 50 to 60 hours per week. I am juggling all the time. I frequently feel like I am in crisis management rather than in proactive management. When I set my schedule to be part time, I arranged it around my ability to drop off children at the bus and my need to leave to be home when the bus arrives. Unfortunately, I rarely can leave when I should. Thank goodness for terrific neighbors!"

The key learning here is that you need to learn to live with the feeling of never getting everything done. Most likely, Vickie would still feel like she could never get everything done even if she worked full time. Go back to Chapter 3 if you need a reminder about boundaries.

People who sometimes work from home really need to set clear boundaries. Nancy has a home office that she only enters when she intends to work. When she is there she is incredibly focused and does not get distracted by household tasks or other activities. She says she gets so engrossed that she often forgets to eat. Once she leaves the room, she closes the door and shuts out that part of her life.

Last, be sure to spend time on whatever it was that caused you to go part time in the first place. Think back to the circle chart exercise in Chapter 2. What slices in your pie did you want to increase? What priorities do you want to make sure you include? If it's spending quality time with your children, you aren't going to feel very fulfilled after a day jam packed with errands and doctors' appointments.

One way to make this happen is to add it to your schedule — it sounds rather cold but it works. When Carolyn's daughter was napping, she knew that was the best time to have some quality time with her son. And even though it was hard for her to just sit on the floor and play Tinker Toys, she felt good about the day if she was able to take herself off the "to-do list" track and give her son her complete attention. She tried hard to create more of these moments because she wanted her children to have these memories instead of one of a rushed mommy who was always dashing around the house trying to get one more thing done.

"She Just Works Part Time" and Other Potential Perceptions

Most of this chapter has been about how to manage your relationships at work and how to be perceived in the most positive light possible. But your spouse's or significant other's opinion of your part-time work also has an enormous impact on whether you feel successful — and it also impacts your personal relationships. Partners may develop opinions on how your reduced paycheck and increased "free time" will impact them and your family. In fact, depending on why you have chosen part time, the term "free time" may be a total misnomer. It is a good idea to help manage these opinions and to set expectations before you start a part-time schedule.

This is something Carolyn wishes she had done before starting her part-time schedule. She assumed that her husband would realize that she faced a challenge in managing her work within a reduced schedule. It seemed obvious to Carolyn that he would understand that some days would feel extremely stressful as she tried to ensure she had met her commitments at work. But one day when she was explaining a complicated adjustment in the week's child-care plan so that she could go to an important meeting on a day that she was normally at home, he commented "Why are you going in? I thought you were only supposed to be working part time!"

Carolyn was surprised by his reaction, but explained that there were certain key meetings that she couldn't miss and that she couldn't always get them scheduled on one of her office days. She added that on this particular project, it felt like a few people were looking to use her schedule as a scapegoat for failure and that she didn't intend to give them that chance. By being at every one of these key meetings, she knew she would never have to worry about someone being able to blame her schedule for any problem or delay. Her politically savvy husband instantly understood.

Other part-timers aren't quite so lucky. One woman told us, "I feel like my spouse thinks my job is not a 'real' job because it can be worked part time. If there is an occasional need to work on my day off, or bring work home to do over the weekend, he seems to be frustrated by the impact on our family time. But he does not hesitate when this requirement comes from his job." In addition, when you work part time there is often heightened pressure to be there and be productive on all of your scheduled days in order to be the consummate professional.

Luckily, many people are proud of the part-time careers of their friends and loved ones and support part-time work as a way to keep a career alive. Kate works three days a week as a human resources specialist and says, "My husband respects my work abilities. He has an inflated view of where I would have been professionally had I stayed on a full-time schedule. He appreciates that I gave it up and I let him think he should."

Vicki also talks about having a partner who is proud of her career. "My spouse is extremely supportive. He is the person who urged me to go part time as he could sense the stress and the lack of family unity due to my job. Fortunately, money isn't an issue, so we didn't have to consider any lack of income in reducing my hours. However, I have also considered a career change. One of the areas I have considered is teaching so that I could be home when the kids are. But my husband is proud of my work and my 'title.' I have met some resistance from him in changing careers into an area that he perceives as lower in status and subsequent income. However, his bottom line is that I am happy and our family is taken care of."

Whether you have a very supportive partner, or one who is a work in progress, you can avoid many misunderstandings by having a conversation about what you expect to be the impacts of your part-time schedule. Below are five discussion points that you should ideally cover with your significant other prior to negotiating a part-time position.

You still have a career and a real job

Because many people do associate part-time work with retail work or, heaven forbid, "pocket money," you may need to create an updated vision for your family. Use some examples from this book of people who are working part time and still maintaining a career and a responsible position. It's very important that your partner still values your work and doesn't just see your new schedule as some sort of pastime or way to get out of the house. You need to know your work is valued since you will probably lose in the power game when it comes to income.

Flexibility about the exact schedule

Explain that there will be times when you need to go in on your day off or rearrange your schedule for the week. To help your partner understand, explain that to be viewed as a professional and to maintain your credibility, you will need to be very creative to meet your commitments at work and to be seen as a team player. Be sure to get his or her agreement if you anticipate impacting your partner's schedule more than in the past.

The reality of occasional work on your days off

Let your partner know that you expect to occasionally have to do some work from home. You can provide an estimate of how much time and what the impact will be at home, but be sure to explain that this is not easily quantifiable until after you have worked the part-time schedule for a few months. Reassure your partner that you are clear on your boundaries and don't intend to work excessive hours beyond your paid schedule.

The financial balance of power

Like it or not, the figure on your paycheck is a factor in your relationship. It may not be a huge issue in all relationships, but for most people, the scorecard on who brings home the bacon can become a sore spot when life gets challenging. Although we are not advocates of these attitudes, we are realists, and society tends to place more value where the money is earned. Working part time definitely means less money. During your discussion on this topic, be sure to highlight the benefits your part-time work will bring to your entire family. This could include things like a less stressful family life, more parental time with the children, and reduced child-care costs.

Managing expectations about your stay-at-home days

You'll want to make sure that your partner doesn't misconstrue your new part-time schedule with becoming June Cleaver. Working part time outside the home does not mean you will be able to keep a perfectly clean house, catch up on years of projects, and cook gourmet meals every night. You should be careful not to expect this of yourself either. Talk with your partner about how you plan to spend your days at home so he or she has a realistic view of how your days are likely to unfold.

Remember why you wanted to go part time in the first place. Whether that reason was to spend more quality time with your children, to look after elderly parents, or to pursue a new hobby, recognize that you can't meet these goals and create domestic perfection at the same time. This would also be a good time to talk about keeping some housecleaning help if possible, or at least deciding on who will perform which household tasks. When Beth decided to begin job sharing, she and her husband agreed that they would get rid of the housecleaning service to help offset the decrease in income. Then she ended up spending both of her newly gained days "off" cleaning and doing errands. It soon became clear that she wasn't gaining anything by job sharing. The purpose of job sharing was to spend more quality time with her children. Instead, she was even more frenzied and short tempered with them than she was when she worked full time. The cleaning service was brought back.

By discussing these issues with your partner prior to committing to a part-time schedule, you have greatly increased your chance of professional and personal success.

You may also need to manage some of your friendships differently. Although this doesn't require quite as much planning and discussion as with a partner, you may have to help your friends understand your new schedule. Your neighbor who is a stay-at-home mom may be hoping you are more available for get togethers and play dates. While this might be true, you could also find yourself very protective of your "at home" days and how you spend your time. Your parents or in-laws may also view you as more available for family gatherings and responsibilities. Just be aware of the possibilities in how others view your time, and make sure you feel good about how you are spending your time.

Working part time can be a wonderful way to make your chaos more comfortable. You get the best of both worlds — working, making a contribution, and earning a paycheck, with more time to enjoy the priorities in your personal life. For specific help with creating a part-time schedule and all the supporting elements, see Part IV where you will find assistance with finances, child care, and creating an alternative work schedule proposal.

f o m C
o r t
a l b e
C h
a o
s

Job Sharing: The Power of a Partnership Has Endless Possibilities

It's a beautiful sunny Friday morning and Judi is happily absorbed teaching art in her daughter's classroom. The kids are enjoying their painting project and Judi is admiring the budding talents of her daughter and her classmates. She glances at the clock and realizes it's almost 10:00 a.m. and the huge job of setting up for a wedding at the hotel where she works has begun. But Judi isn't the least bit worried or anxious — her job share partner is covering the event, and all the planning Judi did in support of the wedding is in good hands.

Judi is a catering manager for a large, well-known, high-end hotel chain. To be successful at a managerial level in the hotel industry would normally require working at least 55 to 60 hours per week. But Judi turned her position into a job share and has been very successful, consistently exceeding her sales goals every year.

She is a job sharing veteran of nine years and has had four different job share partners. Currently, she works 8:00 a.m. to 2:00 p.m., three days per week, and then one long day of 10 to 12 hours, which is quite common in the catering business. Her partner works full time, 8:00 a.m. to 6:00 p.m., five days per week and alternates Saturdays with Judi. This allows Judi to be home in the afternoons four days per week when her two children, who are in elementary school, get home — and to teach art in the classroom occasionally.

There are endless possibilities in a partnership. For many people, a job share is the best of both worlds when it comes to combining family and career. While there are many similarities to part-time work, job sharing is unique because of its collaborative nature.

The Unique Benefits of Job Sharing

Job sharing is a way to work fewer hours while maintaining a career track. Job share partners can actually benefit professionally through collaboration with another highly invested person. When a job share is successful, stress is diminished for both partners as a result of the shared workload. The work gets done even when you are not in the office since your partner is there to handle any crises.

There are also benefits for the employer. In a job share situation, both partners are usually much more productive in the time they have to be at work. There are several reasons for this. First of all, if a company is allowing a job share situation (or any other alternative work arrangement), any conscientious person feels intense pressure to be there on his or her specified days, on time, and to put in at least a good solid day's work if not a little more.

Jennifer, who successfully job shared an outside sales position in the wireless communication industry for six years, said this about her arrangement: "We really wanted the job share to succeed and therefore did what it took to meet that goal. We rarely caused problems due to our situation and we communicated very well."

Beth job shared a senior marketing position for two years with another Judy and they had a similar approach to Jennifer's. They spent almost no time chatting with coworkers. They walked briskly around the office and rarely attended birthday luncheons or other optional celebratory events. In a sense, they got their social interaction by working with each other. It also didn't bother them to work intensely on the days they were there, as well as spending some time on the telephone or doing work on their days off. This gave them each a sense of personal competency and a warm sense of accomplishment when they left for their "days off."

Another plus for the job share situation is that often people are more productive out of a sense of responsibility to their partners. Beth and Judy were both driven to work harder and follow through on obligations so as to not leave extra work for the other person.

But before we get into the details of creating a job share and making it successful, we will cover some of the potential negatives. We wouldn't want you to have any surprises!

The Downside of Job Sharing

The main risk in job sharing is the potential of slowing your career track. This is not unlike the risks involved with going part time. However, if your organization and managers are open minded enough to allow a job share, hopefully they will be open minded enough to allow you to be promoted either separately or as a team.

Unfortunately, this is not always the case. Beth and Judy were senior managers and they applied for two different director level positions for which they were qualified. In both cases, they were not even granted an interview. We call this the "glass ceiling of alternative work schedules."

Beth and Judy felt that there were some deeply held perceptions that since they were a job share team, they were not as serious about hard work and success as were others. In fact, they often worked longer hours than many of the directors did. In one case, they believe that their direct manager, who was the mother of two young children, was struggling with her own choices. She was perhaps a little envious of their situation or inadvertently projected some of her own struggles onto Beth and Judy.

As you consider a job share, take some time to honestly evaluate the culture of your organization and your own expectations before moving forward. If you believe that the risks are low, then go for it. If you determine that as a job share, you may not be viewed as extremely promotable, you may decide that you can feel okay about that for a few years. We are not condoning what many books have referred to as the "mommy track," but to deny that it exists in many companies would be foolish. Certainly it is a worthy goal to work to change perceptions by doing an excellent job of being professional and seamless in your job share partnership. However, as we discussed in Chapter 10, you need to think about how you would feel if others who are less experienced and less qualified are promoted around you.

The other risk with job sharing is similar to the "full time creep" that we covered in Chapter 10. Jeri, an elementary school teacher, considered this factor and chose not to job share although it had been approved and she was ready to go. Her principal was requiring both her and her partner to attend every major school-related event. This included things like parent-teacher conferences and other events that occurred both during school hours and after hours. It became clear to her that she would be working 60 to 70 percent at 50 percent pay, so when another full-time position opened up right before the school year started, she decided to continue working full time. Like Jeri, be careful in your eagerness to have your job share approved and appear seamless, that you don't end up working almost full time for part-time pay.

Is Job Sharing Right for You?

What is it like to share your job with another person? It means that you share the burdens and the workload, yes, but you also share all of the praise, responsibility, and accountability. You totally live and die together as a team or it will not work. Jennifer commented on this fact. "One of the obstacles I learned to overcome was to set my own sense of personal accomplishment aside and share in the glory or loss of nearly everything. I also felt awkward when it came to writing styles as mine is fairly different than my partner's. Over time, I learned my partner was open to constructive criticism, and it became easier to suggest changes."

When Beth and Judy were job sharing, they committed to their manager that they would have total accountability as a team. Therefore, if there was a performance issue of any sort, it was with "them," not one or the other. If there were accolades or bonuses to be had, they would be for both of them, even if they had to decide how to split them. Both felt strongly that if they did not conduct themselves in this manner, then it would be easy to become divided and thus not effective. The old adage, "together we stand, divided we fall," is imperative here. Squabbling or backstabbing of any sort between partners would ultimately end the job share and reflect badly on both people. So, for those of you who are great individual achievers and love that feeling, you may want to investigate other alternative work arrangements. The first I, *individual,* knowing yourself, is critical when thinking about a collaborative work arrangement.

If you are someone who thrives on collaboration, then this could be the perfect arrangement for you. It is like having a cohort — a partner in crime. Rarely is there someone else who cares about your job as deeply and passionately as you do. You can share the ups and downs and strategize together on how to handle difficult coworkers and customers or daunting projects.

Judy would leave Beth a voicemail the evening before Beth's first day of the week so she could listen to it on the way into the office and feel prepared for the day. In the voicemail Judy would often jokingly say, "This is who I pissed off this week, sorry!" This was actually a very effective way to vent if some interaction or meeting had gone awry and also to strategize about how to handle the situation going forward. She would also update Beth on her schedule. Beth would then start her week feeling prepared and even cared for.

But there is one caveat here on partners commiserating about difficult coworkers or situations. If you, or your partner, are the personality type that can easily sink into negativity, this is not a good thing. The purpose of the partnership is to collaborate, encourage each other, and offer perspective, not to feed each other's negative attitudes.

Schedules and Structure

The most common way of sharing a job is for one person to work Monday through Wednesday, and the other to work Wednesday through Friday. This scheduling allows for Wednesday to be an overlap day for continuity. However, you may both work a full overlap day or not, depending on how many hours you have negotiated with your employer. Although Beth and Judy did use Wednesday as a day to sync up, they were careful to also be very productive separately on that day. They would schedule meetings and other things that required both of them, such as team meetings and performance reviews. But they often were double booked for most of the day, each heading off to different meetings.

When you job share you must always be cognizant of the fact that people are watching you to see if both of you are pulling your weight or if you have simply negotiated a way to do everything with "your buddy." In other words, make sure that your arrangement is a value for everyone — you and your organization. If it looks like you are just doing everything together and having a tea party when you overlap, this will breed trouble. Beth and Judy were always very careful to not cause the company to spend extra money just because they job shared. They took turns traveling and only once, because of special circumstances, did they travel together.

There are other ways to structure the schedule. One word of caution; your goal is to appear seamless and *not* to add complexity to anyone else's life. Creativity in scheduling is fine, but beware of too much complexity for you or for your manager and coworkers. Your schedule should be simple and predictable.

Judi, our catering manager from the beginning of the chapter, has an unusual schedule since one partner works 60 percent and the other works full time. However, this is effective because this catering position requires working Monday through Saturday. This situation fills her needs and those of her department, so it is a win-win situation for both parties and she has been working this schedule for a couple of years. In the past, she worked a traditional job share where each partner worked 35 hours per week, alternating three-day and four-day workweeks. As the needs of her department grew, the demands of her family also changed, and she adjusted her schedule accordingly.

Could Your Job Be Shared?

Some positions lend themselves more naturally to job sharing than others. If you think a job share is for you and are considering turning your position into a job share, ask yourself the following five questions.

Can the work be divided or can an effective plan for managing the work be created?

One major detail that needs to be thought through is how you will divide the work. There have been many successful job shares between teachers, school nurses, and other jobs where each partner can essentially cover certain days and there is not a huge amount of overlap. In many jobs today there is no "clean break" that will make job sharing a piece of cake. The key is to realistically look at how you will orchestrate duties, tasks, and responsibilities. It is quite common for partners to talk to one another on the telephone every day. For an example of how two partners divided the work, see Chapter 15.

Does the job have complex communication requirements?

Ask yourself if there is an intricate organizational structure, such as a matrix reporting relationship, in place? This may not rule out job sharing but think through how you will handle coordinating with both a functional manager and a customer-based manager. This situation is becoming more common. The functional manager manages a specific area of expertise. For example, computer programmers often report to the information technology manager. But programmers may also report to one or more customer-based managers. These are the managers of the various departments, who need, and often pay for, the programmers' work.

Other examples of complex communication requirements are positions with heavy face-to-face customer requirements. Again, it could be done but how will you manage customers so that they don't have to build relationships with both job share partners?

Lastly, think about communication if you have a large number of direct reports. At one point in her career, Beth was a sales manager with 15 people reporting to her. She considered making the position into a job share, but the communication necessary to manage 15 high-energy, high-powered salespeople would have been a nightmare. Certainly, these types of situations can work but if your goal is to have less stress and more pools of calm water, then be careful to not inadvertently create a situation with less pay and the same or more amount of stress.

Does the job require heavy travel?

Jobs with a huge amount of travel required may be poor candidates for job shares. If two people are looking to job share as a means to have balance in their lives, then travel may not be appealing to either partner. If the travel involves developing relationships with customers or coworkers then it may become tricky to have only one person that has traveled and met the people. It would not be feasible to have the company pay for double the number of airline tickets so that the two of you can "tag off" on Wednesday!

None of these situations are insurmountable, however. The key is having an employer who is open minded, and for both partners to be able to be flexible with which days they work. Some of these situations could be worked out if the partners are able to shift the number of days and their schedule when a trip or a particular project comes up. This would not work if either partner is locked into working only specific days due to childcare constraints or other commitments. That is one reason why it is important to thoroughly think through how you would divide the work.

If the job includes supervising people, can you develop a realistic plan for sharing management responsibilities?

If you are a manager or a supervisor with other people reporting directly to you, a job share can still work, but may be a tougher sell since there are fewer precedents. Beth and Judy had three direct reports. Once the employees adjusted to having, as they said, "two bosses," things went very well. They had to learn that their bosses were one unit and that they did not have to repeat things to one of them if they had already told the other. That's because Beth and Judy communicated so well between the two of them that their employees never had to repeat things or engage in other rework. Also, Beth and Judy's people management styles were very similar and complementary. It would be very difficult if you were constantly disagreeing on how to handle employee situations. When two partners have the same basic values and are open minded, they can both learn a tremendous amount from the other and it is a plus for everyone.

The same logic would apply if you were a classroom teacher. Instead of having employees, you would have students that would need to adjust to having two teachers. Once a paradigm shift is accomplished, it could actually be refreshing for students to have two energized teachers rather than one somewhat burned-out one!

Of course, since we are all human, there will be times that a detail or two will fall through the cracks. Both Beth and Judy felt strongly that less fell through the cracks as a job share team than it would have if either one of them had been working the position alone. The job share forced them both to be more organized in their thinking, note-taking, and follow up. It was also nice for them to have each other to discuss delicate personnel matters regarding their employees. They felt that they handled situations better as a team than when they were managers separately since they had a more rounded perspective on things.

Are there quantifiable benefits to sell to management?

In Judi's case, job sharing is perfect for her position. However, when she originally sold the idea of a job share to her upper management nine years ago, it was a tough sell. Fortunately, her company had the statistics on turnover that illustrated clearly how high the burnout rate was for her position. By referencing a precedent at another hotel property within her company, Judi was able to show that if she left, it would be more difficult for her company to find someone who was skilled and qualified and was willing to work six days a week long term.

Judi's longevity in her position has turned out to be very important in the social catering market. She had additional experience catering numerous weddings and had done annual events for several years for a number of different organizations. The general manager of her hotel understands how valuable she is because of her past success and longevity. This is not always the case. In many organizations, things like longevity are viewed as intangible. You must try to back up your claims with numbers whenever possible. This is much easier to do if you are in some type of a revenue-producing position like sales or if you have what are known as billable hours such as lawyers or consultants.

One company we worked with had data that showed that a newly hired salesperson took 18 months to ramp up before they were fully productive. In a situation like that, you could calculate lost revenues during the ramp-up period. On the positive side, Judi and her partner also were able to commit to increasing their sales goals in order to offset an increase in the company's cost of paying for benefits for both partners.

Now that you have assessed your particular position by asking the five questions above, there are other factors beyond your particular job that also need to be considered.

Assessing Your Company's Culture

In order for any alternative work arrangement to be successful, the organization must understand the value of its people and be receptive to creative options. Much of what we covered in Chapter 10 also applies here.

The key point is to make sure that your organization has a culture that realistically will support you in a job share arrangement. If the organization strictly measures people by how late their cars are in the parking lot, this should be a red flag. Much of your job share communication is not, and should not, be visible to the naked eye. If your company measures people by how well the work gets done, you are in luck.

Also, in many companies, employee satisfaction is taken very seriously. If your company regularly measures employee satisfaction and incorporates key initiatives from a survey into its strategic plan, this could fit nicely with your desire to create a job share or other alternative work arrangement. If the openness in your company culture does not exist, you may end up putting a huge amount of work into a proposal only to be unsuccessful and angry in the end.

Assessing Your Manager

A unique obstacle to selling a job share is the fact that many managers are concerned that it will be more work to manage a team of two than just one employee. This is a valid concern. Jeri has been an elementary school teacher for 30 years. When she proposed a job share she did the necessary planning because, "principals are generally okay with job shares as long as you don't make more work for them."

You will need to address this concern in your proposal. Remember that the onus is on you and your partner to make your job share successful and not to make more work for others. You should spell out how it will work for your boss to manage the two of you. Show him or her how you will avoid added complexity and work. Assure your manager that you are a team and that you understand that you must communicate impeccably well so that he or she doesn't have to repeat things.

Also let your manager know that when any business/project issues arise, he or she can meet with whichever one of you is there that day. Otherwise, work would not get done efficiently. Your manager will never have to think about which of you to talk to and when. If you and your partner are comfortable with the idea, also suggest that your manager do performance reviews with the two of you together so that he or she does not have to schedule double time.

Finding and Selecting the Right Partner

Job sharing is like a marriage. If the two of you are a good fit, it can be absolutely blissful. If you are not a good fit, it can be sheer hell. As in life, often you're not thinking at all about marriage or a long-term commitment in a personal relationship until you meet the person of your dreams. Job sharing often comes about in a similar manner. Perhaps you are at work chatting with a coworker when you both realize that you have a lot in common. One of those commonalities is the desire to create a more balanced life for whatever reason through a reduced work schedule. The two of you are now in the early phase of considering becoming a job share team.

What if you want to create a job share and have not stumbled onto that coworker who would make the perfect partner? There are really two different ways to pursue it. The first way is to make your own proposal to your manager and then ask for his or her help or at least blessing to search for a partner. You could then post the position as half of a job share using the same processes you would use for any other open position that needs filling. Your manager or coworkers may even know of someone who would fit the position.

The other way to go about your search is to advertise for a partner on your own in local trade publications, parenting publications, or business journals or on the Internet at one or more of the job search sites. Once you select a partner, then the two of you approach your manager together with your proposal in hand. It is most realistic to find someone local since it would throw off your cost benefit analysis to ask your organization to pay moving expenses for your partner. Depending on your organization's culture and your business, it may or may not be generally accepted to bring someone in from the outside versus finding someone who is already a coworker. You certainly need to have a plan if a long ramp-up time will be necessary for your new partner.

Once you have found a potential candidate, what qualities should you be looking for in that person? Compatibility should be the biggest factor. Beth and Judy agreed philosophically on most things. Their management styles were very similar but their personality types and strengths and weaknesses were different enough to make them excellent complements for one another. For example, Beth was good at starting project plans, memos, and other documents. Judy had trouble starting, but was an excellent editor. Beth's background was more heavily in sales, her partner's in marketing. Beth is a high CFC while Judy is a midrange CFC. They complemented each other well because Beth sometimes spurned Judy on to work faster, while Judy sometimes calmed Beth down. If one of them felt quite emotional about an issue or situation, the other would be more level headed. They were truly the two halves of the perfect employee.

The second biggest factor of a successful partnership is the love of collaboration and willingness to commit to sink or swim together. If you are worried that your partner isn't handling situations appropriately or keeping commitments on your days off, it will be a nightmare. You must have an agreement that no matter what, you will never throw the other "under the bus" and never disagree in public. Like good parents, you each back up any action or decision the other has made and then discuss it later in private if there are issues. If you basically agree philosophically and have a strong spirit of collaboration, there shouldn't be many issues.

Jennifer had a similar arrangement with her partner but it took her some time to reach the same point. "The 'one voice' representation in meetings was difficult for me as I felt as though I wanted my own opinion and not a shared opinion. This became easier as I let go of my own ego a bit and cared less about what others thought."

In Beth and Judy's job share, a couple of managers tried to play them off each other by calling one of them in to a meeting and saying, "You are much better at this than your partner; she made some serious mistakes when she...." There were times when it was clear that the partners intimidated coworkers and some others up the chain of command by being "two on one" in some meetings. But when dealing with some unpleasant political situations, there was a lot of comfort in being a team. There would not have been comfort had they not been straightforward and honest with each other or had either of them had doubts about the other conducting herself with integrity.

Another criteria to look for in a partner is someone who has comparable values. When Judy was asked what she felt had made the job share successful, she replied, "I think that choosing a partner who shares similar values and is equally successful in her career is crucial."

Sharing a common work ethic and professional goals enabled Beth and Judy to be a good team and to support each other professionally. Since their whole goal was balance, the fact that they also shared similar values in their personal lives was important. This helped them to each keep good boundaries about not working too many hours per day, or working on their days off. It also gave them the ability to remind each other, when necessary, that balance was the primary reason that they were job sharing and that they needed to keep their priorities straight. This doesn't mean that you and your partner have to be exactly alike. Instead, your values as they pertain to conscientiousness at work, how you deal with people at work, and other relevant areas must be similar.

Jennifer says, "I believe, and I have said this many times over the years, that it truly comes down to work ethic, integrity, and consistency. My partner and I became very good friends, but we weren't close at the start. In fact, we had very different styles, yet we complemented one another very well. We both encouraged one another and respected one another along the way. We were reliable yet flexible. We set our personal egos aside and attempted to work as a team to achieve our goal of balancing work/life with what is most important to both of us — our families. We laughed a lot, and over time cared about each other very much because our commitment to one another was very strong. We considered ourselves 'spouses' which is essentially what we were during the five work days." Jennifer and her partner even had a tradition of celebrating and giving each other gifts every year on their partnership anniversary.

When you are meeting with a prospective partner, you should be very honest and forthright about your work style, your management style, your strengths and weaknesses, and your personal and professional goals. Beth even made it clear to Judy, who was pregnant when they started job sharing, that she too intended to have another baby. As part of their proposal process, they worked out how they would cover each other while on maternity leave. In addition to the CFC quiz, there are also several personality type indicators, such as the Myers-Briggs, that you could use as tools to determine if the two of you are a good fit. If you do not have access to these types of tools, career counselors are trained on how to use them and can usually administer them for a reasonable fee.

We would recommend asking any prospective partner about any incidents she may have had in the past where she had difficulty working with a coworker and also about any successful collaborative experiences she has had. The way people have reacted to similar situations in the past, and what they tell you they have learned from them, are often the best indicators of how they will react in the future. If your prospective partner went through a painful layoff in the past when business was lean, she may become insecure and even adversarial in tough times.

Another key ingredient for success is finding someone who is an "equal" when it comes to career experience and status. Several years ago, Judy considered job sharing with one of her employees. She does not believe that it would have worked because she would always have been considered more of the expert and her partner could have been considered somewhat of a second string by coworkers, rather than an equal, at least for a while. This would not have allowed them to achieve the goal of being "interchangeable" as she and Beth were.

Which Job to Share?

Once you find the right job share partner, you will need to decide whose job is best suited for a job share, or whether you will need to seek a position that is new to both of you.

In Beth and Judy's situation, they decided to apply together for a new position within the same company. It worked out that way primarily because a new position came about and they were perfectly qualified between the two of them. At the time, they were both trying to turn their respective positions into job shares. Neither of them was quite qualified to share the others' existing job. In reality, they were each also feeling a bit possessive about their current positions where they had worked hard to achieve competency and success. Applying together for a new position diffused all of that.

While this is not always necessary, be on the lookout for situations that could potentially create a playing field for the two of you that is not level. In many situations, it would end up creating a feeling of imbalance if one partner worked more hours than the other, had more responsibility than the other, or was paid more than the other. Certainly, these things can and have been overcome by some job share teams, but beware. Power balance issues can be subtle and insidious. For instance, you must never say anything to your partner that would cause him or her to feel that you are more "in the know" because of some event you witnessed or meeting you attended on his or her day off. You will inevitably each have those experiences where your partner had an exciting day and you received the news or information second hand from him or her.

In some cases you can find the position and the partner all at once. Jackie has job shared for a year and a half as an interstitial lung disease nurse coordinator at a prominent university medical center. She provides support for patients and families to effectively use resources and provides disease state management across the continuum. She applied for her position, which was one half of an existing job share. The person who had held the position as a job share already, had lost her partner. It was posted as a 50 percent position, one half of a job share, as we suggested earlier. She says, "I was lucky because my predecessor did all of the legwork to convince them that the position could be done as a job share." She then just had to interview for the position and make sure that she could partner effectively with the other person.

The Importance of Being Seamless

Your motto as a job share team should be that no one should ever have to think about whom to call when. You should be thoroughly seamless and interchangeable to everyone you work with. In Beth and Judy's job share, many coworkers were caught up in the idea that they had to tell everything to each partner. The partners had to repeatedly assure all of them that that was not the case. They had one telephone number that they both answered and linked their e-mails so that no matter what, any call or e-mail would get taken care of. They felt strongly that since *they* wanted to job share, the onus was on *them* to do all of the communication behind the scenes so as not to make anyone else's job any harder or more complex. The bottom line is that is why they were successful. Excellent communication is key! Judi in catering agrees with this and said that her communication plan changed with different partners and new technology.

Beth and Judy experienced some technological bumps in the road, but they remained steadfast in their belief that being seamless was critical. There were a few times when it felt like it was taking a tremendous amount of extra work to communicate behind the scenes so that they did not impact others. They persevered and constantly looked for ways to improve how they were doing things. Techniques such as linking e-mail boxes and passing voicemails through from office voicemail boxes to their respective cellular voicemail boxes were high tech and successful.

Some of their other communication methods were surprisingly low tech but extremely effective. They developed a form that was used for taking notes at meetings. It included time and date of the meeting, a list of attendees, action items that they were assigned, and next steps. After the meeting, the form was stapled to a file folder with the name of the project or issue. Their main tool in the office was simply a spiral notebook that contained a running list of "to-dos." They would each cross off items as they were completed and add new ones that came up.

Jackie has achieved seamlessness with her partner through the very nature of her position. "The nature of our job allows for successful job sharing. There are only two clinic days and we each are in charge for one of those days, so it's imperative that we attend on our day. Other days are spent on research activities, telephone triage, or other things that can easily be done from home if needed. Also, if we need to switch days for some reason, we work it out ourselves."

She also said that she and her partner talk on the telephone every day — this was a common theme for all of the people we interviewed. This reinforces that being seamless and having excellent communication are critical to success.

Getting Started

So, if you want to create a job share, how do you go about it? You have decided that it is the right arrangement for you and have found a partner or have a plan to find one. You now need to put together a proposal that includes a cost benefit analysis and sell it to your employer.

The key thing to keep in mind is to go into this as if you are a salesperson selling this concept to your employer and the other stakeholders in the decision. These other stakeholders could be your employees, external customers, internal customers, and coworkers at various levels.

Jennifer, the sales professional, relates her story of selling her boss. "Once the pros and cons had been determined, we drafted a brief, yet succinct document that we presented to the current sales manager. He liked the idea of being an open-minded and fair manager and helped us spearhead it through upper management and human resources. One of our selling points was to make him look good along the way." Jennifer also had a strong reputation built on several successful years at the company to assist her case.

We provide much more detail about creating a proposal in Chapter 15. We also used a job share as the example, so there are lots of ideas you can borrow. Once you know what you want to create, roll up your sleeves and get going. It's up to you!

Part IV

Ready to Make a Major Change? À la Carte Help Provided

12 Chapter

The All-Important Affordability Question: Can Your Finances Support Your Dreams?

Lisa is at a crossroads. After taking a one-year leave of absence from her high-stress, frontline job at a company that is growing exponentially, she wants to return to work part time but doesn't know if she can afford it. Working full time was necessary while her husband started his own business. She now anticipates that his business will become profitable within the next year and she would love to be at home with her two small children at least two days of the week. But she worries about working part time — will the money be enough?

Lisa sought the help of a financial planner and after working through a comprehensive process she is now working part time with the peace of mind that she can meet both her short-term and long-term financial goals.

Oh sure, we can hear you saying, "That might work for her but there is no way I can afford to cut my hours — and I can't even afford a financial planner!" You are certainly not the first person to react this way but we want to challenge your thinking. If you are dreaming of a reduced work schedule, leaving the paid workforce, or becoming an independent worker, then please don't rule out the possibilities before getting all the facts. This chapter will help you understand your choices and provide the steps needed to eliminate any financial roadblocks.

Even if you are not interested in a schedule that could reduce or eliminate your income, this chapter can still be very helpful. Whatever your personal work/life choice, it's helpful to have an entrepreneurial spirit. You are taking charge of your schedule and your life and there is just no way to separate those from your finances. Ignoring this aspect of life planning is like leaving out one major piece of the puzzle and you will have a nagging feeling until you shine some light on what may be one of your least favorite topics.

It's really not so bad! We will show you how other people have gathered the facts about their financial situation, weighed the trade offs, and then made conscientious choices about money in order to work their ideal schedule.

Gathering Your Financial Facts: The Critical First Step

You can probably guess by the title of this section what we are suggesting you do. Yes, it's true, you really do need to track your spending in some form or fashion. Resist the urge to skip ahead — we know how you feel! When we first started working on this chapter, both of us were resistant to this idea. After all, we have a general idea of where our money goes; isn't that enough? And the thought of recording every latte just felt too tedious and depressing.

After we met with Jennifer Easley, a certified financial planner, we changed our minds. As Jennifer says, "It's not about someone telling you how to spend your money. It's about evaluating where your money is going and either validating those choices or deciding to allocate your resources differently."

This really makes sense in terms of deciding whether or not you can work your dream schedule. At least do the work of gathering the facts to get your arms around your current situation.

Like Jennifer says, "Why assume you can't have something when you haven't gathered the facts? It's a matter of priorities."

Jennifer makes a great point when she says it's not about someone else judging your spending. But for many of us, money is very emotional and we grade ourselves, and feel judged by others, on the way we spend money. Maybe we are afraid of seeing the truth once we have the facts and not liking it. But a strange thing happens when you know exactly where your money is going. You feel better — not worse. That's because the fear of the unknown, and the fear of tackling the often overwhelming topic of finances, is much more draining than knowing the pure facts. Seeing it on paper gives you a feeling of control and then you can make choices about future spending with certain objectives in mind, instead of just general guilt.

Track your spending

So how do you start tracking your current spending? There are a variety of tools now that make it easier than it used to be. Software packages such as *Quicken* by Intuit, and *Microsoft Money* can be wonderful solutions. Both allow you to download your bank statement electronically, which saves you from having to key in all the entries from your checkbook. Then you can create categories and assign each item to the appropriate category. For example, all of your grocery store transactions would count towards "food." You would also add in food purchased from other sources, and probably track eating out separately under "entertainment."

If you are not comfortable with learning one of the software tools, there is nothing wrong with using a simple *Excel* spreadsheet or doing it the old-fashioned way using a notebook with columns for the various categories of spending. Or you can save all of your receipts and make notes on them to indicate the category of spending and then add them up on a monthly basis. Choose the method that is most palatable to you. It will be a far less onerous chore and you are more likely to follow through. Exercise 10 provides you with some sample household spending categories that you can use to get you started.

EXERCISE 10
TRACKING YOUR SPENDING

	Jan	Feb	Mar	Apr	May	Jun	Jul	Aug	Sept	Oct	Nov	Dec
Mortgage or rent												
Car payment #1												
Car payment #2												
Credit card payments												
Home utilities												
Cell phone												
Car maintenance												
Insurance												
Gas												
Groceries												
Dining out												
Entertainment												
Haircuts & personal care												
Clothing												
Child care												
Gifts												
Travel/vacation												
Medical expenses												
Health insurance												
Life insurance												
Disability												

Document your net worth

Once you have tracked your monthly spending, the next step is to document your net worth. Net worth is simply the value of your total assets (including cash) minus all your liabilities. To gather the total picture, list the amount in your savings accounts, 401K, investment portfolio, and any other funds you may have. Be sure to also include any benefits provided by your employer such as health insurance, life insurance, disability coverage, and a company car. All of this information will be critical as you get further into the process.

The most important thing is to get started — this will give you the feeling of taking a step toward more comfortable chaos. No matter what you choose to do in terms of a work schedule, the information you gather now will be invaluable for planning a secure future. Use Exercise 11 to get you started.

Assessing the Short- and Long-Term Impacts of Change

One of the biggest mistakes people make is to think only of the short-term ramifications of the change they are considering. For example, if you are thinking of reducing or eliminating your income, you need to look at much more than whether you will still be able to pay your bills. Jennifer Easley lists eight key factors to assess as you consider any change that impacts your earnings, or future earnings, and the associated benefits.

Meet current expenses

This is the obvious short-term consideration, and an important one. Looking at your now well-documented monthly expenses, will you be able to meet them with your new income? You may be able to reduce some of your expenses (we cover this later in the chapter), but you probably have a good idea of your hard and fast expenses.

EXERCISE 11
DOCUMENTING YOUR NET WORTH

Assets	$
Savings accounts	
401K	
Investments	
Health insurance benefits	
Life insurance benefits	
Disability benefits	
Company car	
Total assets	

Liabilities	$
Mortgage	
Credit cards	
Line of credit	
Total liabilities	

Meet future expenses

If you have built a lifestyle that is expensive to maintain in the present, don't forget to factor that in for the future. If it is costly to maintain now, it will also be costly to sustain it — and you must plan for the resources to support it. You also need to factor in any large expenses you expect in the future such as college tuition for your children or nursing home care for your parents. You may have saved some money for these expenses, but be sure to calculate any additional savings needed.

Medical and dental insurance

This is important for both the short term and long term. If you receive medical insurance through your current employer, you may not have thought much about the value of this benefit. Good medical and dental coverage is far from a given in this day and age. If your employer provides coverage, you can safely estimate its value to be at least 20 percent of your salary. If you are without coverage or are paying for it on your own, you know the high cost of health care and insurance policies. Even if you are not a big user of health-care services right now, keep in mind that this can quickly change as you have children, experience a health problem, or just plain get older.

If you are considering becoming a freelancer or consultant, you will have to explore obtaining benefits on your own. Look into the cost of this sooner rather than later because you may get sticker shock. Be sure to check the historical increases in cost each year so you can plan for the cost to escalate over time.

If you are considering reducing your hours at your current place of employment, then you need to investigate how your benefits will be impacted. Some employers offer full benefits as long as you work a certain number of hours a week. For example, full-time benefits may continue for employees working 27 hours or more. In that case, you may want to revise your earlier plan of working 25 hours and find a way to add in two more hours. Other employers prorate the benefits based on the number of hours worked. For example, if you work 25 hours a week, they may provide you with 50 percent of the benefits and you pay the difference. This can mean more money out of your check so be sure to research whether you can opt in on some benefits and opt out on others.

If you are fortunate enough to be covered by your spouse or domestic partner's plan, check on any additional costs of being added to his or her plan.

Life insurance and other company-provided benefits

Many companies provide a minimum amount of life insurance and also give you the option to purchase additional coverage along with other benefits such as long-term disability. If you are considering leaving your position or reducing your hours, determine the amount of life and disability insurance you will need to purchase on your own.

Life insurance can feel like a huge guess but Jennifer suggests a question that can help. Each person in a partnership should ask, "What would I need if my partner were to pass away?" For example, if your husband died, maybe you would not want to work for two years and then be able to replace his income for five. You might also want to be able to pay off your home mortgage. Don't forget to consider life insurance for stay-at-home parents. If the stay-at-home parent passed away, the working spouse would need to hire child care and household help. Lastly, you may want to add a comfortable cushion to cover bereavement counseling.

Pension plans

If you are lucky enough to be vested in a company's pension plan, you will need to understand the future income loss if you were to leave your job or reduce your hours. This doesn't mean you are stuck in a job you hate, but if your pension benefits are lucrative, it's worth doing some scenario planning. Some companies will even provide you with a tool to help with the planning. You can enter various retirement dates, make assumptions about your income growth, and receive estimated pension payments for each scenario. The information will help you determine if it's worth staying a few more years.

401K plans

If you have been contributing to a 401K plan, you can project what the plan will be worth when you want to retire. You can then compare this with the impact of making your desired work schedule change. You may lose out on company-matched funds but you could decide to increase your own savings rate. If you leave a company, you can directly transfer your 401K balance to an IRA without any income tax or early withdrawal penalties. Be sure to understand the ramifications of any potential change to this very important piece of your financial future.

Stock options and bonuses

This is a form of income that isn't guaranteed, but needs to be considered. If you have stock options at your current company, you will lose any vested options if you resign. Check and see if you would pocket any gains by exercising any options before, or shortly after, you leave. Your vested options often need to be realized soon (i.e., within 90 days) after your separation date. On bonuses, review your past bonuses and make an educated guess on your future bonuses. Again, this isn't meant to be a reason to stay attached to a particular company, but you need to account for any lost future income in order to make an informed decision.

Social security

If you have been earning income, you should be receiving a social security statement every year a few months before your birthday. The statement lists your income for every year you have worked. It assumes your current earnings continue in making projections for your future benefits. All this happens after you have earned a minimum number of "credits" based on total income.

Social security pays more than retirement benefits — it also pays disability and survivor benefits under certain circumstances. It's worth getting out your statement to become familiar with the benefits and make sure the yearly income is recorded correctly.

If you decide to dramatically change your income, you can go to the website listed on the form to calculate benefits with a new income assumption. Keep in mind that by 2038, it is estimated that social security will only be able to pay out about 73 percent of benefits owed. So the younger you are, the less of a factor social security should be in your decision-making — you can treat it as gravy. If you are only a few years away from retiring, your benefits projections are more accurate and social security may be an important part of your plan.

Creating a Financial Plan

Now that you have tracked your current spending, have an idea of your work schedule goals, and have considered the eight short- and long-term key financial factors, you are ready to start working on a financial plan. "Creating a financial plan provides a blueprint to see if your dreams can become a reality," says Jennifer Easley. This blueprint lays out all the important elements of getting where you want to go.

If you were to go to a financial planner, he or she would list your resources (which you would have had to collect and provide), spell out any assumptions made, and then provide an analysis. The analysis usually includes several scenarios. For example, if you were considering working part time, the financial planner would probably run one set of numbers assuming you continued to work full time until age 55, and then run the numbers for part time so that you could make a comparison. The financial planner will probably also make recommendations about your investment resources such as diversification and other issues once he or she has asked you about your risk tolerance.

You could certainly do the same thing without a financial planner. (We will talk more about financial planners later in the chapter.) Depending on your number crunching ability, you can get a very detailed estimate or just get a rough estimate. Either way, doing the "what if" planning is what's important. You will most definitely learn whether you can meet your goals or will need to make some adjustments.

Casting Your Votes Differently

As you work on your financial plan, you may start to see how you could make adjustments in your spending and other short-term choices to help you realize your goals. Jennifer says, "Spending a dollar is like casting a vote." Maybe you will decide to cast your votes differently.

Another way to view spending is to calculate the trade-offs. When Carol, the consultant who manages technology and computer-related projects you met in Chapter 8, left her traditional corporate job, she prepared herself financially. "I've completely changed my approach to managing money. In the past, my paycheck was 'fair game' to spend. Even if part of the plan was to put some of it into savings, everything else was 'available.' Now everything goes into savings first, then I take out just what I need to live on. Since all the income I bring in also has to cover down time, vacations, sick time, and time between contracts, the priority of saving is much higher. Also, I now make different decisions on spending money. The question to myself is not 'do you have the money for that,' but rather 'how many days/weeks of free, nonworking time will it cost you to buy that?' Even if you have the money to buy something, when you think in terms of 'if I buy that, I'll have to find a new contract two weeks sooner,' basically calculating the cost in free time rather than dollars, it's amazing what you're willing to pass up buying!"

Whether you think of spending as "casting your votes differently" or view it as a trade-off for free time, sitting down and deciding how much to spend in each of your spending categories is the only way to ensure you are making conscious choices that honor your current priorities and long-term plans. If you find yourself shocked at how much you spend on certain categories such as groceries, eating out, clothes, gifts, or even lattes, you are not alone. At least you are now aware and can make adjustments if needed. Some changes may not even be very painful. You can use strategies such as buying on sale, shopping at consignment stores, using the library, and cooking from scratch more often. Even if you use techniques like these just some of the time, you can make a meaningful reduction in your spending.

In addition to experimenting with new strategies, it also helps to be aware of the seductive lure of spending. We are bombarded with images in the media about the things that will make us happy — everything from what our homes should look like, to what we should drive and how we should dress. It's so easy to fall into that "must have" mentality because it is constantly reinforced and often it seems like our friends, neighbors, and coworkers are doing the same thing.

But it's really such a false promise. How often have you bought something you really wanted only to find it leading to yet another "need"? Buying something is a short-term fix that quickly wears off. Real satisfaction comes from living your priorities and working toward long-term goals.

Besides the media, there is another factor that tends to lead to spending — stress and exhaustion. We live in such a fast-paced and tiring world that it's easy to buy something as a treat because "we deserve it." And of course there are a multitude of convenience foods and services designed to take advantage of our overtired state. The key to reducing this type of spending is to modify your lifestyle to reduce stress and tiredness. We know this is no easy task, so at a minimum just be aware of the buying impulse when you are feeling run down. Instead, think of some other ways to nurture yourself so that when you find yourself tempted by a shopping pick-me-up, you have some other ritual you can turn to.

Here is one last note on the subject of spending. By consciously choosing how you will spend money and by being aware of the emotional aspects of choosing your purchases, you will be passing on an important lesson to the children in your home. If you teach them that every time a new "want" comes up, they don't have to rush out and buy it, you are doing them a huge service and helping to tame our immediate gratification society. Show them how you are saving for the item, and teach them how to research alternative ways of meeting that need. The value of buying something second hand is more than the lower cost. There are environmental benefits too, because no new resources were needed to make something new. Talk about your choices with your children and you will be preparing them for a successful financial future as well as creating educated consumers.

Spending Plans: One Piece of the Financial Plan

So many of us are turned off by the idea of keeping a budget because it feels like something you do when you are young and poor. But having a budget isn't about austere living. It's about empowerment: knowing where your money is going and aligning that with your priorities. "Budgets are not about depriving yourself," says Jennifer, "They are about awareness and trade-offs. And they are a key element of your financial plan."

But since the word budget is still hard to love, let's call it a spending plan instead. The good news is that once you have tracked your spending, creating a spending plan isn't too difficult. You have already determined your spending categories so now it's just a matter of deciding what maximum amount each category should receive for monthly spending. Use what you know about how you have typically spent, and then factor in any planned changes on how you will cast your votes. The result shouldn't be a plan that is so constraining that it doesn't allow for some fun. The point is to manage your spending so you are preparing for both short- and long-term goals. Another way to think of it is in terms of trade-offs. You may decide to reduce your spending on eating out so that you can put that money towards a new car.

Getting Professional Help

If tracking your spending, creating a financial plan, and establishing a spending plan still seems too overwhelming, you may want to consider getting help. But how do you know which type of professional is right for you? Here's a summary of some of the most common types of financial professionals. Keep in mind that some people will offer a combination of these services.

Financial planner

Financial planners offer a range of services that help you to wisely manage your finances in order to achieve your goals. Most will follow steps that are similar to the ones explained in this chapter: understanding your current spending, documenting your goals, and creating a financial plan and spending plan. Look for someone who is certified and therefore has the initials "CFP" after his or her name. This designation is earned after passing a comprehensive exam and demonstrating related work experience. Certified financial planners maintain their designation by meeting continuing education requirements and adhering to a code of ethics.

You may want to interview several planners to find the one you feel most comfortable with. After all, you will be disclosing some very personal information. For information on finding a financial planner, how financial planners charge for their services, and a checklist of questions to ask, American residents see the website for the Financial Planning Association at <www.fpanet.org>. Canadian residents see the website for the Financial Advisors Association of Canada <www.advocis.ca>.

Many financial planners also offer to manage your investment portfolio. If you choose to engage these services, make sure the planner also has the qualifications listed under "Investment manager" below.

Investment manager

Investment managers oversee and maintain your portfolio. They make recommendations or decisions, depending on the authority you give them, to move your money between different investments and are paid a fee for the counseling services they provide. In the United States, they are regulated by the Securities and Exchange Commission (SEC) along with state securities regulators.

Some investment managers also provide financial planning. The planning may not be as complete as a true financial planner, but it's helpful to know that you can get some of these services from an investment manager.

Stockbrokers

Stockbrokers are paid a commission for buy-and-sell transactions. In the United States they must be registered with the National Association of Securities Dealers (NASD). Stockbrokers follow the market carefully and make recommendations on particular stocks. This may be a good choice if you only need help with this particular part of your portfolio. If you are a stock market enthusiast, consider trading through one of the discount brokerage houses where you will pay a lower commission.

Personal bookkeepers

Personal bookkeepers aren't much different than the bookkeepers used by small businesses, except that they handle personal finances. They can organize your files, pay bills, track your spending, help document a budget, and provide you with monthly reports. This may be a good choice if you need help getting your finances organized, and you wouldn't necessarily have to continue long term with the bill paying and maintenance. Remember that bookkeepers do not perform the same functions as financial planners and investment managers; you will need to take charge of these aspects of your overall plan.

It's Worth the Effort

Taking charge of your finances is one of the most important actions you can take in creating your Comfortable Chaos plan. You are choosing empowerment instead of stress. It may be helpful to know that almost all of the people interviewed for this book took this step sooner or later. They realized the importance of understanding their finances and making educated choices in order to work in the way that was most satisfying to them.

Jennifer Easley also points out that after her clients have completed the process and have a financial plan, they feel great relief. Many have commented that they wish they had done it sooner because it's such a huge weight off their shoulders.

Planning your financial journey is an enormous step in realizing a rich and fulfilling life and there are no real short cuts. But aren't your dreams worth it?

f o m C
f o r
a l b t
C h e
a o
s

Chapter 13

Creative Child-Care Solutions: How to Create the Support You Need

Michelle relies on her mother three days a week to take care of her children and a nanny for the other two days. Carolyn created a three-pronged child-care plan that included her mother-in-law, a long-time family friend, and a trusted in-home daycare provider. Carol has a network of "carpool moms" that pick up and drop off her children. Sandra employs a teenager to pick up her children after school and help them transition to homework and play time.

What do all of these parents have in common? Creative child-care solutions! Child-care challenges can be overwhelming whether you work a traditional schedule, work from home, or work part time. But don't despair! You can find excellent child care that meets your quality standards and fits your unique schedule.

Finding and keeping good child care is such a critical part of keeping your chaos comfortable. As you probably know from first-hand experience, there is nothing more stressful than child-care challenges. Whether it's being ready to go out the door to an important meeting when your nanny hasn't shown up, learning that your beloved child-care provider is quitting, or having a nagging doubt about whether your child is really thriving at day-care, child care can cause major anxiety and sleepless nights. You may end up questioning your work and sense of self when you are less than confident and relaxed about your child-care plans.

But when the opposite is true, when you have a child-care plan where your children are thriving and you feel good about your choice, then other aspects of your life seem to run more smoothly and you can thoroughly enjoy your work and your time with the kids. This is yet another example of the third I, *inter-related*. The success of one area has a carryover effect to the rest of your life. This chapter will help you find successful child care by exploring various options and demonstrating the importance of always networking for your future child-care needs.

If you are planning to implement an alternative work schedule, child care is a pivotal element for your overall plan. That's why we are covering this topic before you learn how to write a proposal for your employer. Research your child-care options thoroughly so you know the possibilities and the potential impact to your schedule. Imagine how it would damage your credibility if you sold your employer on a part-time schedule, and then couldn't find child care that would work? Start thinking right away about your child-care options and use the ideas from this chapter to formulate your plan. You could even go as far as to hold a space in a child-care program or hire a nanny or child-care provider with the understanding that it is tentative until you secure your new schedule.

Five Keys to Finding Creative Child Care

Finding and keeping great child care is rarely a quick and easy process. We wish we had better news for you, but some of the best solutions come from long-term planning and a constant vigilance when it comes to seeking, and keeping, the right caregiver. There are five keys to unlocking the door to the happy child-care kingdom.

Networking, networking, networking

Finding child care may be the biggest networking topic on the planet. Unlike job hunting, where you at least have a résumé to send out, you are your own personal calling card for child-care needs.

The word networking can bring up painful images of standing at a business function with cocktail in hand, forcing yourself to walk up to someone and introduce yourself. But networking doesn't have to be that hard. When it comes to child care, it really just means letting people know that you are searching for child care. Tell them a little about your schedule needs and what you are looking for, and resist the temptation to get too specific on the details of your perceived solution. That's because there may be options that you haven't even heard of or considered. It's best to leave the solution possibilities open, but widely broadcast your needs.

Networking with other parents can be extremely beneficial. They may have researched some of the providers you are considering or may be able to give you new ideas. Also talk with people who aren't parents. They may know of someone, or some place, that could be your perfect solution.

Get creative about your advertising sources

If you are searching for a nanny or an in-home provider, you are probably familiar with the traditional methods of advertising. You can register with nanny agencies or do your own advertising in newspapers and other publications. These sources certainly can work and you should consider them. But you also want to think outside the box and strategize on where your potential candidates may hang out.

If you are looking for a teenager or college student, advertise at schools. Every school has some type of bulletin board and many have websites and student employment centers. Call the schools in your area and ask how you can advertise. A bonus of this strategy is that students are often attracted to jobs that are close to school. They benefit from an easy commute, and you have a better chance of keeping them if the convenience factor is high.

Another potential source is retirees or stay-at-home moms who would like to supplement the family income. Advertise for these people at health clubs, libraries, and stores that cater to kids. Look around your neighborhood for other places that may attract moms and grandmotherly types. It might be the local craft store, a certain coffee shop, or even a hair salon. Again, use location in your favor. Sometimes people will consider an opportunity just because it would easily fit within their daily routine.

Don't be afraid to combine options

When looking for child care, it's helpful to stay open-minded and not locked into one particular type of solution. What if you found the perfect nanny but she could only work two days a week and you need three? Don't give up yet — look for a solution for the third day. Maybe there is a neighbor or friend who would gladly watch your children since it is only one day a week. Look for the "win" for that person. It could be income or it could be playmates for her children. One-day-a-week situations are often also the perfect match for grandparents who want to spend quality time with their grandchildren but do not want to provide full-time care.

For Carolyn, combining child-care sources became the norm after her first child was born. She couldn't find a child-care center that was right for her and kept longing for a way to leave her son with family. With her parents living four hours away, it didn't seem possible but she created a short-term solution that helped her make the major transition back to full-time work. Her very energetic and giving mother agreed to come every other week and babysit for three days. The alternate week would be covered by a trusted, loving, long-term family friend. Both women realized that three days a week was a significant commitment, but liked the every other week approach and knew that the arrangement was temporary. Thankfully, Carolyn's mother-in-law signed up for one day every week, and Carolyn's husband provided the final day of coverage.

The arrangement worked beautifully and Carolyn had the added benefit of being mothered by her own mother who often cooked dinner and did the laundry, as well as the care and support of the other two women on her child-care "dream team."

When the winter weather started five months later and Carolyn's mother could no longer make the drive without worries of snow, Carolyn found an in-home provider through the power of networking and continued with the family friend and her mother-in-law. People often asked her if her son was confused by the arrangement. On the contrary, he thrived with his loving caregivers and bonded with women who were going to be an important presence in his life.

Another benefit of combining child-care sources is that it creates an instant back-up plan. The two-day-a-week nanny may be willing to work an occasional third day when your one-day-a-week provider is not available. Just be careful that you don't ask either party to cover additional days very often. It's important to respect their original schedule constraints or they could end up feeling used.

Know yourself and your children, and trust your instincts

All the creativity in the world won't mean a thing if the plan doesn't feel right for you and your children. Once again, knowing yourself and remembering the importance of *individual*, comes into play. You know the type of environment that makes you the most comfortable and the elements your children need to feel secure and happy. Also take your child's CFC into account. You probably have a pretty good idea how much chaos your child can tolerate without giving him or her the quiz in Chapter 2. Consider your CFC and how the child-care plan will support, or detract, from your overall chaos factor. For example, if you are a mid-range CFC who has to deal with a high-paced and stressful job, you may need a very secure, stable, and consistent child-care plan in order to balance that out. The example of Carolyn's three-pronged approach could seem ideal to you, or could drive you crazy, depending on your personality and the other elements of your life.

Once you have made a choice and have checked references and done a background check, you still should listen to your gut instinct. Do not ignore any nagging doubts you have about a potential child-care provider or an existing arrangement. Play detective if necessary. What is it exactly that doesn't feel right? Is it something that can be corrected? This is one of the most important relationships of your life — do whatever is necessary to make it right.

Always be thinking about your next phase

Once you have found your ideal child-care solution you can relax, right? Think again. As much as you want to believe that you have found a wonderful and stable long-term solution, it may not last. Unfortunately, long-term child-care providers are not the norm and there is a good chance you will be looking again within a year. For that reason, keep your ears open when you hear of great child-care providers. Keep a potential providers' list and note the name and telephone number of the person, along with how you heard of him or her. If you interviewed someone you loved, but for whatever reason he or she didn't take your position, stay in touch. Send this person an occasional e-mail asking how it's going or sharing some information that he or she may find helpful. You never know when this person might become available, and you may need someone.

It's also critical to be thinking ahead to your next child-care phase. For example, if your child is in the preschool years and you have researched preschools, child-care centers, and other providers and have it all figured out, don't get complacent. It will all change dramatically when your child hits the school-age years.

When our children were babies and toddlers, we often thought this had to be the toughest child-care challenge. It is difficult, but now that our children are school aged, we think this might be the toughest phase! Once they hit school they start to have their own little social lives, which include after-school play dates and activities. Plus, the school day does not exactly match up with the hours of the workday. So you may be faced with finding quality before- or after-school care, which is not entirely easy. Your school may have a program, but if your child needs to get to swim lessons, or just does better unwinding at home, you may need a nanny-type person for a few hours after school.

One of the most helpful things to do is to talk to parents in your area who have children a few years older than yours. Ask them what their challenges are, what programs they have found, and what is working well. You don't have to line up your exact solution yet but you do need to get an idea of what you may be facing. This is a good habit to start since your children will always be changing and growing and your child-care plans need to keep up with them.

Lastly, we have what we call "the summertime nightmare." For working parents, summer can become a time of stress instead of the happy, carefree days we remember as kids. If your regular program will be closed in the summer or if your child-care provider will be taking a vacation, start planning for the summer no later than January. There are hundreds of kids' camps out there but you have to research them, figure out if the hours will work, and consider the cost, which is often astronomical. If you do find a camp that will meet your needs, register early. Each program has a registration period, and if you need to be sure of a spot, mark your calendar and register on the first day of enrollment, or soon thereafter. Typically, the most popular programs fill up fast, which can be a good sign. It means lots of parents have researched that camp and are voting with their checkbooks. But do still conduct your own research. Not every camp has well-trained staff members with a good staff-to-child ratio.

Another possibility for summer is to hire a student as a helper or nanny. Depending on his or her age and experience, the student could do everything from watching your children when you work from home, driving your kids to camps and activities, or taking them for outings in the park. The caveat is to make sure that the student is truly qualified, dependable, and ready for the responsibility. Ask if he or she is CPR certified, and check his or her driving record if he or she will be driving your children around. You will also have to give detailed instructions on your rules in the house and safety precautions.

Eleven Creative Child-Care Solutions

Here is our list of child-care sources based on our experience and the creative solutions of the people interviewed for this book. Some of the solutions are traditional, and others are more innovative. But we wanted to create one master list so you could be sure you are considering all your options. Don't forget that some of the best overall solutions are combinations of one or more of the different options.

Daycare centers (full time)

This may be the most familiar option. There are thousands of daycare centers in North America and they typically cater to parents who work full time. The benefit is that you are not at the mercy of an individual provider's schedule and health — the daycare center is open and ready to receive your child five days a week. If you are working full time, this can be a reliable and comfortable solution.

You can also opt to pay the full-time rate and use the center on a part-time basis. This of course can be expensive but if you can afford it, the flexibility and convenience are well worth it. Karen, the part-time assistant attorney general, chose this option. "Full-time daycare is a wonderful arrangement. I use it for my scheduled work days and also as on-call babysitting on days off while I need to run errands or just have an hour or two to myself."

Daycare centers (part time)

If you don't need full-time care, some daycare centers offer part-time options. If you are in the proposal phase of a part-time schedule at work, it is important to investigate the child-care possibilities early because not all centers offer part-time care.

Many of the full-time daycare centers will allow you to sign up for fewer than five days per week. Be aware that you may pay a premium for this "privilege." Rarely will you pay the exact percentage of the time you use. Sometimes costs are prorated reasonably for part-time care and other times it seems as though you are paying almost the full-time rate. For example, you may need 50 percent usage, but the center will charge you a minimum of 75 percent. Depending on its fee schedule and scheduling rules, it could still prove to be a good option.

At some centers, you have to choose either a Monday, Wednesday, Friday schedule or a Tuesday and Thursday schedule. If this doesn't fit your work schedule, it can be a problem.

However, if it's a great daycare, you may want to consider modifying your work schedule — another reason to decide on daycare before writing an alternative work schedule proposal.

Other daycare centers will let you pick your schedule. For example, you can request Monday through Wednesday, but then you are locked into those days and if a critical meeting comes up on a Thursday, you are out of luck. Occasionally, a daycare center will let you pay for part-time usage and not make you specify the exact days. This was the case for Kate, who found this solution to be ideal since she often had to change her schedule to accommodate important meetings. "During the first years, I had a part-time arrangement at the daycare that I could bring my child in any three days that I chose. It was wonderful. We paid part-time but had a full-time slot."

Unfortunately, the ability to change days every week is pretty rare. But at some places, even though you are locked into specific days, you can pick up an extra day when needed if they have space. You will of course pay extra when that happens but having the flexibility is often worth the price.

In-home daycare providers (full time)

This option is similar to full-time daycare centers with some advantages and disadvantages that are hard to quantify since there is such a wide variety in the types of in-home daycare situations. Potential advantages of an in-home daycare are the home setting and usually fewer children than at a traditional daycare facility. The disadvantages are that you may have less flexibility on hours and vacation schedules, and you are on your own when the daycare provider gets sick or goes on vacation.

Some in-home providers only offer full-time care and you may face the same dilemma and need to consider paying full time for part-time care. The costs can be less, so it may be an acceptable option.

In-home daycare providers (part time)

Many in-home daycare providers prefer to work part time themselves and only take children a few days a week. This can be a perfect situation if you can sync up your working days with theirs.

Carolyn was fortunate to find a fabulous in-home daycare provider who helped her family on two different occasions. When her mom had to end the drive across the mountains to provide care three days a week, Kathy was the ultimate solution. She preferred to provide care to one baby four days a week and was looking to add a second child three days a week. Later, when Carolyn needed child care just one day a week for two children, again she was fortunate that her needs meshed with Kathy's. "I felt so entirely comfortable and trusting of Kathy and knew that having her for my unique one-day-a-week requirement was a complete gift." Carolyn continued this arrangement until her son started kindergarten and Kathy was ready to return to the traditional workforce after having run the daycare to be available for her own children. Talk about a win-win situation!

Nannies (full time)

A nanny can be a great solution since she comes to your home and your children's normal routines can be maintained. The option isn't cheap but for many families it brings peace of mind and freedom from hustling children out the door in the morning. It can also be a huge help in terms of getting to work on time — something that is critical if you are working an alternative schedule.

Many nannies need to work full time and earn 40 hours' worth of pay. The good news is that you may be able to find one that fits with your schedule, even if you are not working the traditional 8:00 a.m. to 5:00 p.m. If you are working 4/10s or 9/80s, ask your potential nanny candidates if they would be interested in a similar schedule. They may jump at the chance to have one day off per week, or every other week, while maintaining their full-time pay.

Once you find a nanny, your job is far from done. You now officially have an employee to manage and this can take a lot of time and effort. Even if your nanny is fabulous, you still will have management responsibilities such as setting expectations, communicating on the day-to-day issues, and administering pay and benefits. This doesn't make it a poor choice but you do need to be aware of the extra time commitment. If you have someone who does your income taxes for you, you may be able to pay him or her to do the nanny tax-withholding piece and prepare the W2 and other documents.

There is one last factor to be aware of when employing a nanny. When you arrive home in the evening, your house may show some wear and tear, and your refrigerator could be empty. Even though you may have some expectations that the toys get picked up before you get home, it's unrealistic to expect that the house will look exactly as it did when you left in the morning. Be aware of this issue when deciding whether to hire a nanny, and if you do hire one, work with her to set reasonable standards for the care of your home.

Nannies (part time)

Nannies come from all walks of life, including professional nannies, students, and retirees. If you work part time or job share, you should consider searching for a nanny who also wants to work fewer hours. Be sure to ask about their schedule restrictions when interviewing. Some students can be very flexible, while others are locked into a more rigid structure. If you fall in love with someone whose schedule is not quite a perfect match, keep talking. You may be able to cover the schedule gaps some other way and will gain a qualified nanny who will likely be willing to give and take on schedules in the future.

Nanny share

Nanny sharing takes some major coordination but can be a wonderful solution. We hired a nanny together and the nanny spent three days at Beth's house and one at Carolyn's. This is one way to share a nanny. It takes time and networking, but can work for a part-time solution.

The other way to nanny share is to have the nanny care for your child or children along with another family's child or children. Debbie, the part-time pharmaceutical sales representative, teamed up with a neighbor when they both had newborns.

They advertised and found an ideal candidate who became a beloved nanny for both families. The nanny would care for both infants at the same time, and would alternate between houses each week. Debbie and her neighbor were lucky to enjoy a three-year journey with their nanny before their children moved on to preschool.

This type of nanny share is not just about finding the right nanny. Your relationship with the family you will share with needs to be a good fit. Both families should have similar values and parenting styles because this will influence your choice of a nanny and the house rules you establish. In many ways, nanny sharing is a lot like job sharing. Make sure you are compatible. Sit down and talk about expectations and how you will communicate with each other and with the nanny. In a nanny share you not only have to manage your employee, the nanny, but also your relationship with the other family.

Relatives or family friends

Relatives and family friends are a popular option for many reasons. Your children get to spend time with grandparents or other people who already love them and will hopefully be in their lives for many years to come. Using relatives can also be a financial saving, and they may be very flexible about your schedule and caring for your children when someone is sick.

The caveats are that you need to have compatible parenting styles and be able to discuss problems in an open and professional manner. You won't have the same relationship you would have with a traditional daycare provider, so you will need to think through potential issues and envision how you would resolve them. If you are still unsure, consider a trial period where either party can renegotiate at the end of the period.

Relatives and family friends can be a wonderful solution for you and your children. Even if you or your relatives don't opt for full-time care, they may be the perfect solution for a part-time schedule or for one or two days a week.

Other parents

If you work part time, you may be able to team up with other parents with similar schedules — as long as they also have similar values and parenting styles. Maybe you can watch their kids two days a week and then they watch yours two days a week. This takes a very good relationship with the other parents, as well as some serious thoughts about whether this is how you want to spend your "day off." Caring for other peoples' children in addition to your own may interfere with your original goals for working fewer hours. But it could be a great solution when your kids are school aged and you trade off on the before- and after-school care.

You may also be able to find a stay-at-home parent who would like to supplement his or her income and care for your children a few days a week. It's worth asking around just to find out your options. The perfect solution could be right across the street!

Babysitting co-ops

Co-ops can be formal arrangements with point systems that you set up with other parents, or they can be a more casual network of people who trade off child-care duties on an as-needed basis. Darcel, who works from home doing temporary assignments for her former employer, has created a community of moms from her playgroup who help each other out. "We do a lot of scheduled babysitting swaps to help us all get things done. I typically work to have three families ready to go — when one drops out I start grooming another one."

This option typically works best if you only have a few hours per week that need coverage because most parents that participate are expecting short time commitments. But you never know, it could work for longer periods of time — you just need to find a group of people with needs and parenting styles that are compatible with your own.

Coworkers with opposite schedules

Yes, it does seem like a stretch but it can work well for job-share partners or part-timers at the same company. A coworker with a schedule that is different from yours may still be facing the same child-care challenge as you. As long as your parenting styles are similar, and you agree on how to care for each other's children, one person could work while the other provides child care and then you would switch.

Jean and Linda did just that. They created their job share with the understanding that the partner who was not at work would be at home with the kids. Jean and Linda each had two children who played well together so they felt like even the kids were benefiting.

Why Finding Great Child Care Is Only the Beginning

Earlier we talked about how you don't get to relax even when you have found the perfect child care. Not only do you need to be thinking about the next phase, but it's critical to spend time building the relationship with your current child-care provider. One of the worst mistakes you can make is to put lots of charm and energy into finding and attracting the right caregiver, only to treat him or her as a second-class citizen once he or she is in your employ. Instead, provide the caregiver with lots of positive feedback and words of thanks. We have always believed that the only way our child-care providers can care for our children from their hearts is for us to truly care for them from our hearts! In terms of showing your appreciation, you can also incorporate small gestures like bringing your caregiver a card, flowers, or a favorite treat such as a latte or a muffin.

Treat your caregivers as valued members of your parenting team. Ask for their suggestions and feedback on how your children are doing and anything you could do to be more effective. Caregivers often have a fresh perspective that you are unable to see. One of the reasons Beth enjoyed having a nanny was the opportunity to collaborate with her and gain new insight. "We would sit down and problem solve whenever there was a behavior problem. Then we would all agree how we would handle it so we would be consistent."

In addition to maintaining your relationship with your current caregiver, you also need to create a back-up plan for when he or she is not available. Start by asking yourself what would happen if your child-care provider was sick or your child was sick. Chances are you will be impacted by at least one of those situations. Make a list of your back-up options. Could you call on your parents or other relatives? Is there a family friend or neighbor who could help out? Don't just assume that these good folks will step in and save the day — make a point to ask them ahead of time.

Be specific with your request about back-up care. A sample conversation opener could go like this: "Aunt Sarah, I'm concerned about what I will do on the days my nanny calls in sick and am looking to create a back-up plan. I certainly recognize that you have commitments and plans. Would you be willing to be a back up on an occasional basis?" You should then define what occasional may be to the best of your ability and let Aunt Sarah know if she is your only back up or whether you have others. Having at least two back-up options is highly recommended. Also ask whether you can pay your back-up person, and if so, how much? Lastly, when you do need to call on your back up, some type of special thank-you is in order.

Back-up plans are important, but you can create even more safety, comfort, and peace of mind by developing an overall support network. Think of it as something richer than a back-up plan — it's all the people who support you in your role as a parent and worker and will step in to help in any way they can. It might just be a conversation where you feel listened to and encouraged that you have made the right choice for this period in your life. Or it could be more tangible help like when your car breaks down and you call your neighbor and ask if she can meet your child at the bus.

Creating a support network isn't all about the benefits and a safety net. It also connects you to the larger community by defining, and continually growing, your circle of friends and neighbors. It's a wonderful gift to yourself and an important lesson for your children that we are not meant to live in isolation.

Relationships with other people enrich our lives. When you provide help or support to a friend or neighbor, you are making a difference and living life beyond your own four walls. So get to know the people in your neighborhood, the other parents you see at school and activities, and the people who provide you services like your mail carrier and delivery person. You will gain more than you realize.

We wish you great success in your search for child care and hope that you are blessed with people who love your children and strengthen your family's life.

f o m c
f o r
a l b e
C a h
a o
s

14

Chapter

Strategies for Re-Entry:
How to Return to the Workforce
after a Break

Let's say you have stepped out of the workforce to raise your children, go to school, or care for an aging parent. Does that mean you have forever said good-bye to your former career or are too stereotyped to pursue a new field? Absolutely not! The Comfortable Chaos approach recognizes that change is normal and desirable, and there are numerous strategies you can use to control how quickly, or slowly, you wish to develop your new work life.

Thankfully, the concept of coming and going from the workforce is no longer unusual. But it is rather recent. Re-entering the paid workforce after taking a break to care for children is a relatively new phenomenon. It's only been in the last few decades that people started getting married later and delayed having a family. Often, they are already well established in their careers when the baby arrives and they decide to take some time off. Many want, and expect, to return to the work they invested in and enjoyed.

However, in past generations, it was women who almost always stayed home with the children and typically only returned to the workforce if they got divorced or widowed — and then they were usually faced with starting at an entry-level position. Since women often got married and started families at a younger age, in many cases, they either were not well educated or had not been in the workforce long enough to develop many career credentials. Not to mention the fact that women were given far fewer opportunities for career advancement as compared to today. In a sense, they didn't have anything to go back to, so unless it was financially necessary or they wanted to follow a passion later in life, there wasn't much of an incentive to return to the workforce.

In today's environment, many women and men who had a career prior to stepping out of the workforce eventually want to go back to the sense of competence, autonomy, and intellectual stimulation that work provides. One woman we interviewed said, "I'm noticing a real boost in self-esteem now that I'm working again. I didn't really expect that since I totally value full-time parenting too. I guess it's nice to actually accomplish concrete projects and be rewarded in addition to the intangible rewards of parenting."

It is still somewhat of a challenge to re-enter the workforce in a position that is at a level commensurate to the one you left, but it is possible if you do your homework. It may take a while and be a little difficult to ease in to your dream job but don't lose hope. It's also possible that your definition of a dream job has changed. You may find yourself interested in a completely different line of work, along with a different schedule and environment.

In either case, you need to create the on-ramps that prepare you for re-entry. Just like an on-ramp onto a freeway, you will need a pathway to use to get back into the career arena. And having more than one option is nice. The on-ramp should also allow you time to accelerate to freeway speed, and even then you may choose the slow lane over the fast lane.

These on-ramps are something that you need to be thinking about as soon as you leave the workforce. If you have already stepped out and haven't been planning for re-entry, then the time to start is now!

Catherine is a great example of someone who built on-ramps just in case she needed them. She was a stay-at-home mom for six-and-a-half years after leaving her job at a television station to focus on her two children. She hadn't intended to use her on-ramp so soon but the perfect job with a flexible, part-time schedule became available and it was too good to pass up. She is now the public information officer for a large metropolitan school district. The job is interesting, pays well, and still allows her to create the mix of work and home that is right for her. She works 20 hours per week, but only goes into the office two hours per day.

Not only did Catherine return to work after a break, but she was able to choose the part-time hours she desired and work mostly from home. Even though it is much easier to craft your customized alternative work arrangement when you have a proven track record within an organization, Catherine is proof that it can also be done when you are new to a company or organization. So what did Catherine do that allowed her to not only re-enter the paid workforce, but step back into a wonderful situation?

While she was a stay-at-home mom, Catherine worked heavily on a school bond campaign with her school district. She did an excellent job as a volunteer and worked closely with the school district superintendent and public information officer. When the public information officer became pregnant, she identified Catherine as her first choice to fill in during her maternity leave. This is definitely an unusual situation, but it proves that skill can matter more than already being on the payroll. Catherine expressed an interest in the position but outlined her very stringent schedule constraints to the superintendent. "I thought that would be the end of it," she says. But, because of her prior credentials, excellent track record with the bond campaign, and the rapport she had built with both the superintendent and the public information officer, the superintendent was willing to work with her. "The superintendent is a male with no children but he was very supportive." Catherine believes that this is because he felt confident she was the right person for the job. After the public information officer returned from maternity leave, she and Catherine continued on as a job share team.

It's also important to know that Catherine was already familiar with how to make a job share successful. She had created an alternative work arrangement in her job with the television station prior to going on maternity leave with her first child. At that time, she was the host and producer of a public affairs show. She was good at her job and valued by her employer. When she returned from maternity leave, she didn't want to work full time but was not quite comfortable with stepping out of the workforce altogether. She proposed a creative solution to work half-time. She knew a coworker whose job as a producer was a half-time job but who really wanted to work full time. Catherine proposed that her coworker keep her current half-time position, which was two days per week, and then take over Catherine's duties on the other three days. The company benefited because skilled employees were covering everything, and her coworker got a full-time job with new and interesting duties.

Catherine successfully worked that schedule until she became pregnant with her second child and decided it was time to leave the workforce for a while. Her experience with job sharing and creating the schedule she needed definitely contributed to her ability to negotiate her later position with the school district.

Strategies for Returning to the Paid Workforce

If you would like to return to the workforce — whether now or in the future — there are some strategies you can use to maximize your chances of success. You may not use all of the strategies, but do think about which ones are right for you and start taking the appropriate steps.

Find the right volunteer position

As illustrated by Catherine's story, the right volunteer position can be a ticket back into a fabulous position in the paid workforce. It's never a guaranteed conversion, but you certainly can seek out volunteer positions that feed both your passions and/or social consciousness *and* build your skills and credibility at the same time. If the position doesn't fit one of these criteria, think again before volunteering. It is one thing to volunteer in your child's classroom, which allows you to build rapport with your child's teacher and help insure your child's success in school. But if you are asked to take on a huge project at school or anywhere else, be discerning in how you spend your time. Make sure that you get something personally out of the deal. Maybe you will choose to be the leader of a group at church because it entails using your group facilitation skills. Perhaps there is a legislative issue that you are passionate about and the volunteer work would also give you access to a network of key people in the community who share your views. Or maybe you will work within your current volunteer groups but ask to be involved in a different capacity.

Another thing to consider is how an organization or a volunteer position would look on a résumé. How could you utilize the experience to highlight your skills and marketability? While stuffing envelopes can certainly be a good way to help out once in a while, it will never be a résumé builder. Instead, look for something that showcases your skills.

Ann is a former marketing manager who is now a stay-at-home mom with two children. She wanted to volunteer for the PTA and made a purposeful decision when she chose to take on community relations. She organized a high-profile benefit concert and worked with a musician and local community leaders. Since her background is marketing, this project allowed her to utilize her skills and gave her a sense of fulfillment. It also gave her accolades from everyone involved, an experience she could use on her résumé, and recognition from a number of powerful people in the local community. She could later turn this into a networking opportunity — which leads to the next strategy.

Network with both new and former contacts

Ann has made some great new contacts in her children's school and the community. To keep her options open for future work opportunities, she should periodically initiate some communication if she doesn't see these contacts on a regular basis. In the case of the community leaders, she could e-mail them occasionally with a link to a news item they might find interesting or send them a congratulatory note when they receive publicity. Ann reflected later, "Although I am going in a different direction now, I can easily see how I could utilize the contacts I made through the benefit concert to make an on-ramp back into the paid workforce."

The other key part of an effective networking strategy is to keep in touch with former colleagues and business contacts and continue to network with them. This is often quite easy and even fun since in our busy lives, our coworkers and other business associates often end up being friends as well. It does however take effort and initiative to stay truly connected. If you have stepped out of people's daily lives, you may not be in the forefront of their minds even if you were once close. The old adage, "out of sight, out of mind" really is true. Staying in touch by telephone and e-mail is easy and is absolutely a must. And getting together in person is a good idea. It may take some coordination on your part to make the time and accommodations, but it most likely will be well worth it in the long run.

Jill is an example of someone who kept in touch with a former manager with great results. She is an aircraft structural engineer who left the paid workforce for five-and-a-half years. She recently started a new full-time position without feeling any financial ramifications for having been out of the workforce. When asked how she found such a wonderful position so quickly, she replied, "I worked my contacts for all they were worth. I received lots of contacts and suggestions from my fellow female engineers. They understand the necessity of staying at home for a few years with my children and were uniformly supportive of my attempt to re-enter the work force."

When she first got serious about looking for a job, she contacted her old boss who wrote a strong letter of recommendation for her. He then referred her to the manager in charge of hiring her engineering discipline at her old company and she e-mailed her résumé and the recommendation letter to him. That manager informed her that his company was not hiring for the remainder of the year but he sent her to two smaller, local companies that he subcontracts with. Jill then wrote letters to those two companies, using that manager's name as a lead in (e.g., "Mr. P. recommended I contact you..."), and of course included her letter of reference. The power of Jill's first contact led her to a series of referrals that ultimately resulted in securing a job.

Find a full-time professional who is interested in job sharing

If you are interested in easing back into the paid workforce with a part-time schedule and thrive on collaboration, job sharing might be ideal for you. Job share positions are occasionally posted and advertised but it may take networking to find someone who is just in the planning stages of cutting back.

Susan is a third grade teacher. When she had her first child in May a couple of years ago, she took off the rest of that school year and the next one to spend time with her baby. Then, friends of hers in education introduced her to Karen, another elementary teacher who was teaching full time but wanted to job share so that she could spend more time teaching at the university level. Susan and Karen started talking and realized they could possibly job share Karen's position. Karen already had a strong reputation and was trusted by the parents at that school. She used her reputation to recommend Susan, and after a great deal of preplanning to ensure success, Susan stepped seamlessly into the position as half of a job share. The team has not experienced even an ounce of parent resistance.

If you are interested in job sharing as an on-ramp back to the paid workforce, start talking to people who are doing the work you are seeking. As you build rapport, you can find out if they are satisfied with their work schedule and hours. Their desire to cut back may be your ticket into the game.

Take a class in your field or do something else to keep current

This can also be a great way to get out of the house! Take a class at the local community college or university. Or, if getting to a class is too much of a scheduling hassle, look into a web-based class. You can find a class on practically any topic with a little searching.

Jill, the engineer who returned to work did something even simpler. Before starting the interview process, she refreshed her skills by obtaining a demonstration copy of a widely used software package in her field and played around with it at home. It turned out that her new company uses that software and during the interview they were glad to hear she was "familiar" with it. This type of initiative goes a long way in showing prospective employers what an excellent job you have done of staying current, as well as how serious you are about re-entering the professional world.

Read industry and general business/economic publications

This will keep you up to date on current trends, both in your industry and in the business world. You can make it enjoyable by reading in a coffee shop, and you can keep it cheap by getting your materials at the library. Simply using buzzwords and showing that you understand them sounds trite, but can actually go a long way. The reverse is also true because you can look outdated if you don't understand the current lingo that people are using.

Participate in professional associations

Like it or not, opportunities usually come about because of *who* you know. *What* you know comes into play after that. The best approach with professional associations is to get involved with the organization even though your main intent is to stay current and network. Take on committees or projects, then follow through, keep your commitments, and do a good job. If you are merely there to schmooze and see how these people can be of benefit to you, they will see through you in no time and you will not be regarded in high esteem. So do it right with the goal of helping the professional organization and yourself.

Evaluate your former industry and consider a new industry if the pace of change requires up-to-the-minute skills

Before Beth left the wireless industry she would sit in meetings and hear people say, "Boy, I wouldn't hire him. He has been out of the industry for two years and it changes too fast!" Other highly technical fields will have the same problem — it's just not probable that you can leave for a few years and then slide back in.

If you do want to return to the same field, you will need to make a huge effort to stay up on the technology. This can be done by reading industry periodicals, working on a contract basis, attending conferences, and even volunteering to demo new products. Be ready to share these experiences in an interview so you can easily rebut any questions about your loss of skills.

If you decide that keeping up with the industry while you are out of the workforce is not for you, look at your transferable skills and apply them to an industry that is not constantly changing. For example, your managerial skills can be applied in any number of fields.

Consider going back full time even if your preference is part time

This can be an effective strategy only if you are relatively certain you can move to a part-time schedule after a period of time. Assess the culture of the organization to make sure that part-time work is both utilized and embraced. Are there other employees working a reduced schedule? Talk to some of them and ask about their experience and perceptions of part-time work in the company. Then, depending on your rapport with your hiring manager, you could request a trial period where you work full time, with the understanding that you can move to part time after you have proven your worth. If you are not comfortable making this request up front, it may still be worth taking the risk that you can negotiate a change later.

Jill is planning to propose a part-time schedule when the time is right. She went back full time because her husband is not currently working but her goal is to scale back to part time when he goes back to work. She said, "My plan is to use this time to prove my worth. When I interviewed, we did discuss the possibility of part time and also stressed flexible work schedules. I had a choice of working as a normal salaried employee or as contractor with full benefits. I chose to contract so I can basically work whatever hours I want and just charge accordingly with a minimum of 33 hours per week. If I need to work fewer than 33 hours, we will discuss prorating benefits."

Jill is well positioned in both the short and long term to adjust her schedule to best meet her needs. Look for, or create, these same conditions when you are targeting potential companies.

View your transition as a time to reinvent yourself by finding your passion and identifying your skills.

For many people, this is the scariest and also the most exciting option! What better time to really think about what type of work best meets your priorities and provides a new challenge?

Nancy was a television advertising sales executive before leaving the workforce to stay at home with her children full time. When her children were six years old and two years old, she realized that while she valued full-time mothering, she yearned for adult stimulation and was ready to return to work. She didn't want to return to the very demanding profession she had prior to having children. She knew the hours would be long and she would have to travel frequently. Instead, she took inventory of her strong transferable skills such as relationship building, follow-up skills, self-motivation, independence, and organization. She realized she still wanted to be in sales but needed a different industry. After thinking through some possibilities, she decided real estate sales met all her objectives. She then took night classes and studied for her real estate license while her youngest child was napping.

Real estate was also a good choice because she could use her many contacts to get started in the business. Her contacts came from both her previous professional life and those she established while networking with other mothers and doing volunteer work.

She now works three weekdays, the weekends, and some other time at home on the computer. That still makes at least a five-day workweek, but she and her husband do their best to stagger their hours to minimize child-care costs.

Combining Strategies

Whether you have a set goal in mind or are exploring several possibilities, you will benefit from using more than one of the above strategies. Each one can take you down a different path, and you could end up some place even better than you imagined.

Ann, the stay-at-home mom with the marketing background we talked about earlier, followed a series of leads that gave her more than contacts — they helped her discover what exactly she wanted to do. As she looks back on her process of discovery, she realizes that she instinctively laid the groundwork for her re-entry by always networking with former contacts, being active in her graduate school alumni group, and in the volunteer work she chose.

She also did a very small amount of marketing for friends on a "trade out" basis. One friend was starting a jewelry business and she did some marketing for her in exchange for jewelry. The "trade out" way of doing things felt a lot less risky for her and although the work was minimal, she used it to keep her skills strong, build her résumé, and, probably most importantly, maintain her own confidence in her skills and personal marketability.

Today, almost serendipitously, she is involved in a start-up company with two other people. Her interest in marketing caused her to strike up a conversation with a window installer who had designed an innovative product. After numerous conversations, she started working with this person, brought in another partner, and is slowly working on developing a marketing plan. This is allowing her to work at her own pace, with the possibility of a lucrative endeavor a few years down the road. Ann says, "If I hadn't kept networking and doing some things to keep my skills sharp, I am sure that this opportunity would not have materialized for me and I would not have had the confidence to pursue it!"

Résumé and Interview Tips

Okay, let's say you have identified some opportunities and need to prepare for an interview. There are five résumé and interview tips that are important when returning after a break from the workforce. Let's take a look at them.

Make sure your prior work experience is strategically placed on your résumé and is specific and quantifiable

Don't be a slave to the chronological approach on your résumé — this would force you to list your time away from the workplace right at the top. Instead, consider the format where you list your key skills and provide examples from your work history. This allows you to list your strongest work experiences in the order that best displays your strengths. You would still note the company and the date but you are no longer making that the focal point of the résumé. For an example of this type of résumé, see Sample 1.

Also, make every point quantifiable — hiring managers always look for specifics. For example, if you are claiming an excellent sales record, they will want to see an exact number. Otherwise it is just a "motherhood and apple pie" statement that means nothing. Did you increase market penetration by 40 percent? Did you increase your sales by a certain percentage?

Obviously it is easier in some positions, such as sales, to be more quantifiable than others. But it's critical to find a way to quantify your work successes if you have spent time out of the workforce and are banking on that prior experience to make some points. If you were in the training department, cite how many people you trained, how many classes you designed, or ultimately any improvements in business that could be attributed to the training. If you were in marketing, did you increase market share? What size was the budget you managed? Were you responsible for a dollar amount of cost savings for your company? If you claim you have excellent written and verbal communication skills then bring a writing sample and demonstrate your verbal prowess.

Don't try to hide your time out of the paid workforce

If your résumé is organized by key skill, include some experience from the time you were out of the workforce. This is where your volunteer or community achievements come in handy. But if you

SAMPLE 1
SKILL-BASED RÉSUMÉ

SALLY ANN JOHNSON
2254 ELMWOOD DRIVE
DES MOINES, IA 55555
1.555.555.5555
SALLYANN@ELMWOOD.COM

Education:

Bachelor of Science
MAJOR: Exceptional Educational Needs
EMPHASIS: Early Childhood
MAJOR: Elementary Education
May 1994 GPA 3.57   Years Attended (1990 – 94)
University of —

Masters Degree
Masters in Adaptive Education Assistive Technology
Certificate acquired summer 2000
Expected completion Spring 2005
GPA 4.00   Years Attended (1999 – present)
University of —

Certification:

Department of Public Instruction
Birth–8 years
Elementary Education Grades1–6 Assistive Technology add on   (Summer 2000)

Professional Experience:

EC:EEN Teacher   Years Employed (1994 – 01)
School District —

- o Revamped the Early Childhood program by engineering the classroom
  environment in order to meet the needs of each child.

- o Met needs of children with disabilities such as Autism, Down's syndrome, Prader
  Willy syndrome.

- o Collaborated with other professionals such as OT, PT, and SLPs.

- o Utilized various technologies throughout the classroom to increase the students'
  ability to participate within all aspects of the Early Childhood curriculum.

- o Initiated a building assistive technology committee to review the needs of the
  district.

- o Developed and coordinated a new child find program that screened 120 children
  and included a community resource and information fair for parents.

SAMPLE 1 — Continued

EC:EEN Teacher   Years Employed (summer 1995)
YAW (Young Artist Workshop)

- o Provided a unique Early Childhood environment that allowed children with special needs opportunities to express themselves through the arts.
- o Activities included computer-based art, music, dance, and art during a three-week summer camp.

Assistive Technology Specialist Consultant

- o Provided consultative assistive technology services, which included full assessment and training students, teachers, and parents in order to allow the students independence within all environments.

Volunteer Activities:

First Presbyterian Church Care Center Developer   2000 – 01 School Year

- o Created and implemented the children's center by developing the physical space and creating fundraising opportunities to provide funding for purchasing of equipment and materials.

Mothers & More Leader   February 2003 – Present

- o Developed superior leadership skills by reorganizing and reviving a struggling local chapter into a thriving women's group that provides support, education, and advocacy to its growing membership. Membership was 26 and is now 145.

PTA Science Chair   2003 – 04 School Year

- o Supervised and reorganized the execution of the local elementary school Science Fair, which allowed more than 250 students the opportunity to develop advanced knowledge of the scientific method and science-related activities.

Continuing Education and Skills:

- o Developed PECS Training (Fall 1998)
- o Therapeutic Listening
     Listening with the Whole Body (February 1999)
     Samonas & Sonas Core Training (August 2000)

References:

Available upon request.

are asked in the interview or asked to fill out a form with a chronological list of experience, then simply state "Family leave from x date to x date." Be matter of fact about that time period just as you would about anything else. It is not something to be swept under the rug. Be strong, self-confident, and proud.

During the interview be the consummate professional

This is always important but especially if you are trying to impress a prospective employer that you are indeed a professional who is serious about the job. You don't want to reinforce the parent stereotype by having spit-up on your shoulder and a purse over-flowing with snacks and toys. Instead, invest in one new interview suit or outfit that isn't too trendy but is stylish and up to date.

Avoid talking about your children unless specifically asked

One time Beth was interviewing a woman who had taken time off to raise her children and she used being a Girl Scout leader as an example in answering several of the interview questions. While that certainly does take significant organizational skills and leadership, it is better to use examples from past work experience unless you absolutely draw a blank on the question. Look over your résumé and think through your prior work experience *before* the interview. Remind yourself of situations in which you excelled. It may take a while to get your head back into that time period and frame of reference.

Demonstrate your up-to-date knowledge of the industry

As we mentioned above, it is particularly important in the re-entry situation that you know, and use correctly, current buzzwords, industry terms, and concepts. This is also the time to emphasis anything that you have taken the initiative to do to hone or update your skills recently — like Jill having obtained and worked with that new software. If you aren't asked specifically, then bring it up on your own. Talk about what you have done to stay up-to-date in the industry and keep your skills fresh. By demonstrating your initiative you have just made yourself a more attractive candidate.

You are now armed with the strategies for re-entering the workforce, as well as résumé and interview tips. Feel confident that you can find or create the work situation that is right for you!

f o m C
o r t
a l b e
C h
a o
s

Chapter

15

Creating an Alternative Work Schedule: How to Think Like an Employer and Pitch Your Proposal Like a Pro

Most of us have had a fantasy about walking into our boss's office and demanding a raise or a new schedule or we will quit immediately! The daydream continues as our boss begs us to stay and promises to do anything possible to keep us. While there may be a few situations where this actually happens, it's more likely we would be told in no uncertain terms to not let the door hit us in the behind on the way out.

If you want to create a sellable alternative work arrangement, you need to put a lot of work into correctly positioning yourself. Most of the successful transitions to an alternative work schedule occur within a person's existing company. People either modify their existing position to create what they need or seek a new position within the company. Their reputation in the company is often the key to getting their plan implemented.

The same is true for you. Your best opportunity is within a company where you have a proven track record that you can, and should, reference. If you are unsure about your reputation or need more information on your strengths, do some information gathering. Your company may even have some feedback tools that you can use to gather data, such as a 360-degree review process. You will need to illustrate in your proposal that you are an asset to your company. This is definitely a sales process.

Karen, from the attorney general's office, used her well-established reputation to do just that. After eight and a half years of full-time work, she had her first child and decided to go part-time. She said, "I presented a proposal to my division chief. I did not have to fight for it because our office has policies that allow telecommuting and part time. While granting those work schedules is discretionary, I had positioned myself so I was confident it would be approved."

Jennifer, an outside sales representative who implemented a job share with a partner said, "I firmly believe that without our length of tenure, the high level of responsibility, our demonstrated customer commitment, and the success we had each achieved individually, the arrangement would not have been as easy to realize. It's clear that local and corporate management trusted us to implement this new idea seamlessly and beneficially to our customers, and knew they could retain high energy and productive employees along the way."

As we discussed in the job share section, it is also important for your position to be viewed as key to the company. Without this factor, a solid alternative work schedule can be at risk. Even though Beth and her partner both had years of valuable experience and impressive track records, the strategic focus of their organization shifted during their job share. In the end, their position was not considered to be critical, and that injured their ability to negotiate further benefits and to progress further in their careers.

Although implementing an alternative work schedule within your current company is certainly the most common path, that doesn't mean it is the only way. Catherine, who we profiled in Chapter 14, went to work for a new organization after taking a break from the workforce and was still able to negotiate a job share situation. She used her past experience, along with the reputation she had built as a volunteer, to create what she needed. The key really is to have a solid reputation that you can leverage to your advantage.

Once you have positioned yourself effectively, you are ready to start thinking about the specifics of your proposal. Your task is to put together a comprehensive plan for a creative solution that works for you and benefits your employer. To do this, think like an employer. What would you want to know if you were the boss? What benefit is there from the company's perspective? Getting clear on these answers early on will make it much easier to write the proposal.

The proposal itself can take one of many different forms. Assess the culture of your organization before choosing and customizing a format. If you work in a very traditional industry such as banking, accounting, or engineering, a very formal and detailed proposal would probably be in order. If you work somewhere that is more casual, then you should adjust your format accordingly. You still need to have a well thought out plan, but might present it verbally and reference some simple bullet points.

The proposal is also a sales tool for you and it's your chance to state your case. It may be appropriate to use catchy sales phrases, humor, and buzz words from your industry. It is always smart to use key phrases from your company's strategic plan. Whenever possible, link what you are trying to create to the company's strategic direction and ultimately to the bottom line. The goal is to create a win-win situation and in order to do that you must put yourself in the shoes of your employer.

Ten Elements of a Comprehensive Proposal

In this chapter we will take you step-by-step through the ten elements of a complete and detailed proposal. We will stop and discuss each aspect of the proposal and show pieces of a real life example. A job share proposal was chosen for purposes of illustration because it can be the most intricate and complex. Your proposal may, or may not, need to be as comprehensive, but it is certainly better to err on the side of thoroughness. Much of the sample job share proposal is also pertinent to the other alternative arrangements.

Introductory statement and needs analysis

To start the proposal, you need a clear and compelling statement about what you are proposing and why. This isn't the place to list all the specific benefits. Instead, give an overarching explanation that clearly shows you are thinking in terms of the employer's best interest. A good way to do this is to talk about how the arrangement fits with the company's overall strategic direction. What is the business reason that makes this a viable proposal for the company?

Example:

We are proposing a job share in a senior management position in order to retain key skills and maximize productivity in a critical position. A job share is a nontraditional way to retain valued, experienced employees and use the synergy created by having two highly motivated employees with different strengths and backgrounds collaborate on the same objectives.

Implementing alternative work schedules helps our company to compete in the marketplace by attracting and retaining talented, qualified employees — a key to our strategy for both short- and long-term business success. By implementing a job share at a senior level, the company demonstrates and makes visible its commitment to work/life balance.

Job title

Rather basic but important — simply state the title of the job.

Example:

Position to be shared: Senior Marketing Manager, Western Division

Schedule specifics

These are the details of the days and the hours you plan to work. If you intend to work part time, outline what hours you will work. If you are proposing to telecommute, thoughtfully lay out which days you will be remote and when you will be in the office for "face time." If it is a job share, document who will work when.

Before completing this section, check to see if your company has any policies about alternative work schedules pertaining to vacations, sick time, disability, and holidays. In this section, you should also spell out how your schedule will work in relation to these benefits.

Example:

Partner 1: Monday: 8 hours, Tuesday: 8 hours, Wednesday: 8 hours = 24 hours

Partner 2: Wednesday: 8 hours, Thursday: 8 hours, Friday: 8 hours = 24 hours

Work allocation during vacation and sick leave: Employees are available to back each other up in the case of extended absence. During one partner's maternity leave, the other partner will work in the office four days per week. The fifth day will be for handling any urgent issues by telephone and e-mail from home.

Vacation and sick leave will be prorated. During a vacation or sick leave of one partner, the other partner will be accessible by telephone, checking voicemail and e-mail at least twice per day, and will make herself available to the best of her ability to come into the office for any crucial meetings. Any extended leave, such as short-term disability, will be handled the same way we handle any others (i.e., backfilling with an "acting" person).

Benefits to the company

This section describes the specific benefits for the company in allowing this alternative arrangement. This could also be called the "what's in it for them" section. This is a critical section to include when proposing any alternative work arrangement. Some of the benefits will be intangible, but be as concrete and detailed as you possibly can.

Example:

The senior marketing job share will result in the following benefits:

- *Increased employee loyalty and satisfaction.*
- *Ability to retain experienced, valued employees and avoid recruiting/training expenses.*
- *Full utilization of employees' skills.*

- *Increased productivity — energy level is higher due to improved balance and focus.*

- *Increased effectiveness due to the combined skills and experience of each employee and the synergy of having two people brainstorm on difficult issues (i.e., double the skill set in the position, often complementing skill sets).*

- *Double the network/contacts/resources available to the position.*

- *The ability of the job share team to take on additional projects/tasks due to having 1.2 full-time equivalent, due to the proposed schedule of 48 combined hours.*

- *An extra 0.2 resource to increase customer satisfaction and positively impact the bottom line by having additional time to proactively address customer issues.*

- *An extra 0.2 resource to increase employee satisfaction and retention by having more time to spend one-on-one with employees and also going out on customer calls with salespeople. This will also allow for additional coaching and training of the salespeople in conjunction with the customer calls, which in turn has a positive impact on both customer satisfaction and employee retention.*

- *Enhanced job satisfaction of direct reports and coworkers on the team as well as better performance due to having two managers, which allows more time for one-on-one coaching of team members (i.e., there will always be a manager available).*

- *Allowing manager-level employees to job share is an extremely positive statement for our company to make in support of work/life balance. It sends a strong message to our employees as well as our customers. Balance was one of the top employee satisfaction survey action items from this year.*

Benefits for the employees in the job share

This section describes the benefits for the employees, but you will notice that many of the benefits are also a plus for the employer. That's an added sales feature for your proposal so play up those benefits if possible.

Example:

The senior marketing job share will benefit the partners in the following ways:

- *Flexible work schedule allows the employees to achieve the desired balance between family and work.*
- *Both employees maintain their career track.*
- *Diminished stress as a result of balance.*
- *The fun and enjoyment of sharing ideas and creative strategies with someone equally interested in the marketing department's success.*
- *Overall increased job satisfaction and loyalty to company.*

Cost benefit analysis

A detailed and realistic cost benefit analysis is the most important element in selling your proposal. Although the title, cost benefit analysis, sounds complex and onerous, it does not have to be rocket science. This section just needs to be realistic and logical. In fact, simple is often better, especially if you are not a numbers person by nature. Don't try to do anything that you may not be able to fully explain. If your organization has a standard cost benefit or business case format, definitely put it to use. Also check with your human resources department for any data.

In addition, many companies have a standard dollar figure that they use for burden. Burden is the additional cost the company incurs above and beyond your salary for things like health insurance, office space, and your reimbursable expenses. Most companies also have a predetermined figure that they use for recruitment, training, and ramp-up time for a new employee when they incur turnover.

If you are in a sales position or other revenue generating position, this is the place to illustrate the financial impact to the company of losing experienced successful employees. Some sales organizations recognize that there is a minimum 18-month ramp-up period for a new sales person. This translates to hard dollars in lost revenue, in addition to the recruitment and training costs associated with the new salesperson.

If you are in a profession where you are not on salary but get paid for hours worked, this whole process can be simplified. You won't have to negotiate each partner's salary; instead each partner is paid for the hours worked.

If you work for a very small company, they most likely will not have any standard numbers such as the cost of retraining. The upside is that they also may be much more willing to be creative and flexible and may appreciate how important it is to retain a valued employee.

One way to start the cost benefit analysis is to present the proposed salary and benefits plan. In this job share example, one partner wanted to work 24 hours per week and didn't need benefits because her spouse had good benefits through his company. The other partner would have liked to have had the benefits but decided to rely on her spouse's. The job share partners both opted to eliminate their benefits to create a strong cost/benefit analysis.

Example:

- *The employee who currently holds the job will reduce her base salary of $70,000 to $42,000 (0.60 for 24 hours). Because the partner opts not to take benefits, the burden amount will be $0.*

- *The second partner will also work 24 hours per week. She will also reduce her current salary of $70,000 to $42,000 (0.60 for 24 hours). Because the partner opts not to take benefits, the burden amount will be $0.*

- *Net saving is calculated as follows:*

  Current situation: $70,000 salary + $24,180 burden = $94,180

  Job share situation: $84,000 for both salaries + $0 burden = $84,000

  Net savings to the company = $10,180

- *Additional benefits are listed in section 4, and costs associated with hiring and training will be avoided.*

You will notice that it is very attractive for the company to not have to carry burden on either person. That counters a common objection that companies have about job shares that they will have to pay double the burden. Let's see what this same example would look like if the partners were asking the company to carry burden on one of them.

- *The employee who currently holds the job will reduce her base salary of $70,000 to $42,000 (0.60 for 24 hours). Burden will be prorated to a rate of $14,508 versus the old rate of $24,180.*

- *The second partner will also work 24 hours. She will also reduce her base salary of $70,000 to $42,000 (0.60 for 24 hours). Because the partner opts not to take benefits, the burden amount will be $0.*

- *Net increase is calculated as follows:*

  Current situation: $70,000 salary + $24,180 burden = $94,180

  Job share situation: $84,000 for both salaries + $14,508 burden = $98,508

  Net increase to the company = $4,328

  The $4,328 increase will be offset by the benefits listed in section 4. Also, costs associated with hiring and training will be avoided.

In this example, there will not be a cost savings, but the additional productivity benefits listed earlier can make up for the additional cost. Costs will also be avoided for recruiting and training as well as lost opportunity if turnover is incurred. This is the inverse effect of retaining qualified, experienced employees through alternative work schedules.

If your cost benefit analysis turns out like this second example, include the intangible savings in your proposal and make an effort to quantify them by using some comparable examples.

This may take some research, but remember that for most employers, numbers speak louder than words.

Another way to make a strong case in the cost proposal is to offer to take on something new. You could tackle a key problem for the company that isn't getting addressed, or you could commit to increasing your sales goals or your workload in some way to offset any increase in cost that the company may incur.

If your cost benefit analysis still is not favorable, you may need to start thinking about other ways to cut your company's costs or increase your productivity. As you saw in the cost benefit examples, one approach is to reduce or eliminate your benefits. If you already have benefits through a spouse or domestic partner, this may be a great solution. In a job share situation, one partner may require benefits and the other may not. If neither of you required benefits it would be even more attractive to your employer.

However, if benefits are important to you, as they are to many people, then you just need to be creative in your proposal and try and find ways to justify or offset the cost to the company. Judi job shares a position in catering and has a husband who is self-employed. One of the major reasons that she continues to work is to carry benefits for her family. She negotiated full benefits for both her and her husband, but in return, Judi and her job share partner agreed to increase their sales goals proportionately.

Cutting down on travel or other types of expenses is another way to change the outcome of the cost benefit analysis. If you want to telecommute, you might offer to purchase a high-speed data line at your home or a laptop out of your own pocket. Be creative in offering win-win solutions so that both you and your employer gain something positive.

Example:

We have an average monthly revenue per customer of $30.32. If we subtract $13.00 for support costs, that yields $17.32 per additional new customer unit and $207.84 per additional unit per year of profit. To offset the additional $4,328 in expenditure for the job share, we will add an additional 21 customers per year.

In other words, the job share partners are committing to increase their customer acquisition goals by 21 customers per year. That comes out to 1.75 customers per month, which is very achievable.

Successful precedents

Using successful precedents or examples can be a great tool, particularly if they are within your company. If there are no useful precedents within your company, then benchmark other organizations. Try and find some that are relevant to your situation. If you are proposing part time in an unconventional way, look for another unique part-time situation that has been successful. If you are in the corporate realm, try to stick with a corporate example that is as close to your industry as possible. The same goes if you are in education, nonprofit, or government. One thing that came out loud and clear in our research is that every decision maker thought their industry or type of work was unique and tended to discount things that worked in other types of organizations.

Sources for researching outside your company are newspapers, business, trade, and parenting publications, web searches, and networking locally or within your industry. There is much that can be learned by benchmarking other industries or professions and applying innovative ideas to your own situation.

Strategy for managing/allocating responsibilities

This is imperative in a job share proposal, but also is quite helpful in part time, flextime, or telecommuting where there may be meetings that are missed because of schedules. In this section, you will explain the nuts and bolts of how the work will get done.

Example:

Overall, the key to making this successful will be excellent communication and coordination between the partners so that no balls are dropped or decisions delayed due to the job share. Following is specifically how each of these responsibilities will be managed/divided in the job share:

- *To ensure success against our metrics, we have identified clear targets. The progress towards the targets will be tracked as closely as our available reporting allows with both partners reviewing the progress together every week on the day they overlap. Motivation and direction of the team towards the targets is accomplished jointly through employee performance reviews, plans, and team meetings. Team meetings will occur on Wednesdays (overlap day) as will one-on-ones (done together) with our managers. Both partners will be accountable for staying focused on the targets and making decisions accordingly.*

- *The subordinates will report to both job share partners. After collecting data from others who have job shared and from a few of the team members, the overwhelming consensus is that employees need to report to both people. That way, they have a manager available every day and benefit from more "face time" with their managers. If the team were split in reporting between the two job share partners, half of the team would always have two days per week without a manager.*

- *In order to provide the best assistance in the development of tactical plans for accounts, each partner will have a few strategic account/projects that she is the "lead" on. The lead will be responsible for initiating the planning and strategic decisions, but will communicate them to the other partner and may utilize the other partner to brainstorm solutions and take advantage of the opportunities for synergy. For smaller and day-to-day tactical planning and coaching, both partners will assist when appropriate. In both of these cases, e-mail will be used to document plans and decisions and to communicate between partners. The partners will have e-mail folders for each employee and each strategic account/project.*

- *Marketing plans, forecasts, and objectives will be done jointly whenever possible. In the event that a quick turnaround is required for a forecast or plan, one partner will have the knowledge and authority to make decisions, and will have the ability to contact the other partner on her days off if necessary.*

- *On the issue of staying within budgets, as with the financial metrics, the budgets will be clearly defined and tracked to the best extent that reporting allows. Therefore, each partner will have the knowledge and authority to make decisions and communicate to the other partner.*

- *Managing a team of people will require excellent communication between the partners. With this communication, the team will actually benefit from having two managers who will be available to them more and will be less stressed/ fatigued because of increased balance in their lives. Direct reports will never feel like they have to repeat themselves because the partners will keep excellent logs for one another utilizing e-mail and voicemail. The partners are aligned philosophically and therefore will support each other's decisions even if they don't thoroughly agree on all of the details.*

Detailed communication plan

The communication plan addresses a number of different communication issues. It documents how you will stay connected to the office on your days off or tied in with your partner in the case of a job share. Keep in mind that you should not plan to be 100 percent dialed in to work during your time off or you will have defeated the purpose of the alternative work arrangement.

If you plan to telecommute, this is more important than it seems. As we mention in Chapter 7, if you wish to protect your career track, you need to make sure that your manager doesn't think of you as "out of sight, out of mind" when opportunities arise for special projects or promotions. Have a detailed plan to stay in touch and toot your own horn a little if your accomplishments aren't totally obvious.

This section of the proposal is also important for illustrating how coworkers and other associates will communicate with you. Remember, the key here is not to make it more difficult for others to communicate with you or they may simply choose not to!

Example:

- *Our e-mail boxes will be networked so that no one ever has to think about which one of us should receive the* message. All messages will be received by both of us and everything will be handled seamlessly. We have a system for re-marking messages as unread so the other partner knows which messages they need to read.

- Both partners will share one office telephone number and voicemail box. This again will prohibit anyone from having to think about whom to call when. All messages/calls will be received and handled seamlessly.

- We have developed a form for taking notes at meetings that will be filled out by the partner who attends the meeting and then stapled to the appropriate project folder.

- We will keep a notebook with a running list of action items that both of us use on our days in the office.

- The partner in the office will pass important voicemail messages through to the other partner's cellular voicemail box on her days off.

- The partner in the office manages the joint schedule. This includes scheduling things for the other partner. Then, the evening before the other partner's first day of the week in the office, the partner that has been in the office will leave her schedule on voicemail so that she is prepared for her day.

- We will talk on the telephone daily or as necessary.

Potential issues and solutions

Anticipate anything that could be an issue with the situation that you are proposing and then outline your solutions to the issues.

Example:

- *Potential issue: Confusion (particularly initially) among customers, direct reports, and internal coworkers.*

- *Solution: Schedules will be posted on our office door. For strategic accounts and projects, one partner will be designated as "lead." In the event of "hot" customer or employee issues, one partner will either follow the issue all the way through (even on a day off) or, if possible, bring the other partner thoroughly up to speed.*

- *Potential issue: Different knowledge bases.*

- *Solution: The partners have a strong combination of the required skills and knowledge. It is also acknowledged that initially there will need to be quite a bit of communication between partners even on the days that they don't overlap.*

- *Potential issue: Communication breakdowns.*

- *Solution: Each partner has a cellular telephone with text messaging and a laptop with virtual networking capabilities so that the partner who is not at work on a particular day can be reached to handle issues in the case of an emergency. E-mail logs will be sent on important issues between partners at least daily.*

- *Potential issue: Partnership issues.*

- *Solution: The partners have done a through analysis on their compatibility and work styles. The outcome suggests a very productive partnership and both partners are conscientious and success oriented. Both partners are also committed to put forth the energy necessary to make the partnership work and be seamless to team members, coworkers, and customers.*

- *Potential issue: Compensation.*

- *Solution: The additional cost of compensation will be offset by the reduction of recruiting/training costs caused by turnover since alternative work schedules are a powerful retention tool. It will also be offset by additional customer acquisition goals.*

Getting the Right Equation

Once you have drafted your proposal, it is important that you feel good about what you are about to negotiate. If you give away too much and end up with reduced compensation for a lot of work, you may end up feeling angry.

When Beth and Judy were negotiating with their company, they both volunteered to give up their benefits. At the time it wasn't necessary — the company was willing to provide benefits to one of them but not both. Judy did not care about benefits and Beth did, but they wanted to start their partnership with equal conditions.

The complexities of the benefit policy drove a particular outcome. In their company, the policy stated that if an employee worked fewer than 30 hours per week, the company did not have to pay them any benefits. If one of them received benefits that would mean that one partner would have to work 20 hours per week, with the one receiving the benefits working 30 hours per week since the company was not willing to pay for more than a combined 50-hour week. The partners did not feel like they would both be equally invested. Their agreement was that they would initially each work 24 hours, three eight-hour days. Beth was somewhat concerned about the benefits piece. Her husband had benefits but she wasn't sure how well they would serve her family. The door was left open to readdress her benefit concerns later if it became an issue for her.

In actuality, because the partners were salaried, each worked at least 30 hours per week if not more. Their compensation was reduced to 60 percent of what it had been to reflect the supposed 24-hour workweek. Meanwhile, Beth was discovering that her husband's benefits were not nearly as good as hers had been. Health care was costing them significantly more for a family of four than she had anticipated. Beth then re-approached their director to see if she would entertain increasing her hours to 30 per week so that she could receive full benefits. By then, the climate had changed in the organization. She informed Beth that it was no longer up for discussion. This caused Beth to feel angry and misled.

The lesson here is to make sure that you negotiate what you need upfront. Most of us have examples somewhere in our careers where things are left open to be revisited later and then it doesn't play out that way. People often change roles within organizations and the business climate can change. There are many logical reasons why long-term verbal commitments aren't kept.

At the same time, it is also important to negotiate a situation that is not too rich for you and too stretched for the company. This could feel like a victory in the short term, but beware — it could end up being a career-limiting, or even a career-ending, move. In times of cost cutting, this could put your situation, and even you personally, at more of a risk for losing your job. At the very least it could keep you from receiving promotions if you are not viewed as being a "team player."

Preparing for Possible Objections

Any good salesperson will probe to gather all of the possible objections he or she may encounter before a big presentation. If you can, interview as many of your key stakeholders to gather their objections prior to presenting your proposal. They may bring up some things that you had not anticipated. Jeri, an elementary school teacher presented her proposal for job sharing to her principal. He asked the partners, "What will you do if a child starts telling her parents that she doesn't want to come to school on a specific day because it is a different teacher from the day before and she prefers one over the other?" Jeri and her partner were prepared for this question and gave a thoughtful, detailed response.

A stakeholder is anyone who will be impacted by your situation. The most important ones are your managers, customers, and coworkers with whom you work closely and cooperatively. When Judi put together her proposal to job share in catering, she knew that there were a couple of people on the executive committee who were opposed to the job share. She interviewed them ahead of time and then made sure to cover their objections in her proposal and presentation. If you are in a position that interfaces with external customers, it is very powerful to casually interview a few key customers and include their input.

Making the Presentation

Your presentation may be a formal meeting with a large group of internal stakeholders or it may be a quick one-on-one meeting in your boss's office. It is important to know this ahead of time. Also evaluate your company culture. Will it be solely your boss's decision? Will the human resources department be involved? Many of the part-timers and people who work compressed workweeks that we interviewed said that their positions just evolved over time. Some started by asking to telecommute one or two days per week.

Will your boss need to present it to his or her boss or a board? If so, can you be present? If your boss has to do the presenting, make your proposal extremely thorough and check that he or she has all of the visual aids and documentation that you can supply.

If you are able to give the presentation, not only do you need your visual aids and documentation, but you can add some creativity. When Judi and her partner presented their job share proposal to their executive committee, they made gingerbread cookies in the shape of people and made them two different colors. The cookies were two pieces that fit together perfectly to form one whole person. When the committee members entered the conference room there was a cookie at each of their places as well as a copy of their formal proposal.

Be just as professional as if you were interviewing with a new company. Don't assume anything is a given. Even if your company has policies that allow for alternative work schedules, they are often at the manager's discretion. Also remember that you have been thinking about this for a long time and it makes perfect sense to you. Your work schedule proposal is probably one of five meetings that your manager has that day so you need to spell things out in a clear, concise, and straightforward manner. Even if you work for an extremely small company and know the owner well, err on the side of being very professional and respectful.

The proposal is the place where the rubber meets the road. It takes work, but it is worth it! Many of the details that you work out in the proposal stage will assist you in being successful once your proposal is approved. If you prepare a detailed proposal and find out in the end that it wasn't all necessary, it still is not wasted effort. The nuts and bolts pieces about communication and how the work will get done are crucial to a successful alternative work schedule. You now have a comprehensive blueprint to guide you in implementing your new alternative work arrangement!

Part V

Living in Comfortable Chaos

f o m C
a o r t
a l b e
C h
a o
s

Chapter 16

Your Ever-Changing Journey

For the longest time, 18-month-old Mason thought that the movement that went with "the wipers on the bus go swish, swish, swish" was the motion his mom made when she put on her mascara in the rearview mirror while stopped at a traffic light on the way to driving him to daycare in the mornings. Judy, Mason's mom, found joy in singing on the way to preschool and thought once again how perfect it was for her to work three days a week and have the other two at home with Mason. For her, it was the best of both worlds.

Hopefully, this book has helped you decide what is right for your world, and you are able to turn down the chaos volume in your life to just the right level. If you are still falling in bed at night exhausted with the only good thing being that you got through your busy day, then where is the joy? As a sentient being, you were meant for so much more. Comfortable Chaos has illustrated that joy can be seized during the exhilaration of the white-water raft ride and can also be found within those pools of calm water that you manage to paddle to now and then.

We have suggested that you use the three "I"s of Comfortable Chaos: *individual, imperfect,* and *interrelated* to make everything from work/life choices to scheduling decisions. Like Judy, we hope you have found, and embraced, what is truly right for you. Just keep in mind that this doesn't mean everything is wrapped up in a neat package. Ericka, one of the interviewees from Chapter 6 put it well, "People generally want to have the perfect experience on all fronts, but it's just messy." How true. Comfortable Chaos will always be a little messy and it is very freeing to delight in the disorder.

But this isn't the end of the story because Comfortable Chaos is not a destination. Comfortable Chaos offers tools for the ever-changing journey because with each kink in the river, a surprise may be waiting for you around the bend. Just about the time you become at ease with the work/life situation that you have created, something inevitably changes. The needs of your family will evolve, your work will change in some way, or perhaps something fundamentally will shift within you. Luckily, the Comfortable Chaos ideas and tools are here for you to use again and again.

Let's revisit some of the people we interviewed for the book and see what has changed for them in the last three years. Karen, the assistant attorney general, continued to work part time and telecommute until her workload increased dramatically and she went back to a full-time schedule for nine months until a major case was completed. She is now happily back to her part-time schedule.

Debbie, the pharmaceutical sales representative, had a second baby and opted to continue working three days a week in the part-time division. Once again, she decided on a nanny and was hoping to set up another nanny share situation. She found one through the most serendipitous of situations. Her former nanny, Tori, was at a coffee shop and had left on her nametag from the child-care center where she now worked. A woman came up to her and started asking questions about the child-care center because she was looking for care for her newborn daughter. Tori gave her some information but also mentioned that she knew of a family that was looking to nanny share. She gave the woman Debbie's telephone number and the two women completely hit it off. A second wonderful nanny share situation was born.

Lou Ann and Ian from Chapter 8 are still enjoying their lifestyle and have successfully integrated the care of Ian's 80-year-old mother into their lives. They have just moved her from another state and although they realize the time commitment required for her care, the independent nature of their work inherently allows them to be flexible.

Jan, the graphic designer who was freelancing, opted for a different work arrangement once her baby was born. She discovered that caring for her daughter and working from home was too isolating. She found a part-time position that allows her to work as part of a team, and continues her graphic design business on a smaller scale.

All of these people had to adjust to an external change — whether it was a change in workload, a parent that now needs assistance, or the arrival of a new baby. But there doesn't have to be an external change in order for you to do something differently. Don't be afraid to admit that some changes you made may not have played out to your satisfaction. As we said earlier, Comfortable Chaos is a process.

Michelle, who found part time to be frustrating because she gave up her ability to be "in the know," decided to go back to a full-time schedule. She now flexes her hours and puts in longer days in the office Monday through Thursday so she can work fewer hours on Friday and telecommute from home. Fully aware of the challenges, she used the abutment strategy and made some very helpful changes on the home front. She and her husband sold their view home in the city and moved to a family-friendly neighborhood that also shortened both of their commutes. The home has a separate space for her mother who comes three days a week to watch the kids. Michelle's husband works four days per week and is home with the children for one day. On Fridays, Michelle's telecommuting day, she uses a variety of creative approaches to cover child care and only occasionally has to lock herself in the garage to complete a telephone call.

Judi, after successfully job sharing for ten years, went back full time for several months. She thought this would be the right solution but discovered that she wanted to spend more time with her adolescent and preadolescent children. Although she is finding that the adjustment to the stay-at-home role is taking longer than she thought, she is confident it is the right choice at this point in time. She is able to pursue a passion that has been dormant for a long time. Painting is her new love and now has a place in her life.

In addition to not being afraid to admit that something didn't work, it is important that you share your learnings with others. Whether you have a success story or a "lesson learned," pass on the wisdom. Life is short and many people struggle with the same issues. It's only by talking openly that we have any hope of making substantial changes in our culture of all-consuming work.

It's interesting that many of the people interviewed for this book who are working alternative schedules said that they felt like they had to keep their schedules extremely low profile. One woman, who was allowed to work a flexible schedule for a few months in order to transition back after maternity leave, referred to her schedule as "my secret, dirty deal." Why should this be a secret, and worse yet, be labeled as something not quite right? Let's get alternative work schedules and other sane approaches out of the closet! You can do your part by highlighting your success, instead of trying to hide it.

There is another reason why it is important to share your ideas and dreams with others. It's how creative solutions are born. When we held a focus group last summer, the evening yielded unexpected benefits. We got some great information, ideas, and opinions from the participants just as we thought we would. The surprising part was that the evening proved to be both empowering and cathartic for the participants. Everyone enjoyed talking about their work/life balance struggles so much that they wished we could do it on a regular basis.

As we have been busily putting the finishing touches on this book while trying to walk our Comfortable Chaos talk, we were reminded that we shouldn't take our frenzied daily lives too seriously. We were meeting with a man who was telling us that he enjoyed extreme sports because, "A tough day in my neighborhood is when Starbucks is out of half and half!" There are a lot